The Concise Guide
to
BRITISH
CLOCKS
Brian Loomes

The Concise Guide
to
BRITISH CLOCKS
Brian Loomes

BARRIE & JENKINS
LONDON

First published in Great Britain in 1992 by
Barrie & Jenkins Ltd
20 Vauxhall Bridge Road, London SW1V 2SA

British Library Cataloguing-in-Publication Data.
A catalogue record for this book is available from
the British Library

ISBN 0–7126–5187–X

Designed by Dennis Barker
Line drawings by Neil Hyslop

Typeset by 🅵 Tek Art Ltd,
Addiscombe, Croydon, Surrey
Printed by Kyodo Printing, Singapore

Front cover picture: Lantern clock with alarm
mechanism by William Bowyer of London
(*reproduced by Courtesy of the Trustees of the British
Museum*).

CONTENTS

APPENDICES

For Joy

About the Author

Brian Loomes has been a professional writer for over 25 years of mainly non-fiction antiques-related books, and is a regular contributor to specialist antiques magazines. For many years he has been a dealer in antiques, specialising in antique British clocks, working from his home, a former farmhouse in the Yorkshire Dales. He was for many years a professional genealogist and a Fellow of the Society of Genealogists.

PREFACE

Yet another book about clocks. Why? Surely there are enough books on the subject already – I've written fourteen of them myself!

Oddly enough, there are very few general books on clocks in print today. Of course there are coffee-table books, but these are of little help to those who wish to study the subject in greater depth. There are also reprints of books written many years ago, but as our knowledge of the subject has advanced greatly even in the last ten years, there is little point in taking instruction from any but the most recent books.

The collector of clocks today is in a very difficult situation. The sheer amount of space required by longcase clocks has always made it something of a problem to gather together more than a very few examples, particularly in view of the small sizes of today's houses. Moreover, with prices rising almost by the hour most of us cannot afford to build up a collection of any size.

What this means in practical terms is that clocks have become a pursuit for many of us not unlike that of the train-spotter, who never attempted to 'collect' trains, but was content to see them and read about them, especially in a well-illustrated book. The enthusiast has therefore had to become more of a clock-spotter than a collector. What he needs are more books and better books. If he were to buy a well-chosen selection of clock books, the outlay would be tiny compared to the cost of a single clock, and would be money well spent if the books help the would-be purchaser avoid a disastrous mistake.

This book approaches the subject in such a way that the beginner will be able to follow the stylistic and mechanical development of clocks as he meets with them and without becoming bogged down in off-putting minutiae. As a result the novice should soon be sufficiently familiar with the different types of clock to be able to recognise them and to assess both period and quality. At the same time the experienced collector or clock buff will find much here that is new to him. In particular, I have drawn considerably for detail on original documents of the day, using contemporary accounts to illustrate not only the clocks themselves, but the working conditions and practices of the time.

The questions of how a clockmaker learned his craft, where he learned it, where he was able to practise it and in what manner, are all important considerations and are not only of interest in their own right, but are vital to an understanding of how a particular clock or type of clock fits into the overall picture. Aspects such as whether a particular man was an actual maker of clocks or a retailer, whether he did his own wheel-cutting or his own engraving, how you set about recognising such factors and what bearing these have on the value of a clock are topics which are dealt with in very few books, but which are discussed here in some detail.

My intention has been to write a book which will be a good starting point for the novice, whilst at the same time offering an approach that may be refreshing and different for the more experienced collector. The aim is to pack a mass of information into a small space and yet keep it interesting. I hope it succeeds and I hope you enjoy it.

Brian Loomes

Pateley Bridge
North Yorkshire
1992

1 Clockmaker or Retailer, Craftsman or Handyman?

Identification and dating are the main features of any book on clocks, but these alone are not enough. The owner, student, enthusiast or would-be purchaser needs to know more than that. Once he has established any facts he can about the name on the dial, the type of clock, and its age, he then needs to know the following: is it a 'good' clock (whatever that may be), is it a rarity or commonplace, is it superbly made or ordinary, is it desirable, is it a one-off or were these made by the million, is it a rare survival or are a great many similar ones readily available today, was it really made by the man whose name it bears, or by his company or workmen or by a factory . . . and so on. In other words, he needs to understand where his particular clock fits within the overall scheme of three and a half centuries or so of clockmaking.

There is an answer to all these questions, but to the beginner

1. *An engraving of 1748 showing a clockmaker at his workbench. Hanging on the wall behind his back is an Act of Parliament clock, showing the existence of such clocks many years before the Act after which they were supposedly named.*

these aspects are a total mystery and are completely unfathomable, and will remain so unless he knows something about the wider background of the trade. So often does one hear half-baked ideas and notions bandied about which bear no relation to the reality of clockmaking in the past. The number of times one hears tell that this particular clockmaker only ever made three clocks, or six, or two, and that one is in so-and-so museum, and this one is one of the 'others' – such stories are absolute nonsense and are mostly put about by vendors in an attempt to whip up the enthusiasm of the potential customer. All they indicate is that the person expressing such an opinion has no concept of how the trade functioned, and has not even thought seriously about it. How could a clockmaker make a living if he made only a handful of clocks in his life?

There are several well-documented examples of provincial clockmakers whose output exceeds 1200 clocks. Most worked at the trade personally, with maybe an apprentice to assist them, and perhaps a single in-house workman, known as a journeyman. Not all worked equally hard, obviously, but we know that a clockmaker could make one clock every two weeks (longcase clocks, that is, as these were the main output of most British clockmakers most of the time). Twenty-five clocks a year for as many years as he could draw breath, and the working span of many clockmakers exceeds 40 years!

How did he learn his trade? Did he make all the parts himself? Did he do his own engraving? Was he really a clockmaker or a retailer? Well, the world of retailing in the sense of buying-in an item ready-made in order to sell it only begins after about 1820, and for the most part only after about 1840. Obviously, all imported clocks sold in Britain were retailed, not made, here, even when they bear a supposed maker's name. A few 'clockmakers' in this country in the later nineteenth century sold imported clocks, such as carriage clocks, which might bear their own name and town and also be lettered 'Paris', as if they had a Paris branch. This is no more than a sales gimmick used to try to camouflage the fact that the clocks were imported from a French mass-producer. You have only to look at the serial number on an imported clock to see that it can run into many thousands. But let us go back to the beginning of the history of clockmaking, and consider how a clockmaker learned his trade, what he could do, and how.

The usual way in which a clockmaker learned his craft was through an apprenticeship, though this was by no means always the case. Some clockmakers were self-taught and were very proud of the fact, like Thomas Peirce of Berkeley, Gloucestershire, 'whom no man taught', as was claimed on his tombstone in 1665. These self-taught clockmakers began as an offshoot of the early smithing trades, principally in country districts, and often called themselves 'clocksmiths'.

APPRENTICESHIP

The recognised manner of entry into the craft, or 'mystery' as it was sometimes called, was through a formal apprenticeship, whereby a youngster was given a thorough and extensive training by a fully-qualified master-craftsman. The rules of apprenticeship were strict from the earliest times. A statute of 1563 specified that an apprentice must serve a term of seven years under his master, that he was not allowed to marry before the age of twenty-four (in other words till well after he had completed his training), nor could he work before that age either on his own account or even under another clockmaker, which latter method was known as working as a 'journeyman'. This word derives from the French word *journée* (a day), and indicates one who was paid for his work by the day. Before long these age limitations ceased to be applied so rigorously.

A formal contract was drawn up, known as an indenture, which set out the terms of the apprenticeship, and which was signed by the master on the one hand and by the parents of the boy on the other. Sometimes, of course, there were 'apprenticeships' which were merely a loose, even purely verbal, arrangement between master and parents, so that there may not have been an indenture on every occasion. Such a situation might apply, for instance, where a father taught the craft to his son, or an uncle to a nephew. But there was a recognised and proper way of going about it, and it generally suited both parties to have this set out in its official form. Such documents would often be thrown away once their immediate usefulness had become obsolete, though a clockmaker might well have kept such indentures throughout his working life, especially in case he might need to produce proof of his training at some future time.

For instance, in 1630, when Ahasuerus Fromanteel applied to join the Blacksmiths' Company, who controlled the London clock trade before the founding of the Clockmakers' Company, he was turned away until he could return bringing proof of the apprenticeship he had served in Norwich – which he did a month later. Lewis Cooke had practised his craft in York as early as 1614, and when the newly-formed Clockmakers' Company asked him in 1632 to produce proof of his apprenticeship, it is not difficult to imagine the indignation of a master clockmaker of over twenty years' standing. He refused point-blank and left 'with much ill language'. Presumably he did eventually comply, for he entered the Company officially soon after, but found himself having to eat humble pie: 'I did give the said John Harris the lye and told him he was a botcher and that he never made so good a piece of work in his life as that was which he found fault withall; these words being rashly and inadvisedly spoken I am heartily sorry'.

So apprenticeship indentures tend to survive only by chance, and for many thousands of clockmakers of the past no such documents are known to survive today. Occasionally such things come to light in a parish chest, or in bundles of old papers lodged with solicitors. Fortunately there was a period, from 1710 to 1810, when a tax was levied on such contracts, which meant that government officials were certain to record each one and to keep copies of such paperwork as was relevant to it. The indentures themselves were not preserved by government deparments, but only the relevant details such as names of the parties, trade, terms of service, premium and, of course, the tax paid.

There was no set form of indenture agreement which applied nationally, but local custom would determine the precise arrangements. An indenture of 1696, under which clockmaker Henry Harper of London took into service young Richard Allen from Pangbourne, Berkshire, speficied the following points. The period was to be seven years. The apprentice shall faithfully serve the master, willingly obey him, cause no damage or wastage, shall not commit fornication nor contract matrimony, shall not play at cards, dice or any other unlawful games, shall neither buy nor sell, shall not haunt taverns or play-houses, shall not absent himself without leave. In return the master shall teach him 'in the same art which he useth', and shall provide meat, drink, apparel, lodging 'and all other necessaries according to the custom of the City of London'.

This was the basic form of indenture, though conditions varied in different areas. The indenture of Thomas Lister from Keighley, who was apprenticed in 1730 to John Stancliffe of Barkisland, Halifax, covers the same basic points with a few variations: the apprentice was not to frequent taverns or alehouses, play at dice, cards, tables or bowls. In return, the master would teach him in 'the art, trade, mastery and occupation of a clockmaker', would provide him with meat, drink, lodging and washing . . . and allow unto his said Apprentice two weeks yearly to go to School to learn to write and pay unto his said Apprentice yearly during the said term five shillings'. Young Thomas was thirteen years of age at the time. The time off for schooling and the pocket money of five shillings a year were unusual aspects, offering a better deal than that given to most youngsters. It may have been that the terms were generous on account of the fact that Thomas's mother was a widow and would have had difficulty in finding money from her own meagre income.

There is a further indication that Stancliffe was a particularly lenient master. Apprentices were forbidden to sign their work because, of course, any work they performed was the property of the master and was sold under the master's name. Even if this was not explicitly written into the terms of service, it was established practice throughout the trade at all times. However, just occasionally one finds the name of an apprentice, or more usually a journeyman, engraved *inside* the movement, where it would only be seen by some other clockmaker who might dismantle the clock for repair. I myself recall seeing a Stancliffe clock with Thomas Lister's name boldly engraved on the movement frontplate, along with the year, 1731. This could hardly have escaped Stancliffe's notice, so the implication is that he permitted it. It may seem surprising that Thomas was already capable of engraving at the age of only fourteen, but his late father, William Lister, had himself been a clockmaker at Keighley, so no doubt Thomas went to Stancliffe with considerable skills already learned, despite his tender years.

At this period, apprentices were not normally paid anything beyond food and lodging. Moreover, most clockmakers insisted on a fee, called a premium, from the parents (probably to cover variables such as clothing). This fee might be anything from a few shillings, depending no doubt on how famous the master was, and could be as high as thirty pounds or more. The amount was settled by agreement. In 1666, the famous clockmaker Ahasuerus Fromanteel was involved in a legal dispute, having married a widow, whose children he had trained in his trade. In pointing out how much he had spent on his step-children, he argued that he had trained them as his own apprentices 'for which he deserveth to have £20, for he has not had less from any apprentice during these last 20 years'. At that time £20 was a large sum, and equated to one years' wages for a journeyman.

The normal age at which a boy was apprenticed was fourteen. In the early days, however, there were abuses of the system, and youngsters were sometimes apprenticed as young as thirteen or even younger, and on rare occasions as young as eleven. In these cases, the term was often lengthened to eight or even ten years, so that he would complete his service at the age of twenty-one. In the early years of the Clockmakers' Company of London, which was founded in 1632, such abuses of the system occurred, and the Company did its best to stamp them out. It would sometimes order an apprenticeship to be cancelled and the lad re-bound a year or two later, when he reached the appropriate age. Such examples were probably a deliberate ploy on the part of the clockmaker, who often saw an apprentice as a source of cheap labour. The Company tried hard to prevent this, and also regulated the number of apprentices employed at any one time, partly to preserve the good name of the craft, but also no doubt in the interests of helping their fully-qualified members find employment.

Sometimes these situations arose by mischance, as in those days there were no such things as birth certificates, and youngsters, and even parents, were sometimes unaware of their true ages. This could well happen in the case of orphans or foundlings, but also to boys from quite normal families.

About seven years ago I discovered a manuscript volume entitled *A short account of the life and travels of James Upjohn of Red*

Lion Street, Clerkenwell, clock and watch maker and Goldsmith by Company copied into this book by A. Upjohn, 1784. It is a quite amazing volume recording many details of the trade and working methods. I know of no other manuscript of this nature, but as I bought it by way of business, I could not afford to keep it for myself. I sold it to the Worshipful Company of Clockmakers of London, where it will be preserved. The manuscript describes just such a situation, in which James worked under his own father, Edward Upjohn, a clockmaker at Topsham in Devon. His father 'set as many of us as were able to work; for I remember I was obliged to work between school hours and after I came home from school; my father never suffered any of us to be idle . . . I was taken from school at eleven years old, and I can remember five of us (*ie.* his brothers) all at work at one time at Topsham, in making clocks and watches completely within ourselves'.

It happened about the year 1743 that he was working one day with his elder brother, William, when they asked their father when their term of apprenticeship would end. He replied it would be when they were twenty-one. As they were unsure when that might be, the two secretly went together to check in the church registers for their dates of baptism, the only means then available of verifying their ages, only to find they were already over twenty-one. When they mentioned this to their father, he flew into a violent rage, and struck James a blow that knocked him off his workstool. The next day James packed his bags and left home with only five shillings in the world.

The wastage rate amongst apprentices was high, especially in London, where something like three out of every four failed to complete their terms of service, for whatever reason. Poor working conditions, combined with strenuous work over what seem by our standards to be unreasonably long hours, took their toll. Some took sick, and died in service. Others could bear it no longer and ran away. When we hear some of the reports from contemporary accounts, it is hardly surprising. In 1786, apprentice Thomas Mitchell raised complaint against his master 'for not giving him sufficient food, sleeping in the coal hole, not having had clean sheets since last February, repeatedly beating him in a cruel manner and keeping the lad to work from 5 o'clock in the morning till 2 or 3 o'clock next morning'.

Clockmakers often advertised in the local press for suitable youngsters to learn the trade. In 1804, for instance, clockmaker Thomas Shepherd of Wotton-under-Edge advertised for 'an able active Country lad of good character, from 13 to 14 years of age. No extra degree of School Education is required; a disposition in favour of the business, with proper talents and application to it, are qualities essentially necessary. A premium will be expected'. Sometimes the premium was waived, perhaps for a promising lad from a poor background. In 1793 Walter Mayers of Gloucester advertised for 'a Youth of reputable parents, and good natural abilities is likewise wanted as an apprentice. The premium will not be so much the object as his capacity, for he will be expected to work'.

And work they did. Apprentices were traditionally given the most tedious jobs. Filing and smoothing brass plates was a dirty and repetitive job, and apprentices always got more than their share of those. Cutting and filing of clock-hands is another task said traditionally to have been done by apprentices. Another is chain-making, that is, making the winding chains for thirty-hour longcase clocks, where hundreds of wire pieces were cut to length and bent into links by a special tool similar to a pair of pliers. Chain-making is often said to have been done by the female members of the household as they sat by the fireside of an evening, being an alternative to knitting.

For bracket clocks, small chains were made, known as fusee chains, and for watches even smaller ones. Watch-chains were said to have been imported from specialist makers in France before 1790. The first bulk maker of fusee watch-chains in England was Robert Cox of Christchurch in Hampshire, who drew up agreements with various workhouses to employ young girls at this task. They worked as long as seventy hours a week for little over a shilling in wages, which in any case they never received personally for it would go into the workhouse funds. A comment on Christchurch in 1834 runs 'The only manufactory here is that of Watch fusee Chains, by which many poor children are rendered nearly, if not totally blind, that business being extremely prejudicial to the sight, and mostly performed by children'.

By the nineteenth century, apprentices did receive a wage of sorts, albeit a small one. In 1889, Henry Myers Todd was bound apprentice for six years to Edward Hird, a clockmaker at Ulverston in Lancashire, who is said to have 'looked like King Edward, with a little pointed beard'. He received 2s. 6d. (£0.13) in his first year, 3s. 0d. (£0.15) in the second, rising to 8s. 0d. (£0.40) in his final year.

The Clockmakers' Company attempted to regulate the trade in London, and in most cities and larger towns the local guilds did the same. There were very real abuses of the system, which they sought to prevent. In 1641, for example, the Clockmakers' Company banned Francis Starley from the trade, who confessed when challenged that 'he was not served an apprenticeship, but only spent six weeks with Mr Stillinger'. That they were successful seems to be proven by the fact that no clock or watch appears to have come to light bearing Starley's name, the implication being that he did in fact abandon the trade as ordered.

No member of the trade was allowed to practise within the jurisdiction of any guild until he had completed his apprentice-ship, or proved his competence, or both. Some devious characters occasionally tried to dodge the system by using apprenticeship as a bypass. The most flagrant example I have come across was discovered by the Clockmakers' Company in 1691, when 'Abraham Strachan, a Scot, between 30 and 40 years, and no freeman, for several years past has worked here without consent, and avoided prosecution by moving from place to place – hath this July bound himself (apprentice) for seven years to Thomas Warden', to avoid redress. At forty he was probably the oldest apprentice in history, but the Company cancelled it.

Not all apprentices were satisfactory, as we can see from an advertisement in the *Salopian Journal* of 1802: 'Whereas Samuel Pedley, Clock Maker, is under an agreement to Robert Webster of this Town for nearly Two years to come (*ie.* as an apprentice), notwithstanding which he scarcely works one-third of his Time, and that without any just cause but the Effect of Idleness and Drunkenness. This is therefore to warn all Persons whomsoever against harbouring or employing him after this notice, as they will be dealt with as the law directs'. Such a threat was a serious one and was usually effective, as Samuel Pedley's name never again appeared as a clockmaker. This is what was known as a 'runaway apprentice', and such people were blacklisted in the trade.

An advertisement in the *Cumberland Pacquet* in December 1790 runs:

> APPRENTICE RAN AWAY. Penrith 24th of 12th Month 1790. Whereas John Thompson (son of John Thompson of Wigton, Clockmaker) an indentured apprentice to William Wilkinson (late of Wigton) Clockmaker, ran away from his said Master some time ago . . . Notice is hereby given that whoever harbours or employs the said Apprentice, shall be prosecuted as the law directs . . . William W.

However, the apprentice's father was not content to let it pass at that, but took an advertisement himself shortly after:

> TO THE PUBLIC. Whereas an advertisement appeared in the Cumberland Pacquet of the 29th Ult. (*previous month*) under signature of WILLIAM WILKINSON of Penrith, Clockmaker, charging his apprentice John Thompson . . . with having some time ago deserted his apprenticeship, The said apprentice's father will give a sufficient indemnity to any person who may employ or harbour his son and take every method to chastise Wilkinson's insolence; and that the public may not be deceived by his fictitious advertisement, the following facts are laid before them, viz. The young man in March 1787 was

under necessity of leaving his master, for want of victuals and other bad treatment and about that time a Magistrate (the late Dr Dunn of Lowther) on hearing both parties, ordered him home to his parents with a severe reprimand to Wilkinson who has ever since known where the said apprentice was, and whose term elapsed the 5th of April last and shortly after Wilkinson directed the gentleman who had the custody of the indentures to cancel them, without (before or since) making any demand of the young man as his apprentice, till very lately, when he saw him at work with Mr Lough, watchmaker, in Penrith when a jealous and malevolent disposition instigated his insolent advertisement. John Thompson Senr. Wigton. Jan 8th 1791.

Upon completion of his apprenticeship, the fully-trained clock-maker was then free to offer his services to a master. The conditions applying to his employment as a journeyman varied with different regions. For the most part he was at liberty to offer himself for employment wherever he wished, though in some districts, and especially in the seventeenth century, he was expected to work for another year or so under the same master. Completion of his term of apprenticeship also freed him from such restrictions as the inability to marry, and many youngsters married very shortly after their term ended. To 'pass out' as a fully-qualified clockmaker at the end of his service, an apprentice was required in many areas to apply for 'freedom' by joining the local guild. This applied principally in London and the larger towns, and in these places, where the guild control was strong, he was barred from trading in his own right or even working as a journeyman until he had formally received his 'freedom'. In almost all rural areas, the guilds had no powers, and he was at liberty to please himself.

THEORY AND PRACTICE

What did the apprentice actually learn to do during his seven-year training in the 'art and mystery' of clockmaking? In theory, he learned to make every single part of a clock or watch, and generally speaking a master would concentrate on either watches or clocks, but not usually on both. From quite early times a maker would specialise in one or the other, although he had to understand and be able to repair both. There were exceptions, but by and large the two trades were seen as being separate, though overlapping.

First, the apprentice would have to learn how to calculate the mathematical niceties of wheelwork, and for some this meant going back to basics to learn their multiplication tables first. Occasional surviving jotting-books of apprentices have a tables sheet, to be consulted and learned. From very early times there was a considerable degree of specialisation in the trade, especially with watchmaking. The maker had to learn how to do everything, even though in practical, everyday work he would not be required to make everything himself. Spring-making, for instance, was almost always regarded as a separate offshoot, and clock and watch makers would buy-in their springs from a man who did nothing else. The same applied to a varying degree with most watch parts, and even to a lesser extent with clock parts. Clock spandrels for dials were often supplied by brassfounders, and few clockmakers would cast their own – though the apprentice supposedly had to know how to. He would certainly need to know how to cast brass, and what components made up its composition.

Those brass parts which would suffer friction and wear (such as wheels and clock-plates) were hardened by hammering, known as planishing, then filed smooth and polished to try to give a good finish and an even thickness (though cast brass was seldom of uniform thickness). Files played a much more important part in such work in the past, and there were very many types of file for all manner of work which might in later times be done by other means. One inventory of a watchmaker's tools taken in 1600 included 248 different files. Wheel-cutting was done by hand initially, though the spacing of the teeth round the wheel was done by means of a dividing plate, to ensure uniform distances between teeth. Later, a cutting disc was incorporated into the dividing plates and was called a wheel-cutting engine. The teeth at that stage were rectangular, and had to have the tips 'rounded up' by hand filing.

MAKING OR BUYING PARTS

The laying out of the clock's 'trains', as it sets of wheels were called, would be based on well-known formulae, but each master might have his own preferred variations on a theme, which might well be passed on to his apprentice but were probably kept secret from rivals. This would especially apply if he were to invent some unusual feature of his own design. The pinions, which were the smaller gears linking the brass wheels, were made of iron. In the early days these were filed out of the solid by hand, but before the end of the seventeenth century a method was invented of drawing pinion wire. This involved forcing steel rod through a number of cutting plates, until with the final draw the whole rod came out as one long pinion. This could be bought by clockmakers as pinion wire, and unwanted sections turned off to leave the required pinion itself. An apprentice might well learn to file a pinion up by hand, but in his normal work he would almost always be working from pinion wire. As time went by he would rely increasingly on specialists who could produce his parts more cheaply and more efficiently, so that his main time could be spent on constructing clocks or watches, rather than on making each part himself, before beginning to construct the movement proper.

In the year 1747, the *London Tradesman* summarised the situation as follows, with particular reference to watches, but in a lesser degree also applicable to clocks:

> The movement maker forges his wheels of brass to the just dimensions: sends them to the cutter, and has them cut at trifling expence: he has nothing to do when he takes them from the cutter but to finish them and turn the corners of the teeth. The pinions made of steel are drawn at the mill, so that the watchmaker has only to file down the pivots, and fix them to their proper wheels.
>
> The springs are made by a tradesman who does nothing else, and the chains by another: these last are frequently made by women in the country about London, and sold to the watchmaker by the dozen for a very small price. It requires no great ingenuity to learn to make watch chains, the instruments made for that use render the work quite easy, which to the eye would appear very difficult.
>
> There are workmen who make nothing else but the caps and studs for watches, and silversmiths who only make cases, and workmen who cut the dial plates, or enamel them, which is of late becoming much the fashion.
>
> When the watchmaker has got home all the movements of the watch, and the other different parts of which it consists, he gives the whole to a finisher, who puts the whole machine together, having had the brass wheels gilded by the guilder, and adjusts it to a proper time. The watchmaker puts his name upon the plate, and is esteemed the maker, though he has not made in his shop the smallest wheel belonging to it.

So, having learned how to make every item himself, the apprentice watchmaker would spend his time mostly in finishing and assembling, and not in the actual making. With clocks, a far greater proportion of the item was constructed by the tradesman himself. By the early nineteenth century it was possible for the clockmaker to buy in movements ready-made in sets, with only the finishing left for him to do, and, of course, the assembling. In practice, however, a great many clockmakers, especially provincial ones, did continue their own making of parts well into the 1830s and 1840s. The question of how to recognise one from the other, and whether it matters anyway, will be discussed later.

The answer to the question of how much each clockmaker did for himself varies. An extreme instance is perhaps that quoted in a letter of 1755 by a mining surveyor writing about the parish of Asby in Westmorland. The spelling is that of the original. 'In this parish is a coper mine in which a Clock Smith digs all his coper he uses, having smelted it himself: it (*having*) so fine a colour, he makes wach cases & sells 'em for pinchbeck. He is all has overworked (= *always overworked*) being in a remote place 'tis scarce known'. Pinchbeck was an alloy which resembled gold and was used as a cheaper alternative. The maker referred to is probably William Powley.

ENGRAVING

One facet of clock and watch making, and a very important one, was that of engraving, for that was the decoration which adorned the dial of the clock, and, in watches, the case too. Engraving was vitally important, as fine engraving might help sell even a modestly-made item, whereas poor engraving might hamper the sale of even the finest mechanical movement. Apprentices did learn how to engrave, but from the earliest times this skill tended to be a specialist field, and the best work usually came from those who spent their time doing nothing else. Those who made watch

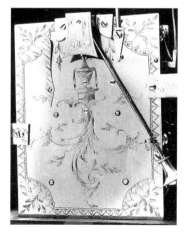

2. *Backplate from a London bracket clock of the third quarter of the eighteenth century, showing typical engraved decoration, the bob pendulum of the verge escapement resting here in its carrying hook.*

cases often also specialised in engraving work. In 1700, Sir William Chaytor wrote a letter from London to his home in Croft, North Yorkshire: 'I am now my dear heart got into a good convenient neat little private lodging first floor at Mr Beekman's, an ingraver at the Golden Ball next door to Mr Maddox . . . My landlord is an ingraver and watch case maker . . . a good-humored man and his

old housekeeper Mistress Hooton a widow.' He refers to Daniel
Beeckman, who was paid forty shillings in 1695 for engraving the
coat of arms of the Clockmakers' Company on a new copperplate.

There were those who specialised in engraving of all kinds from
quite early times, even in the provinces. In 1759, John Butterworth
advertised in the *Leeds Mercury* as an 'engraver in the Bull and Bell
Yard in Briggate, engraves all sorts of bills, clock faces, etc . . .'
Also in Leeds was Sylvester Forrest, who advertised in 1768 as
'seal-cutter and copperplate printer . . . clock faces engraved &
finished'.

William Marston of Shrewsbury was a clockmaker who could
also engrave, and he advertised in 1791 'arms, crests, cyphers, etc.
neatly engraved, either concave or convex. NB Marston scorns to
puff about doing what he is not perfectly master of himself'.

In 1784, John Morgan of Thornbury, Gloucestershire, advertised
that he: 'makes clocks and watches, rings, sundials, electrical
machines and apparatus, thermometers, barometers, etc. Coats of
arms, crests, cyphers engraved on plate, seals, etc . . . will engrave
and varnish for country clock-makers, or serve them with dial-
plates as cheap as in Bristol or London.' In the early nineteenth
century, Charles Blakeway, clockmaker, of Albrighton, Shropshire,
offered: 'wheels cut for clockmakers at 6d. (£0.03) per set and dyal
plates engraved at 2s. 6d. (£0.13). A note about James Simpson, a
clockmaker in the late nineteenth century in Dunfermline, records
that 'he used an engraver, Dawson, who inhabited a Bruce Street
attic, a drunkard. He engraved coffin lid plaques as well as putting
watchmaker's (*ie.* watch retailer's) names on the back plates of
factory-made watch movements'.

James Upjohn relates in his memoirs that, when they worked
as a family at Topsham, his brother, Edward, carried out all the
engraving work – 'he engraved all our watches at my father's
house' – yet Edward died at a little over the age of twenty-one! So
engravers often specialised even at an early age.

PRACTICE ENGRAVING

It is not uncommon to find examples of practice engraving
hidden by the clock dial, only for it to be revealed during cleaning.
It occurs more often on brass dial clocks, naturally, since the rear
of the dial was a large area where there was space for such practice.
Brass was a costly commodity. In the eighteenth century it was
priced at ten pence per pound weight, against one penny per
pound for iron. Cast brass, which had been planished and
smoothed ready for drilling for clock-plates or even for dial sheet
use, was far too costly to provide free for apprentices to practise
their engraving on. So anyone wanting to improve his engraving
or lettering techniques would have to try his hand on any odd
scraps of smoothed brass before they went into the scrap box.

Waste metals, including filings, were always kept, and were known as shruff. Such scrap was either traded in to a metal merchant or melted down for re-use by the clockmaker himself.

The high value of worked metals was probably the main reason why clockmakers were willing to take in old clocks in part exchange for new ones. Old receipts often show a discount given by the clockmaker on the new item in exchange for an old clock. Sometimes the old clock was cleaned up, re-bushed and serviced, and sold again, perhaps with a new dial to 'modernise' it to the fashion of the day. More often, however, its value to the clockmaker lay in its re-usable metal value.

It follows that clockmakers, and probably apprentices too, would sometimes practise engraving on unseen parts of a clock. The hidden back part of a chapter ring was a favourite place, or the hidden front side of the movement frontplate. Such practice work was normally only seen by another clockmaker, when he took the clock apart for repairs. Sometimes such practice was confined to a letter or two, or a flower-head, simply, it is said, as a means of testing the sharpness of the engraving tool. This kind of single-letter testing is often found on a lantern clock dial, on the part of the dial sheet that was covered by the alarm disc.

Sometimes, however, the engraver would really get carried away into what must have been several hours of practice work. A clock of the 1760s which I recently examined had the following lines on the movement frontplate (Plate 3):

> Richard Jackson a plate of brass
> will you go and drink a glass
> hah hah ha.

The clock was made by John Greaves of Newcastle upon Tyne. Richard Jackson was another clockmaker working at nearby Hexham about the same time. Whether Greaves engraved this wording himself as some sort of joke against his rival is uncertain, but this seems likely. Perhaps Jackson was known to be fond of the bottle. Engraved vertically up the edge of the same frontplate is:

> what spels dick well
> it spels Richard sure.

This none too subtle comment that 'dick' is an alternative for Richard, suggests that Jackson was not popular with Greaves!

A longcase clock of about 1770 which I once had, made by Thomas Radford of Leeds, had a movement frontplate simply covered with the most beautiful engraving of scrollwork, flowers, lovers' knots, and lettering, including 'Time Flieth', 'Yorkshire', and *'Labor Omnia'*, (being part of the phrase *'Labor Omnia Vincit'*,

3. An eight-day clock of the mid-eighteenth century by John Greaves of Newcastle upon Tyne, the dial removed to show practice engraving work. The derogatory remarks (see text) are believed to refer to rival clockmaker Richard Jackson of Hexham.

meaning 'Work overcomes everything'). In fact, the practice engraving on the hidden frontplate was far better in quality than the engraved dial sheet itself!

Another example was a thirty-hour longcase clock of the 1770s that I once had, on which the reverse of the chapter ring was filled with practice engraving. There were several alphabets in full, in varying scripts. The clock was by James Head of Evesham (Plate 4), and the practice included several attempts at the word 'James'. I deduced that this was done by the maker himself.

Sometimes one finds an example where a serious slip or perhaps a spelling mistake has happened during engraving, and the clockmaker has turned his chapter ring over and started anew on the blank side. This is not quite the same thing as practice work, but leaves an interesting record just the same.

For those makers who could not engrave, there were ample services of engravers available, even if perhaps at some distance away – and in the early days of provincial clockmaking engravers might be spread very thin. For those who wished, there were clockmakers who would supply them with any or all parts. In 1750 the *Ipswich Journal* advertised: 'Supplied from London. All sorts of clocks and mathematical work also brass plates for coffins, etc. by Mandeville Somersall, Clock-engraver and Varnisher, in Fore Street, near Moorgate, London, where country chapmen may be furnished with all sorts of clock plates completely fitted up; as also

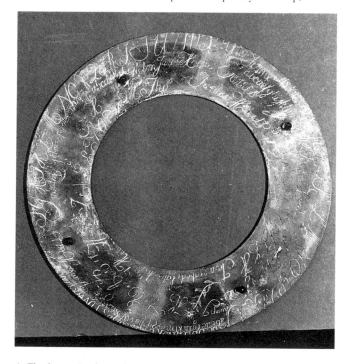

4. The chapter ring from a thirty-hour longcase clock of the 1760s by James Head of Evesham. The back of the chapter ring can be seen to have been used for practice engraving with numerals and alphabets, an indication that brass was too valuable to be used for practice alone.

all sorts of tools or materials for clock and watch making at the lowest prices'.

JOURNEYMEN

An interesting illustration of the degree of specialisation within the watch trade is found in James Upjohn's memoirs. When he left his father's workshop, where he had worked as an unpaid apprentice, he moved first to Crewkerne, where he worked for a family friend, clockmaker John Thomas. There he earned one guinea a week, and was shown balance wheel and fusee making, something he had not done when with his father. In 1743 he moved to London, where he lodged with watchmaker Thomas Dale. 'I told Mr Dale I could make a watch from beginning to end, which he would not believe'; such was the degree of specialisation in London by that time. So James made a watch to prove his point, which Mr Dale bought from him. James found he could earn as much as forty-six shillings in two weeks doing the very same work he had been doing as an 'apprentice' under his father for nothing but his keep.

The journeyman clockmaker, then, once he took up paid employment, moved into a world where considerable earnings were possible.

It is quite difficult to assess the rates of pay of a journeyman, as few examples can be found in old records. Inflation in the seventeenth, eighteenth and nineteenth centuries was very much lower than in recent times, and has little bearing on values. In 1655, William Rogers, a London clockmaker, took Abraham Vanacker as journeyman for four months at five shillings weekly, later six shillings. However this may have been a lower rate than normal, as being a temporary arrangement only, especially as he seems to have been a foreigner who was not officially permitted to work there anyway, and so probably was unable to shop around for a better offer.

From the eighteenth century we have the example of James Dawson, who worked in 1769 for Moses Jacob of Redruth for sixteen shillings a week as a journeyman clockmaker. In 1783, Nathaniel Cavell, the Ipswich clockmaker, advertised for a journeyman, stating that 'a good hand will have eighteen shillings a week and constant work'. From the study of such records as exist, it seems that a self-employed master clockmaker in the provinces was doing quite well to earn one pound a week. James Upjohn thought himself well off as a journeyman in Crewkerne in 1743 on one guinea a week, but, once established as a master in London, he had reached the position by 1768 that he had made £1,251 that year, after allowing for expenses! Within ten years Upjohn had saved over £1,000, and after 25 years he had £8,385. But then, he was a successful watchmaker in the capital, and by no means all such craftsmen were.

From his income of around £50 a year the journeyman had his living expenses. James Upjohn, then a bachelor, took lodgings with a Mr Ward in Berkeley Street for £20 a year. John Hocking, a married clockmaker in Lostwithiel, wrote to his parents in 1824 (as H. Miles Brown tells us in *Cornish Clocks & Clockmakers*) to say he could not help them out financially: 'I ave moor work thin I can fitely do. I can't keep a clock in the shop . . . I have took a house of Mr Lanyon, the rent and outes alltogether is £21 0s. 0d. per year, money enuf for me to get'.

WORKMASTERS

A journeyman worked for a master clockmaker, usually within the master's premises. He might be the only workman in the business, apart from the master himself and an apprentice or two. Or he might be one of as many as a dozen in a larger concern. The famous clockmaker Thomas Tompion worked at the sign of The Dial and Three Crowns, and in 1695 a rates assessment showed that he had five journeymen and eight apprentices. The Clockmakers' Company forbade an employer more than two apprentices at any one time, three in special circumstances. However, there were innumerable ways of bending the rules, or even of ignoring the rules altogether until found out. For instance, Tompion might have done what many did, which was to get someone who had fewer apprentices than his allotted number to take an extra one or two that he did not want, and then pass those over to Tompion.

But that is only part of the picture, because a master clockmaker like Tompion with a large business demand could very well employ separate independent master clockmakers, who may have worked in their own workshops, each with a number of journeymen and apprentices. So in effect, he could have had dozens of people working for him, though not under his own roof.

A journeyman was not allowed to trade in his own right, nor to sign clocks or any other work. Anything he produced was the property of his master and bore the master's name – even if the master himself had never laid a finger on it. In such an extreme case, the master would be no more than an employer, but in the ordinary way of things the master clockmaker was a working craftsman as well as an employer, designer, inventor, shopkeeper, debt-collector, and marketing manager.

It is strange, then, that occasionally we do find examples of the name of someone other than the master inside a clock. A clock by Thomas Tompion is known with the name Harry Callot (or Callowe) engraved inside. Callot is known to have been a journeyman under Tompion, and his name could hardly have been engraved there without being noticed by the master. The assumption must therefore be that a master would sometimes allow a journeyman's work to be credited in this way. Even if the customer would not see it, any future clock restorer would notice it, and the craftsman's talents would not be entirely uncredited or forgotten.

I have seen several clocks by Robert Parkinson of Lancaster with the name Joshua Harrocks engraved inside, and on one occasion with the date 1746 on the movement frontplate. Harrocks set up in business on his own account in 1748, so the implication is that he worked prior to that as journeyman to Parkinson, and that the master allowed him this privilege. On the other hand, a late seventeenth-century wall clock I once saw by Joseph Knibb of London had engraved inside it the name of Francis Stamper, who never at any time (so far as we can establish such things) worked as journeyman for Knibb. The implication is more likely that Stamper was his own master, but did jobs for Knibb as an outworker in his own premises, and delivered the job to Knibb bearing the Stamper name, discreetly hidden away inside the movement so that Knibb could still sell it bearing his own name up front.

I have sometimes seen clocks with a hidden journeyman's name of this sort described as being 'apprentice pieces', ie. some sort of test piece which an apprentice made to qualify for mastership, though while still in his master's employ. This is no more than a romantic notion, and no proof has ever been offered to justify such claims. In any case, how would someone like Harrocks have made so many 'apprentice pieces'?

The step from journeyman to self-employed master clockmaker was one not all clockmakers took. Some were content to work as journeymen for their entire lives. It is likely that they lacked the capital to set up alone, or the entrepreneurial spirit, or simply wanted to take the money without the responsibility. John Philipson, a clockmaker who worked at Winster in Westmorland, was born in 1726 and died in 1788, and spent his entire working life from apprenticeship onwards working for Jonas Barber senior. Many clocks survive with Barber's name, but only a single one with John Philipson's name, and that a complicated musical clock dated 1787. It is believed that he made this clock for himself as his health was failing (for he died within the year) in order that at least one clock would survive which bore his name. This clock is now in Abbot Hall Museum, Kendal.

Samuel Chilver of Halesworth, Suffolk, was a clockmaker who died in 1835 aged seventy-three. His gravestone records: 'He was for 50 years in the employ of Mr George Suggate of this town, and served him honestly and faithfully'. Samuel never made a clock which bore his own name. His son, Samuel Chilver junior, worked for George Suggate junior as journeyman clockmaker until 1844, when George died. He then announced in the *Ipswich Journal*: 'S. Chilver, watchmaker, etc . . . (38 years assistant to the late Mr G. Suggate) . . . has succeeded to the business.' So here is an instance where father and son together spent eighty-eight years as employed journeymen clockmakers under the same concern, before patience was ultimately rewarded and they could finally sell clocks under their own name, or at least the survivor could!

Some clockmakers went from place to place hoping to find occasional or casual work. In 1796 the *Ipswich Journal* records: 'Inquest . . . one Thomas Hagon, a poor travelling watchmaker, who died at the Bell at Kesgrave. Jury's verdict, Visitation of God. It is imagined he was a native of Norwich'. Presumably he never settled in any one place, as his name is not recorded in any of the dictionaries of makers.

We can take it as a general guide, then, that the man whose name appears on the clock dial did actually make the clock himself (even if he had to pay a specialist engraver for that aspect) throughout the period of brass dial clockmaking, which ended by 1790 save for clocks of unusual nature, such as Regulators and occasional late examples of the single-sheet dial. The same men continued the same work into the white dial period until about 1820, after which some clockmakers increasingly bought in parts and did just the finishing themselves. Bracket clocks are in a slightly different category, as provincial makers seldom had the set-up to construct these, and, indeed, even most London makers would tend to have bought them from specialists.

The interesting aspect of those clocks which were made by the clockmaker himself is that each is a unique item (even if he made many of them), and a testimony to that man's skills and ingenuity. But is it actually a rarity, how rare is 'rare', and does rarity in itself make the clock desirable or especially valuable? Well, in brief, value has nothing at all to do with rarity but with demand, and demand is purely a measure of how many people would want, and could afford, to own a clock. As a dealer in clocks, I often like to buy strange clocks, which could be described as rare, yet some are so strange that they prove very slow to sell.

Conversely, there are types of clock which are highly commercial because they fit easily into modern homes and tastes, and even though they were made in their thousands, have no great age, and may be of very mediocre quality, can nevertheless be highly saleable and bring a much higher price by virtue of that demand than older, scarcer, and higher quality items.

All the same, the question of scarcity is one which the owner would like answered. How does his clock fit into the overall history of clocks? Could one hope to go out without a fortune to spend and buy a clock of 100, 200, 300 years old? What exists to choose from? We often hear it said that London-made clocks are best. Are they, and if so, why? Is a provincial clock more or less common than a London one? What is the real difference between them, apart from the mere place of origin? To understand some of these aspects, we need to look closely into how the clockmaking trade was spread round the country, and why.

The relationship between clocks made in London and those made elsewhere in Britain is often misunderstood. In 1500, when one in fifty of the English population lived in London, clockmaking was virtually unknown there. In 1700, by which time one English person in ten lived there, London was the clockmaking centre of the world. The developments in the domestic clock had reached such a point by 1700 in London, that pretty well all later British clocks followed the pattern that was already then established. We shall examine just what those developments were in due course. But the special place of London in the history of clockmaking was not solely on account of the fact that one tenth of the population lived there, though that was one factor. London housed the Court of the monarch and was therefore a centre of the more affluent members of society, both aristocracy and merchants. It had a ready connection with Europe and the rest of the world through its port, bringing both cultural and commercial contact. London was therefore a wealthy centre where a market existed for the very best that could be conceived by the finest craftsmen in the land.

The clock trade in London was strictly controlled to ensure that inferior work was not allowed to enter the marketplace at all. So it was here that the very best in clockwork flourished. The reputation of London work as being of high quality was justly earned and persisted almost as a legend long after provincial makers had arisen who were themselves capable of magnificent work. It is this relationship between London work and that which developed in the provinces which we shall consider in the next chapter.

2 LONDON AND PROVINCIAL, TOWN AND COUNTRY

In London, clockmaking was recognised as a separate craft in 1632, when the Worshipful Company of Clockmakers was established, its function being to control the trade. Previously, clockmakers had worked under the auspices of some other City Company, such as the Blacksmiths' Company. The aim was to prohibit the sale of poor work, and to ban from trading those incapable of the required quality. In effect, the City Companies were a sort of 'closed shop', and no one was allowed to trade unless he had been admitted as a member, even if he were a highly-skilled and long-experienced craftsman. Provided he satisfied the authorities, a maker would be admitted as a 'freeman', which meant that he was free to ply his craft there.

Setting up in business as a clockmaker was not quite as simple a matter as it might sound, even if you were a highly capable craftsman and could survive financially until the money began to come in. There were two basic choices – to set up in town, or in the country. In the country you could do whatever you liked where you liked. The problem there was that customers were widely scattered, and in the very early days of rural clockmaking, which for most counties began about the year 1700, there were no existing customers at all. Country people had always managed without the aid of clocks, other than the local church clock. Sundials had long been in existence of course, but country people lived their lives largely based on the hours of daylight, and could manage their daily tasks without any timekeeper at all. By 1700 country gentry might well have had a clock or two in their homes, purchased no doubt from London or a nearby town (Plate 5). But most country people had no need of a clock of any kind, and for a man

5. Eight-day longcase of about 1710-20, by Thomas Clarke of Bosworth, Leics. The case is of fruitwood, height about 7ft 3in (221cms).

31

to set up in business in the expectation of selling them required considerable optimism – even assuming they had the spare funds with which to buy one.

CLOCKSMITHS

For this reason, the rural clockmaker did not usually set up his business from scratch in quite the same way as happened in the towns. Far more often he was a member of a local family who had worked in the metal crafts trades for generations. Such metalworkers as blacksmiths and whitesmiths had always existed in the country, and had turned their hand to all manner of metalworking and repairing, including even, on occasion, mending the local church clock. From blacksmithing to clocksmithing, as the early country clockmakers often termed their trade, was a relatively small move. Moreover, a man who was a third- or fourth-generation smith already had the goodwill of the local population, who had known his family's work as far back as memory reached. It was from these people that his first clock customers were likely to come.

The smith was a man gifted with all manner of powers. He could beat out crafted objects from raw metal, could make and repair anything of the least mechanical nature, from ploughs to cartwheels, swords to crossbows, even guns. His diversity of talents gave him a certain aura of mystery, and nowhere was this more apparent than in the magical motions of a clock. A man who could begin with iron bars and beat them into a machine which counted hours and days, sunrises and sunsets, full moons and new moons, was one who commanded great public respect. He could regulate Time itself, which in turn controlled everyone's life. The searing heat of his furnace had associations with Hell, Death and the Gods, for Thor himself was a smith. In the sixteenth century, superstitious beliefs still held the popular imagination. An old account of an unusual event exaggerated in the public mind runs:

> This yere, 1533, upon Twelfe day, in Shrewsbury the Dyvill appeared in St Alkmund's church there, when the preest was at High Masse, with great tempeste and darknesse, so that as he passed through the church he mountyd up the steeple of the said church tering the wyers of the said clocke, and put the print of his clawers upon the forth bell, and took one of the pinnacles away with him, and for the tyme stayed all the bells in the churches within the sayde towne, that they could neither toll nor ring.
>
> *Salopian Telegraph*, 1 January 1842

So the country clocksmith was simply adding clocks onto the total of his numerous capabilities, and was using talents he had learnt through generations of metalworking. To increase his clock trade and to attempt to reach a wider audience than his immediate locality permitted, he could attend weekly markets in nearby towns. At least, in theory he could, but much depended on the town, as in most of them, and certainly in all the larger ones, there existed local guilds, whose very purpose was to preserve trade for their own members and to keep out interlopers. They had the power to prevent outsiders coming to steal what they saw as their own local trade, and they used it.

PROVINCIAL GUILDS

Dorchester Borough Records recount that, in 1625, 'John Thomas, a Dutchman, complained against for using the trade of a Clockmaker within this Borough, is ordered to departe this Towne by Munday next'. A craftsman had to be accepted by either the local guild or the Corporation, or both before he was allowed to trade, and they laid down the rules by which he would be accepted into the fraternity. In most towns the guild covered all metalworking crafts, and was known as the Company of Smiths or the Guild of Hammermen, or some similar title.

When clockmaking formed into the beginnings of a separate trade, which for many places was in the first half of the seventeenth century, clockmakers were entered as one category of smiths. Provided they conformed to the requirements of the guild, they were given 'freedom' to trade there. In York, for instance, the first craftsman to become a clockmaker by name was William Kidson, who had formerly worked as a locksmith, but who in 1614 was admitted a freeman as a clockmaker, on condition that he would agree to work only on clocks, watches and dials (probably meaning sundials). The first 'clockmaker' classed as such in Shrewsbury was free in 1701, the first in Ludlow in 1710, Edinburgh in 1646, Glasgow in 1649, Aberdeen in 1672, Dorchester in 1625, Oxford in 1667. Of course, men who made clocks may well have worked in these places earlier, but the dates mentioned are those when they were admitted into the guild by that particular term.

Some clockmakers persisted in attempting to trade without the necessary 'freedom', but they were hounded by the authorities whenever they were discovered. Laurence Leicester of Wigan was denied freedom there in 1703, after which he was repeatedly fined until he eventually died in 1711 without ever having been free to trade there.

Not only did the guilds prevent 'foreigners' (by which they meant non-locals) from moving into the town to settle and ply their crafts, but they even prevented outsiders from coming to sell on a casual basis, such as in a market. In 1715, the Edinburgh Guild of Hammermen exercised one of their rights in searching the market for sign of any goods for sale by non-freemen, and they confiscated two clocks on sale there by John Sanderson, a Quaker clockmaker from Wigton in Cumberland. His clocks were returned to him on payment of a fine of 20 shillings and his written undertaking not to 'import into this burgh' any further clocks.

This requirement of freedom to trade in the towns sometimes resulted in clockmakers who lived and worked some distance away taking out freedom, which they would use on an occasional basis, such as for trading on Market Days. A number of clockmakers over the years took out freedom in Lancaster, although they lived elsewhere, and this was presumably purely for the purpose of attending markets.

GUILD FREEDOM

The guilds controlled the allocation of the right to trade known as the freedom. This in effect meant they also controlled the apprenticeship system in the towns, because the freedom was granted only after having served an apprenticeship which satisfied their requirements. Some guilds would admit those who had not been apprenticed under their jurisdiction, provided proof of adequate skill was provided. This was usually in the form of a piece of finished work, known as a 'masterpiece'. Today this term means something quite different, but originally it meant a piece offered up for inspection by an apprentice to a guild, who, provided they were satisfied with its quality, would then grant his right to work as a master craftsman. Some guilds insisted on a test piece, even from apprentices who had trained under their control. In 1717, for instance, Hugh Barclay, having completed his apprenticeship, presented to the Edinburgh Hammermen's guild what they term his 'essay piece' – 'presented his essay, viz an eight-day pendulum clock and a lock to the door, which was found a well-wrought essay . . .'

The guilds also carried out inspections of the workshops of their members, to check against poor workmanship. The Clockmakers' Company of London carried out regular searches for deficient work, and if they found any, it would be confiscated and defaced, or even smashed with a hammer, before being returned to the maker. The point, of course, was to prevent shoddy work being offered to the public whereby the trade might be brought into disrepute. The Company actually charged a search fee too, so any offending clockmaker not only had his goods confiscated, but also had to pay for the privilege. In November of 1688, for example, they searched the workrooms of Samuel Rosse, a watchmaker, and seized some faulty movements. Rosse not only refused to pay, but he and his wife 'gave them some very evil words'!

In 1652 a search was made at the house of Samuel Davis in Lothbury, and a 'chamber clock' (the old name for a lantern clock) was seized and broken, being deemed of poor quality 'that it might not be put to sale to defraud or deceive the people of the

Common Wealth', and he was fined 40 shillings. In 1682, they confiscated a watch from John Cotsworth, which had an invented name (John Rouden, London) and which they found 'unworkman-like and insufficient'. He pretended that it had been made by 'a little crookback man in Shoe Lane', but they didn't believe this, and he was fined.

FAKED NAMES

There were unscrupulous makers who not only traded without freedom and hoped to escape the notice of the authorities, but who thought nothing of faking the names of reputable makers on their own inferior goods. Faked items were made which bore such hallowed names as Thomas Tompion and Daniel Quare even during these makers' own lifetimes. In 1700, Charles Gretton, a reputed maker of many years' standing, complained to the Company that a Dutchman named Nicholas Vanstripe, a non-free watchmaker, 'hath latly made up a new silver watch and hath engraven theron "P. Gretton, London" . . . and Charles Gretton . . . who hath kept a publick watchmaker's shop above 20 years and sold great quantities of clocks and watches both at home and abroad . . . would know what course is best for him to take to sue the Dutchman'.

Such items bearing fake or invented names were said to have a 'fobbed' name. In 1683, some unfinished watch movements were seized from the shop of Jasper Harmer, 'an ironmonger near Smithfield Bars', which had on them suspect names: Ambrose Smith-Stamford, William Burges fecit, and Jaspar Harbar (sic), London. Not only had he invented these names; he had not served an apprenticeship anyway. We hear more of Jasper Harmer on page 193.

THE CLOCKMAKERS' COMPANY FREEDOM

The Clockmakers' Company of London was an extreme example of a craft guild in so far as their records are well preserved, and, of course, London was a very important centre of the craft, the most important clockmaking centre of the world in the seventeenth and eighteenth centuries. Entry into this company at any time involved the payment, not only of an entrance fee, but of an annual subscription, paid quarterly in fact, and known as 'quarterage'. The Clockmakers' Company differed from most town guilds in having two ranks of members. After satisfying the court as to his training, a clockmaker might enter as a free Brother or as a full Freeman. Technically, a Brother was not allowed to sign his work, and was therefore obliged to work as a journeyman under some other master who was a full Freeman. In practice this distinction was often blurred and its limitations on Brothers were seldom enforced, except perhaps when the administration dis-approved of a particular maker.

It was quite possible for a rural maker to move to London and apply for membership of the Company and to be accepted, provided he could prove his worth with a 'masterpiece', proof of training, and perhaps too a donation or payment of a fee. Strictly speaking, such a man entered with the lesser rank of Brother. In the other towns and cities, his admitted rank was that of a freeman, which conveyed all necessary rights of trading.

A good number of clockmakers, however, deliberately delayed applying for freedom, especially in the London company, as by doing so they could escape the entrance fee and quarterage.

Competition was always strongest in the towns and cities, because these naturally offered the greatest cluster of potential customers in conveniently close proximity. Even rural clockmakers, who may have serviced a widely-scattered community, found refuge in the markets of the towns to supplement what must have been a very meagre sprinkling of country customers in the earlier years of the eighteenth century. This, of course, was why the town and city guilds attempted to protect their local trade from outsiders by imposing the system of freedoms discussed earlier.

PROVINCIAL DISTRIBUTION

There had been pressure on the major English towns and cities since the earliest times of domestic clockmaking (say from about 1650) from too many clockmakers jockeying for privileged and protected trading there. In Scotland, where the population was much more dispersed, we see interesting examples in the eighteenth century of what had happened in English towns at a much earlier time. In Aberdeen, for instance, there had been one or more public clocks from the beginning of the fifteenth century, as was the case with many other towns. These may have been made and installed by clockmakers from afar in the absence of clock makers, and local blacksmiths had done their best to make do and mend as the occasion arose. By 1618, in Aberdeen, the public clocks were in such a sorry state 'for want of skillful men to attend them' that it was decided to 'write south with all diligence and try quhair (= *where*) the best knockmacker may be had and cause bring him upon the town's charges . . . and visit the knokis (= *clocks*) thairof, that such of them as may be mended be accordingly done and sic as will not mend be made new as soon as the same can conveniently be gotten done'.

It is interesting that clockmakers were so few and far between that the authorities did not even know where to send for one, other than to 'write south'. It was not until 1672 that Aberdeen had its own resident clockmaker in the form of Patrick Kilgour, who is mentioned elsewhere (page 50). So, in the early days, and 'early' would vary very much with the kind of region, the towns were only too pleased to have a resident clockmaker. In the case of Elgin, about 35 miles east of Inverness, they still had no resident clockmaker as late as 1756. In that year, the Town Clerk advertised in the *Edinburgh Evening Courant:* 'Wanted at Elgin a skilful clock and watch maker, who might reasonably expect proper encouragement, as there is none of that business here nor betwixt Inverness and Banff, being 50 miles distant. The Magistrates of Elgin would give a small salary for keeping the town's clocks in good order. Any well qualified clock and watch maker who inclines to come here and carry on business may signify the same by letter directed to Mr Patrick Duff, Town Clerk of Elgin'.

Once a number of clockmakers had settled in a town and formed a protective association or guild, then quite the reverse was true, and strangers were actively discouraged from attempting to set up in competition with the locals. An interesting case arose in Edinburgh in 1721, a city where there had long been a guild of Hammermen and in which clockmakers had been included since the 1640s. Langley Bradley was a London clockmaker with a particular reputation for turret clocks, and was based at the sign of the Minute Dial in Fenchurch Street. He had built the new clock for St Paul's in 1707, and was now in the process of building the new clock in St Giles's church in Edinburgh. On 2 December 1721, it was reported to a meeting of the Edinburgh Hammermen that 'Alexander Brownlie, clockmaker, had made a seizure of a part of the dial work of ye town clock, as being wrought by an unfreeman (*ie. Bradley*), and that this day the Magistrates had summarily fined and imprisoned the said Alexander Brownlie'.

Strictly speaking, Langley Bradley was an outsider, and was not permitted to ply his trade in Edinburgh. There must have been strong hostility amongst the local clockmakers, and Brownlie took the law into his own hands by exercising the right of the local guild to seize goods which had been offered for sale without permission from one who was not free to trade there. This same right had been applied in the seizure of two clocks which had been brought to sell in the city by John Sanderson in 1715 (see page 34). So this was accepted practice.

Not surprisingly, the Hammermen agreed with Brownlie and were all for taking legal advice to proceed against the magistrates for their illegal actions. The problem must have been resolved, however, as the clock was duly completed – and by Bradley, the interloper.

It was perhaps a debatable point as to how many workers in the trade could make a satisfactory living in a town at any one time. In 1767, for example, the Perth Hammermen considered the application of David Laing to practise the craft there. His application was rejected because already 'there are three freemen of the calling of that science' in Perth, and the majority refused to accept him. If he attempted to practise as an 'unfreeman', the freeman threatened to prosecute him. Nothing is heard of David Laing thereafter, so perhaps he left the trade for some other means of livelihood.

An interesting occurrence took place in Edinburgh in 1711, when David Mackerson, still an indentured apprentice, applied to the guild to be discharged from his apprenticeship. This happened, unusually, to be a period of eight years, and the youngster was in a very unfortunate position in so far as his master and mistress had both died, yet, being still unqualified, he was unable to obtain work amongst the existing freemen. The guild agreed to admit him as his term had not long to run, but also 'considering there are few watchmakers in this city at present'. There were enough members who worked at clockmaking, but watches were regarded as a separate field with currently more demand than suppliers to meet it.

It is difficult to judge the spread of clockmaking in the provinces. If we consult the books on individual counties (see bibliography), we may well be able to write down a list of several names per county of makers working before the year 1700. These will principally be names culled from ancient records but not substantiated by surviving examples of what they made. Some of these recorded instances will be of men who were 'passing through', and who happened to find their names recorded for some reason or other.

For instance, a clockmaker named William Trippett married at Bristol in 1661. One of this name, and presumably the same man, was at Hull in 1670, when he repaired the clock in Beverley Minster. But no example of his work has as yet come to light, and he was probably a mobile restorer of turret clocks rather than a resident clockmaker producing domestic clocks. Records exist of many similar makers by whom no work has yet come to be recorded.

SURVIVAL OF EARLY CLOCKS

In most counties outside London itself, it is very uncommon to come across a clock made before about 1700, even though there are records of clockmakers and watchmakers supposedly at work there at that period. For convenience, the year 1700 can be regarded as a date when provincial clockmaking was just getting off the ground, and even then the earliest makers will more than likely be those who worked in the larger towns. On the other hand, clocks made before 1700 in London are not at all uncommon: numerous examples pass through the major London auction rooms every year. They may well bring high prices, though not on account of true rarity of survival (for very many survive), but rather on account of their scarcity in the marketplace relative to the high demand for them. Provincial clocks of this same age are many times rarer than the London equivalent, but may bring nowhere near the same price because of the collector's preference for a clock made in London, where it is assumed that clocks were better made. This assumption is not necessarily true, but pertains just the same and probably always did.

QUALITY OF LONDON CLOCKS

An old belief persists today that London clocks are 'better' than provincial ones. Because of the control of the Clockmakers' Company in the past, it is probably true to say that London clocks would be made to consistently high standards. In provincial towns and cities, the guild control also enforced similar standards. In rural Britain the local clockmaker had no one to control his product, and had to live by his own reputation and the goodwill of his customers. On the other hand, the scarcity of customers in the country areas meant that very often the rural maker not only had to give good value, but also had to offer the quality to outdo his town rivals.

6. An early example of a longcase clock, with ten-inch dial (25.5cms) in classic London style, made in about 1695 by Ninyan Burleigh of Pontefract, who left London in about 1693. Superb original hands, tiny minute numbers within the ring, ringed winding holes, engraving between spandrels: all highly typical features of the period.

London clocks tend to conform to a standard – which of course varied over the years – but this standardisation led eventually to a certain repetitiveness and uniformity of style. In country areas makers could do as they wished in terms of style, and much more variety and character may be seen in their work than in London work, certainly after the mid-eighteenth century. The London minimum standard of quality was often far exceeded by some of the more outstanding country makers, and every county had its handful or more of master craftsmen, who could leave London 'quality' far behind. The real answer is to ignore old beliefs, and to learn to recognise quality for yourself.

We shall tackle the problem of how to recognise quality from mediocrity in due course, but first we must look at the clocks themselves, their form and structure, their mechanics and development. In the next chapter we examine the beginnings of English clockmaking as typified by the first truly English clock, the lantern clock.

7. *A typical London eight-day longcase in mahogany, by John Fladgate of London of about 1770. A simpler form of London case with crested top, standing about 7ft 6in (229cms).*

8. *A provincial clock from the later eighteenth century, with characteristic use of oak at that time, by Thomas Richardson of Weaverham. Note the original caddy top, and canted corners to the base. Height 7ft (213cms).*

3 EARLY CLOCKS AND THE PENDULUM

The mechanical clock first appeared in the form of public clocks, or turret clocks, principally in the towers of churches or monasteries or public buildings. Some clocks existed in the thirteenth century, but it was the beginning of the fifteenth century before the turret clock was common enough to be anything but a rarity. Surviving records are patchy from this early time, but from those that do survive it is clear that by the year 1500 a public clock was a feature in many towns and cities.

Very often these clocks were made by clockmakers who were based some way off, and who would be employed by the town to make and install a clock, the maintenance thereafter being left to the local clock winder or maybe the blacksmith. For any serious work, the clockmaker himself had to be sent for, and sometimes considerable distances were involved, so thinly were these skilled craftsmen scattered.

An interestingly late example of this occurred in 1647 regarding the clock in the Magdalen Chapel, Edinburgh, when the authorities decided 'to tak doune the knock (= *clock*) in the steipill and send her away to Londoune, and change her with ane new one or qr (= *whatever*) he sall think expedient'. Even at this late date and in the capital of Scotland, they were at a loss as to where to go for a new turret clock other than London.

FOLIOT AND BALANCE WHEEL ESCAPEMENTS
Early domestic clocks began as miniature versions of turret clocks, made along the same constructional principal. Both were driven by falling weights. Both had their escapements regulated by the

Fig. 1 The Verge and Foliot Escapement

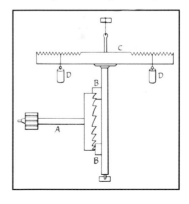

The verge wheel on its arbor (A) is pulled round by the weight and is allowed to 'escape' one tooth at a time by pushing against each pallet (B) in turn. The foliot (C) is attached to the arbor and pallets (B). The time taken for the foliot to swing back and forth determines the speed of running. Cursor weights (D) can be positioned at varying distances to control the rate of swing of the foliot.

verge and foliot escapement (Figure 1). The foliot itself was the iron crossbar, which usually had notches towards its two ends so that small riding weights could be added or removed to speed up or slow down the rate of running. These early domestic clocks were mostly made of iron, as were the turret clocks they resembled. They are today known as Gothic clocks, or sometimes as chamber clocks.

The foliot was not generally used in Britain, nor was the Gothic clock a native British product. These were made on the Continent, and early examples of domestic clocks in Britain were imported ones. It was not until the mid-sixteenth century that British domestic clocks, in the form of lantern clocks, began to appear. These were made principally of brass and their escapements were controlled by the verge escapement with balance wheel. The balance wheel (Figure 2) was a circular ring of brass (though iron was possible) which swung back and forth on a single spoke.

So the regulator on these early clocks was the balance wheel in Britain and the foliot in mainland Europe, both different means of enforcing a controlled speed on the verge escapement, which was weight-driven. The introduction of the pendulum in 1658 meant that both of these escapement forms became obsolete almost at once (Figure 3).

The foliot and the balance wheel were erratic as timekeeping controllers. In turret clocks, the extremes of temperature and the clocks' vulnerability to adverse weather conditions played havoc with a control which was less than reliable under the best of conditions. An error of half an hour in twenty-four was not unknown.

The escapement was that part of the clock's movement which controlled its rate of running, that is, the speed at which the clock

Fig. 2 Principle of verge escapement with balance wheel

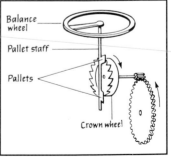

The pull of the driving weight forces the wheels of the clock (known as the train of wheels) to turn, culminating in the rotation of the crown wheel itself. The teeth of the crown wheel push alternately against the two pallets on the pallet staff, thus forcing the balance wheel to swing alternately left and right. It is the oscillation, or swing, of the balance wheel which regulates the speed at which the wheels turn and therefore the pace at which the clock ticks. The clock can be made to run faster or slower by means of a heavier or lighter weight.

Fig. 3 Principle of verge escapement

The short (or bob) pendulum makes use of the verge escapement, just as the balance wheel had done, but now the crown wheel is positioned horizontally, as is the pallet staff with its attached pallets faces. The pallet staff is attached directly to the pendulum.

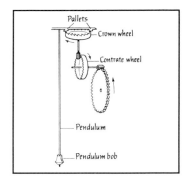

ran down. Without an escapement the clock's wheels would spin round rapidly until the weight reached the ground and the clock ran down within a few seconds. The development of the clock was based in the first instance on the invention and refinement of different types of escapement, beginning with the foliot and the balance wheel. As each improved escapement originated, the older, less accurate forms fell from use, though not always immediately, as we shall see later.

The escapement was in essence a pace-setter, and is believed to be so named because its action allowed the teeth of the wheel(s) to escape one at a time. As the weight forced the wheels of the clock to turn, the speed at which they revolved was slowed down by whatever form of escapement the clock had. The problem with the balance wheel escapement was that it was not capable of being adjusted to run faster or slower other than by increasing the weight itself, which was an unsatisfactory method, and which led eventually to the invention of the pendulum control, which *was* capable of being regulated.

The foliot escapement was to some degree adjustable for loss or gain, and this was done by moving a small riding weight known as a cursor along each of the two foliot arms (see Figure 1), but although one or two rare examples are known, the foliot, as already observed, was not a system generally used in Britain.

LANTERN CLOCKS

The first type of domestic clock made in any serious numbers in Britain was the type which we know today as a lantern clock, though no one really knows how it got this name. The most likely suggestion is that it arose from the clock's vague similarity in shape to an old hand lantern. At the time of their original making they were known simply as house clocks or sometimes chamber clocks, or even just clocks, as there were no other kinds. The term Cromwellian clock was sometimes used to describe them in the nineteenth century, though that term is not used today because it is misleading, as they were made both long before and after Cromwell's time. The construction of a lantern clock (Figure 4) was based on four upright corner posts supporting a top and bottom plate, which held cross-shaped bars between which the wheels were mounted. This method of construction led to them sometimes being known as posted clocks or even bed-post clocks, not (as is sometimes ludicrously suggested) because they hung from a bedpost, but because the frame itself is reminiscent of a four-poster bed in its principle. The term sheepshead clock was

Fig. 4 Frame of Lantern Clock

Drawing showing the constructional frame of a typical lantern clock: upper and lower plates, crossbars, pillars, ending in finials at the top and feet (sometimes called pendants) at the base, and front fret above the top plate, here pierced and of wide scrolled formalised leaf and flower design, with interweaving dolphins.

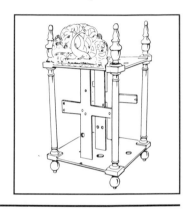

9. *A handsome full-size lantern clock (15in/40cms) from the third quarter of the seventeenth century. The initials HP were probably those of the first owner. The date 1668, added as an afterthought at that time, hence off-centre, is probably the genuine date that the clock was made. The outer shell is all that remains of the original, as the present movement is a late nineteenth-century fusee two-hander (see Plate 20). The hands are late nineteenth century brass replacements for what was originally a single handed clock. The two winding holes cut cruelly through the finely-engraved centre. The clock originally had alarmwork (hole through XI), and the fine Tudor Rose centre is a much later engraved infill covering what originally would have been a plain centre under the alarm disc.*

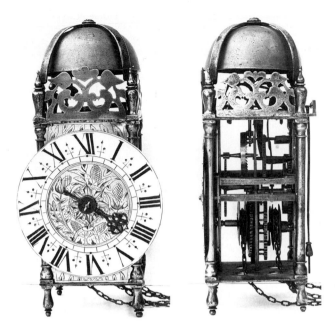

10. Late seventeenth-century lantern clock of extraordinary nature, being made entirely of iron rather than with brass, except for the dial and pendulum bob. Even the wheels, pillars, frets, finials and feet are iron. The top finial may have been broken short. Height 14in (38cms). The engraving is very crude, but charming. The work of a blacksmith or clocksmith of high order.

11. Side view of the movement of the all-iron lantern clock, with original wheelwork throughout. It was made with two clicks for separate train winding, both weights being on the left, but was modified to continuous chain wind for convenience. Such a modification is very minor, and is in no way detrimental to a collector's eye. Both original ratchets were retained, the front one simply being fixed. Side doors now missing.

sometimes used to distinguish late lantern clocks of the broader type, such as were found in East Anglia until the mid-eighteenth century. We can only speculate as to the origin of this name, as it requires a vivid imagination to see the shape of a sheep's head in one, and this term is seldom used today.

All of these varying terms refer to one and the same type o clock, the pattern of which was established by the year 1600 and continued to be produced in London until about 1700, and perhaps for another twenty years beyond that in the provinces. After 1700 changes in the style of its dial gave it a very different appearance, and these modified forms were produced until the middle of the eighteenth century, by which time it fell from popularity as the longcase clock replaced it almost totally.

To a novice, the basic lantern clock looks superficially the same whether made in 1600 or 1700. However, there are considerable differences in detail in the styling, which means that close examination permits accurate dating of such a clock, from these features alone, to within roughly twenty years. Where a maker's name is present, as is the case with the majority of them, close dating is made easier, as it is a very simple matter to check on any clockmaker's name from the reference books available.

Even so, lantern clocks are more confusing than others from the point of view of the beginner. For one thing, changes in style are less obvious than with other clocks. The fact that they were made originally with any one of three different types of escapement (*ie.* verge with balance wheel, verge pendulum or anchor escapement with long pendulum) makes them more complicated to understand mechanically, especially since many have been altered over the years to improve timekeeping. Many lantern clocks were scrapped for the metal value, as it was regular practice for a clockmaker to take an old clock in part exchange for a new one, principally for its metal value. But many such old lantern clocks merely lay partly dismantled, and some were eventually cobbled together again, so that the result is that more lantern clocks are married together from old bits and pieces or simply faked than is the case with any other category of clock. These factors make lantern clocks a bewildering field for many, and even collectors who feel confident about other types of clock will tread more warily with lanterns.

The lantern clock with balance-wheel control had two separate driving weights. The going train (the horological word for a set of wheels) was positioned at the front of the clock. As the single hand was to turn clockwise, the driving weight had to hang on the left. In order to avoid the danger of the clock being pulled over to one side as it hung by its hoop on a wall hook, the sensible thing was to position the striking weight on the right, and this meant that the bell hammer was also positioned on the right. This should mean that the identification of a pre-pendulum lantern clock is made easier, as it will have its hammer on the right-hand side. On the other hand, as we shall see, a pendulum-controlled lantern clock would normally have its hammer on the left, a requirement brought about by employing the Huygens continuous rope-system for winding (see Figure 5). This arrangement is normal, and will account for recognition of one type from the other in most instances. There are exceptions, however, which we will consider shortly.

VERGE PENDULUM

The pendulum was perfected (if not invented) with regard to its use in a clock by Christiaan Huygens of Zulichem in the Netherlands, on Christmas Day 1656. In September 1658, he published his findings to prevent others from copying it and calling it their own work, as indeed he claimed they were already doing. Huygens released his new invention in Holland through Salomon Coster, who had sole manufacturing rights there.

In Britain, the first pendulum clocks were advertised for sale in 1658 by Ahasuerus Fromanteel, a London clockmaker, whose grandparents had been Dutch. It is possible that he still had relatives and connections in Holland, and certainly he had prior contact with Huygens, having sent his son, John, for a nine-month spell of service to work under Coster in 1657.

In 1658, Fromanteel advertised his new clocks that 'go exact and keep equaller time than any now made'. He offered them of one-day duration or to run a week, a month, or even a year at one winding. The new invention was also 'very excellent for all House clocks that go either with Springs or Waights: And also Steeple Clocks that are most subject to differ by change of weather. Made by Ahasuerus Fromanteel, who made the first that were in England'.

The pendulum was the making of Fromanteel. Before its arrival he was just another London clockmaker. By October of 1660, just two years after he advertised his new pendulum clocks, examples of his making were in the collection of the King. John Evelyn recounts in his diary how he went to see the Royal collection, which included a special clock by Fromanteel showing 'the rising and seting of the son in the Zodiaque, the Sunn, represented in a face and raies of Gold upon an azure skie, observing the diurnal and annual motion, rising and setting behind a landscape of hills . . . the Work of our famous Fromanteel'. In May of the following year Huygens himself was in London, and Evelyn

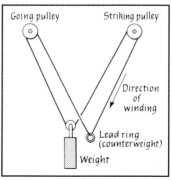

Fig. 5 Endless Rope Winding

The Huygens endless rope winding principle was applied to thirty-hour clocks in this manner. Winding was through the striking pulley, and thus the going train was always in drive even during winding, a simple form of inbuilt maintaining power. Rope or chain was used according to the maker's whim.

recounts: 'and I returned by Fromantil's, the famous clockmaker, to see some pendules, Monsieur Zulichem being with us.' 'Zulichem' was Huygens, whom Evelyn had earlier called 'that great mathematician and virtuoso, inventor of the pendule clock'. Huygens must have been delighted at the success his pendulum device had achieved in the hands of so capable a maker.

In addition to the pendulum itself, Huygens also invented the endless rope winding system of drive for clocks of short duration, such as lantern clocks (see Figure 5). This figure-eight rope joined together the going and striking trains. Lantern clocks which had previously had two separate ropes and which needed winding twice a day, would now run for thirty hours at a single winding. If the mainwheel of the going train was fixed instead of having its own individual winding click (as had previously been the case), then the going train was kept in drive during winding, an added advantage over the earlier system, where the drive power was in effect removed during winding time, a simple form of maintaining power.

So the arrival of the pendulum and, at the same time (or within a year or two anyway – experts disagree about this), the endless rope winding system, meant that the hammer of the lantern clock, which with balance-wheel clocks had been positioned on the right, was now positioned on the left (just visible on Plate 19). If this had been a consistently reliable feature it would have meant that any right-hand-hammer lantern clock must originally have been built with a balance wheel and any left-hand-hammer clock with a pendulum, and this would have been a very useful recognition guide. The reality is not quite as simple as that.

A balance-wheel clock would certainly have had its hammer on the right. However, some pendulum clocks *also* had the hammer on the right: those which had two separate drive weights and which did not take advantage of the Huygens endless rope system (Plate 14). Contrarily, some makers used the left-hand hammer (often regarded as symptomatic of the endless rope pendulum clock) and yet still had two separate drive weights.

The reason that some makers kept two separate weights for individually winding the going and strike trains may have been that this arrangement allowed the option of running the clock to operate without using the strike train, if desired. In other words, it offered a strike or silent option that was not available with the endless rope.

In summarising, it is fair to say that a right-hand hammer usually indicates a clock that was made with the balance-wheel system, but occasional examples may be pendulum versions with separate winding for each train. A left-hand hammer will indicate a pendulum form, normally with continuous wind, but sometimes with separate (two-weight) drive.

ANCHOR ESCAPEMENT

Experts have debated for some years about who it was that invented the anchor escapement. The claims and counter-claims for the various contenders for the title could in themselves fill a book. William Clement of London is the clockmaker most often given credit for this invention, the historical reason for this being that the oldest texts ascribe it to him. In *Horological Disquisitions*, published in 1694, the author, John Smith, in writing about the pendulum, says 'that eminent and well-known artist, Mr William Clement, had at last the good fortune to give it the finishing stroke, he being indeed the real contriver of that curious kind of long pendulum, which is at this day so universally in use among us'. At this time the word 'curious' meant 'made with great care'.

When William Derham wrote *The Artificial Clockmaker* in 1696 ('artificial' used here in its older sense of 'involving craftsmanship'), he stated that 'Mr W. Clement, a London clockmaker, contrived . . . the universal method of the Royal Pendulums'. 'Royal pendulum' was the old-fashioned term sometimes used for what we would today call the long pendulum. Subsequent books repeated what Smith and Derham had said, until before long it became written as fact that Clement was the inventor. In recent years, researchers who thought for themselves have investigated the matter to the best of their abilities and as far as surviving examples of clocks will allow. Joseph Knibb, a fine clockmaker who worked in Oxford prior to 1671, when he moved to London, is known to have experimented in the late 1660s with escapement forms, which may have developed into the anchor escapement as we now know it. So the latest opinion is that the anchor escapement was in use by 1670, its inventor still being undecided.

Fig. 6 Principle of the anchor escapement

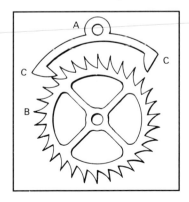

The escape wheel (B) is pulled round by the weight, causing the anchor (A) to sway from side to side by pressure against its pallets (C). An extension to the anchor arbor gives impulse to the pendulum. Thus the rotating escape wheel causes the pendulum to swing from side to side. Sometimes called a recoil escapement, as the locking of the pallets tend to push the teeth of the escape wheel slightly backwards.

The anchor escapement caused the crutch (and hence the pendulum) to swing in a much shorter arc than the pendulum of the older verge escapement, which swung in a very wide arc. Thus it enabled a far longer pendulum to be used, thereby allowing for finer tuning in timekeeping. A single turn of the regulating nut might alter the rate of timekeeping of a long pendulum clock by a few seconds a week: the same turn on a short (verge) pendulum by several minutes a day.

The long pendulum generally had a length of 39.13 inches and would beat once a second, which made it convenient for displaying a seconds dial on the clock dial. Of course, not all were of this length, and thirty-hour clocks may be met with which have considerable variation in pendulum length, as these seldom show seconds on the dial. A few were made with one-and-a-quarter-second beat, in which instances the much longer pendulum hung down into the base of the case – the theory being that, if the long pendulum allowed much finer tuning in terms of timekeeping regulation, then an even longer one would allow still greater accuracy. These very long pendulums proved inconvenient, however, and generally speaking the one-second length was normal.

The superiority of the long pendulum (with anchor escapement) over the short one with verge escapement was such that it became instantly adopted for longcase clocks. Just how quickly this spread throughout the country is difficult to judge, principally because at this very early date (1670) there were very few provincial clockmakers at all, and any provincial longcase surviving from such a very early date is an extreme rarity – hence we seldom have the chance to examine any to form an opinion. The term 'grandfather clock' is that by which almost everyone recognises these clocks today, although this expression itself is thought to be no older than the mid-nineteenth century. In America they are often known as 'tall clocks', but most collectors prefer to use the more correct expression 'longcase clock'.

An interesting illustration, however, of the rapid spread of the anchor escapement appears to be provided by the application, on 16 April 1672, of clockmaker Patrick Kilgour for his freedom to trade in the town of Aberdeen. As a fee, he offered to make a clock of the domestic type, presumably for the council chambers. Kilgour was to 'deliver unto them before Lammas next ane knock (= *clock*) of brass about the bigness of ane house knock, which should be *ane pendulum of the best form*, which should go for aucht days at one winding up, and should strike the hours punctually, and should have a good ɓell with the motion of the day of the month, and should have an pais (= *weight*), and should stand no higher from the floor than the height of an man, and he should oblige himself that the knock should be as sufficient and handsome as any knock made elsewhere . . .' By the description it would seem that this was a longcase clock. At this date such a clock would be a considerable rarity in Scotland, and this must have been one of the very earliest ever made by a Scottish maker. It is not known to survive today, nor any of this age made there.

It is obvious from the detailed description in the council's specifications, that they are setting down in writing such details as Kilgour had given them in his verbal offer, and it is clear that they are not yet accustomed to longcase clocks. Most of the things they specify are common to any longcase clock anyway, but when they specify the height from the floor, they are clearly very impressed with that aspect – a lantern clock, of course, would often have been hung much higher, to allow its drive rope full duration of thirty hours, or even more. Where they went slightly wrong is in specifying one weight, because an eight-day clock which was also a striking clock would have two weights; unless of course they were referring at that point to the going train. But clearly this new type of clock impressed them as being able to run for eight days, whereas the domestic clocks which they had been used to must have been lantern clocks which ran for one day only. Kilgour's clock would run for eight days on one weight, whereas that same one weight drove a lantern clock for just one day.

Many of the details set out provide clear indication of the novelty of the eight-day longcase in Aberdeen in 1672, but what is most interesting in relationship to our discussion of the anchor escapement is the phrase I have set in italics, 'ane pendulum of the best form'. This must mean the anchor escapement form of pendulum, because there were only two forms of pendulum, and the older verge escapement with bob pendulum (the one they may well have been used to in lantern clocks) was clearly regarded as being the lesser form. In other words, within three years or so of its invention, the anchor escapement was known as far away as Aberdeen, where a local clockmaker could offer it as an option of great novelty.

DEADBEAT ESCAPEMENT

So successful was the anchor escapement that it was used from this time on for all longcase clocks made for normal domestic use. One variation was the deadbeat escapement, which is in fact a type of anchor escapement. The deadbeat is usually said to have been invented by George Graham, the famous London clock-maker, in about 1715, though Graham himself never made such a claim. In fact, earlier forms of deadbeat were known as far back as the 1670s. The deadbeat gave a *slight* increase in accuracy of timekeeping, but the teeth of the escape wheel were more prone to damage, and so this form was not often used in household clocks except when the clock was fitted with maintaining power (to keep the wheels turning clockwise during winding).

It might be as well to explain at this point what is meant by

Fig. 7 Principle of the deadbeat escapement

The teeth of the escape wheel (B) and the pallets (C) of the anchor (A) are of different shape from those of the anchor escapement, and the escape wheel (B) turns without recoil.

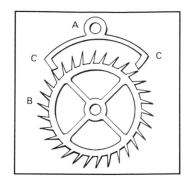

'maintaining power'. When a clock is being wound, the driving pull of the weight is temporarily removed, with the obvious result that the clock hands stop turning during that time, causing a slight loss in timekeeping. However, with many clocks, long-pendulum ones in particular, the continuing swing of the pendulum will actually push the escape wheel *backwards*, causing the hands to go backwards during winding. This was perhaps annoying to the clock owner, but could easily be overcome by setting the clock to run slightly fast, *ie.* by the amount of time apparently lost during the winding.

This might well be less than beneficial to any clock, but with an anchor escapement of the deadbeat type there was a distinct risk of damage to the delicate teeth of the escape wheel. Maintaining power was therefore devised to avoid such damage to the teeth during winding. There were two methods of achieving this.

MAINTAINING POWER

We have already noted that the continuous-rope winding system had its own inherent form of maintaining power (covering lantern clocks and thirty-hour longcase examples). Bolt-and-shutter maintaining power was devised about the time of the first pendulum clocks, for use on longcase clocks of eight-day and longer duration. A lever was pressed (or pulled by means of a short cord) which tripped a spring-loaded bolt into action to press against a tooth on a wheel in the going train, thus keeping the wheels turning in a forward direction during winding time. To avoid an owner taking a short cut and not bothering to trigger the maintaining power, the system was rigged with two shutters, which covered the winding holes and thus prevented the winding key from being inserted at all times except when the maintaining power system was actioned. By this means the owner was forced into using it. On bolt-and-shutter power the shutters themselves gradually moved back into their usual place within a minute or two of winding.

Ironically, the bolt-and-shutter maintaining power on many clocks was removed long ago, perhaps because it was regarded as a nuisance factor. The result is that many such clocks have run for two centuries or more without what was regarded at their time of making as an essential feature.

A different type of maintaining power was invented in 1735 by John Harrison, inventor of the successful marine timekeepers. This system was fully automatic, as its parts were incorporated within the main wheel itself – the winding wheel of the going train. No separate mechanism needed to be brought into action, but the simple act of winding the clock caused the maintaining spring to come into play. This type is known as Harrison's maintaining power, and was used principally with deadbeat escapement clocks of high precision nature, such as Regulators. A Regulator was a kind of clock, usually a longcase, made by the clockmaker for his own use in testing and timing his other clocks, his master clock in other words, made above all other considerations for accuracy (Plate 12). They are often of very formal appearance, being made for his sale shop, not for domestic settings.

REGULATORS

In the form in which we are most likely to meet with it today, the Regulator appears as that type of clock which was used by clockmakers themselves as their master clock. Some, of course, would be made to be sold for use in banks or public offices, or more likely for those to whom accuracy was of great importance, principally scientists and astronomers. The development of the Regulator was an important feature of the endless quest for greater accuracy, and as such its leading innovators were the more famous London clockmakers of their time. A variation in timekeeping of a few seconds a week was of little or no importance in a domestic clock; for a scientist, however, precision was everything.

Thomas Tompion is perhaps the best known name in English horology. Born in 1639 in Bedfordshire, the son of a blacksmith, he rose to become Royal Clockmaker, and by the time of his death in 1713 had achieved a reputation which survives to this day. He made clocks of great accuracy, including some with perpetual calendar work, equation work, and complicated repeating systems. George Graham was Tompion's nephew and successor, and it was Graham whose name is revered as developer of the deadbeat escapement, mentioned earlier.

One factor affecting timekeeping on any clock is that the pendulum may expand or contract from the effects of temperature change. Graham is credited with the invention of the mercury pendulum in the 1720s, involving a jar of mercury as a pendulum

12. Longcase Regulator in fine mahogany case, circa 1835, made by Clare of Preston, Lancashire, standing 7ft 7in (231cms). It has a deadbeat escapement with centre seconds hand and telescopic pendulum to compensate for expansion. The hours show separately in the smaller, upper dial, minutes and seconds from the centre. The brass, silvered dial was often used in Regulators long after its period on normal domestic clocks.

bob. The principle was that, as the pendulum rod expanded downwards in warmer temperatures, the mercury would expand upwards, thus redressing the imbalance in the centre of gravity of the bob. At about the same time, the gridiron pendulum was invented by John Harrison (with his brother James), the man who was to go on to perfect the marine chronometer. The gridiron pendulum had its rod made from alternate lengths of steel and brass, set together in such a way that as one metal expanded in one direction the alternate metal expanded to counteract this. Both mercury pendulums and gridiron pendulums are seldom found on any clocks other than Regulators. A further invention credited to the Harrisons is the grasshopper escapement, a delicate and silent escapement involving little friction, its use again limited entirely to Regulators. Many regulators have special escapements and compensated pendulums, usually maintaining power, and are mainly timepieces only.

Of course, the maintaining power was used on the going train only. It was not needed on the strike train, as that train was active only during striking time. If an owner should be contrary enough to want to wind the striking train during the actual few seconds of striking, then the strike will stop until the key is released, when it will finish its count. Apart from the pointlessness of winding the strike train during the actual striking itself, this practice is not advisable anyway, as with some clocks it may cause the strike to throw out of sequence.

The Huygens continuous-rope system, as I have mentioned, had its own in-built maintaining power, since the rope was wound up on the strike train and power was never released from the going train at any time. This was not planned as an essential ingredient of the system, but came as an added bonus, simply by opting to have the winding ratchet on the strike rather than going train. However, this bonus did provide true maintaining power, and the point is seldom made that even precision clocks, such as Regulators, were sometimes made using pull-wind thirty-hour principles. I have come across several examples where a clock-maker built his own workshop Regulator with this system during the eighteenth century, rather than go to the extra unnecessary expense and complication of making the Harrison type of maintaining power.

The success of the anchor escapement resulted in the verge escapement being obsolete virtually overnight as far as longcase clocks were concerned. Such was not the case, however, with certain other kinds of clock, notably the lantern clock and the bracket clock (see Chapter 9). The verge was retained in these types long after the anchor was well established, the reason being that the short-pendulum verge system was highly convenient for a portable clock. The verge was less fussy about a level position, so for a lantern (especially in its smaller form as a travelling alarm clock) or a bracket clock, either of which might be subject to moving from room to room, or even building to building, this was more convenient.

PENDULUM CONVERSIONS

The pendulum of whatever type (*ie.* with verge or anchor escapement) was a better timekeeper than any earlier form of escapement, and many older clocks were thus converted to pendulum regulation. The town council of Aberdeen must have been so pleased with the longcase clock which Patrick Kilgour had made for them in 1672, with the 'best form' of pendulum, that in 1692 they contracted for him to work on the church clock there, 'to translate the said clock into ane pendulum work conform to the newest fashion and invention done at London for regulating the motion of the said clock and causing her to go just'. In 1699, clockmaker James Anthony of Truro in Cornwall converted the town clock there, 'making it a pendilow'. In 1716, Richard Cornish, a blacksmith at East Grinstead, was paid £3 5s. 0d. (£3.25) 'for turning of ye church clock into a pendall'.

In 1723, Adam Stevinsoun reported to Dunfermline council that 'he had turned the clock in the steeple into a pendulum clock, and desired the council might appoint some person to visit her and report if ye clock be bettered yairby'. Conversions took place in great numbers.

Throughout the land there was a vast quantity of older clocks, which were perfectly sound mechanically, but which would perform better if modified to pendulum control, and ideally to anchor escapement pendulum. Here was a great source of work for the provincial clockmaker, who may in the earlier periods have had difficulty in selling clocks, but may have found it a much easier proposition to offer to alter existing ones to give a better performance. Sometimes this almost amounted to making new clocks out of old. A most interesting example of this is illustrated in George White's massive book *English Lantern Clocks*, where there is a sixteenth-century Continental clock, which had a new dial and movement made for it in 1687, the dial being engraved: 'This Clock new made by William Holloway of Stroud 1687'. In the same book is a lantern clock of about 1650 made by Thomas Knifton of London as a balance-wheel clock. This was later converted to short-pendulum and verge escapement, and on the back of the dial is engraved 'Richd. Roe in Eperston made it into pendelum 1689'. Roe was a clockmaker who worked at Epperston in Nottinghamshire.

An advertisement in the *Ipswich Journal* in 1739 runs: 'James Knights, whitesmith, has taken a shop . . . in Ipswich . . . does all whitesmith's work, cleans and mends clocks, turns old ballance and bob clocks into long pendulum'. It may seem surprising that there were enough balance-wheel clocks surviving by this late date to make it worth advertising the option of converting them, since the pendulum had then been in use for the best part of a century. However, the arrival of the pendulum control in 1658 did not instantly bring to an end the production of balance-wheel lantern clocks, as might have been expected. These were still produced on occasion, as late even as the 1690s, despite their shorter duration and less accurate timekeeping – see page 193. Just why this was so is not really known, but it may have been because balance-wheel examples were less needful of level positions (see page 55) than the verge pendulum forms, which in turn were much less needful of level positioning than anchor escapement forms.

Within a very few years of 1658, the new pendulum, initially of verge form of course, increasingly took over from the balance wheel in all lantern clocks. London was always the major production centre for lantern clocks, simply because there were few provincial makers anyway before the end of the century. In London, the new anchor escapement was seldom used for lantern clocks before the end of the century. In the provinces, surviving lantern clocks seldom date from more than a few years before the end of the century, and here the verge was sometimes used, but quite often the anchor was selected.

RECONVERTING ESCAPEMENTS

The kind of escapement used on lantern clocks can be a guide towards assessing their age, provided it is the *original* escapement. This may be far from a simple matter for the novice to assess. In

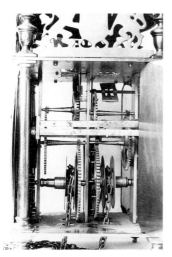

13. *Movement of a verge escapement lantern clock with pendulum, showing wheelwork and tapered arbors. The dial is on the left. This clock dates from the very early eighteenth century, but the tapered style of the arbors is of the kind often used much earlier. Side doors removed. An original verge escapement is an uncommon survivor.*

general terms, virtually no balance-wheel lanterns remain as they were made, and very few verge escapements (see Plate 13). Both types were almost always modified later, usually to anchor escapement for better timekeeping. In recent years, restorers have sometimes converted such clocks back again to the type of escapement they originally had – known as re-converting. So one might meet with a re-converted balance-wheel lantern clock or a re-converted verge escapement lantern clock. If skilfully re-converted it may be easily mistaken for the original, though of course such a clock is not as valuable as one which was never altered from new.

Many people today take the view that a balance-wheel or verge pendulum lantern clock which has been converted to anchor escapement perhaps two hundred years or more ago is better left in its modified form, since conversion to anchor escapement was a normal part of its progression through history. This is a special view taken with regard only to lantern clocks, as other kinds of clocks did not go through such conversions. Others feel that it is preferable to 'restore' the clock back to its original form by re-converting it. If in doubt, perhaps the best advice is to leave things as they are – re-conversion could always be done at a later date if desired.

LANTERN DATING FEATURES

Other features help in dating a lantern clock. Earlier ones have a narow chapter ring with dial-centre-engraving of a repeated pattern of flowers, tulips being popular from about mid-century. The maker's name on these earlier ones tends to be in the dial centre itself, or occasionally on the front fret. Some were not signed at all – perhaps so that they could be sold through retailers or agents 'in the country'. Towards the end of the century chapter rings grew wider, and the floral centre changed in character, usually towards bolder displays of larger and fewer flowers, tulips still being popular (Plate 14).

Many lantern clocks had alarmwork, a central disc in the dial centre being used to set the required alarm time by turning the disc to set the selected hour against the tail of the single hand (see Plate 17). The alarmwork itself would be at the back of the clock, sometimes inside the backplate, sometimes outside it, but usually attached to it. Conversion to anchor escapement almost always involved removing the alarmwork, which tended to be in the way of the long pendulum at the back of the clock. With such conversions, the alarm disc may well remain, even though the alarmwork has gone. A removed alarm disc is usually easily recognised, because the dial centre which was formerly covered by the disc will be left unengraved (Plate 14). A clock which once had alarmwork can also be recognised by a hole in the chapter ring or close to it, usually around the XI number or the I number,

14. Unsigned lantern clock of about 1670 showing typical dial style with tulip theme centre. The blank zone originally carried an alarm disc, the alarmwork being removed when converted from centre verge to anchor escapement. The right-hand hammer here indicates not an original balance-wheel movement, but a verge escapement with separate winding for each train.

15. Back view of the lantern clock in Plate 14. The original iron backplate carries empty holes which formerly carried the alarmwork. The original hoop is riveted to the top-plate, and the original spurs to the backplate. Side frets are usually unengraved, as here. Doors missing.

where the pivot for the trip lever protruded (see Plates 9, 14). So missing alarmwork is very easy to spot from the front view alone.

Other stylistic features which do undergo change through the seventeenth century are the feet and finials and the bell strap style. These, however, tend to look very similar to each other to a beginner, and identifying them at a glance requires experience. On most lantern clocks, the finials and feet are screwed onto the pillars as separate pieces. On some, however, the pillar was integral with these appendages, in which examples the plates fit by pinning rather than being wedged between pillar and feet/finials (Plate 16). This style of pillar integral with the feet and finial was used by French makers of lantern clocks, and by occasional

16. *A lantern clock of the late seventeenth century by George Guest of Aston (Birmingham). An example where the feet and finials are integral with the pillar casting (though the right-hand front finial is a replacement crudely soldered on)*

London makers, perhaps of French origin or influenced by French style. There was also a particular 'school' of clockmaking in South-West England where this method was often preferred. However, the choice of pillar-style was often no more than a fickle whim of a particular maker, and no distinct conclusions can be drawn from it as to the area of origin of the clock, or its age.

Lantern clocks had a single hand which recorded hour and quarters. Time to the nearest quarter-hour was accurate enough for most purposes, and particularly since the clocks themselves were inclined to err by several minutes a day, perhaps by as much as fifteen minutes a day with balance-wheel clocks. After all, the sundial had only a single pointer (called a gnomon), and while a sundial *could* indicate minutes, most were content to register quarter-hour units. So, in a way, these earliest lantern clocks were the indoor equivalent of sundials.

A very small number had two hands, and registered minutes, and these were principally clocks which chimed quarters. More often one finds on examination that a two-handed lantern clock was originally a single-hander, and has been modified to accept a second (*ie.* minute) hand later (Plate 9). These can easily be recognised because the chapter ring is set out to show only quarter hours, and has no minutes numbered on it. Those modified to two hands might have a series of dots drilled on the chapter ring to represent minute positions, but will lack the minute *numbering* which a genuine two-hander would have. By the second quarter of the eighteenth century, two-handed lantern clocks were known, but these were usually of the arched dial type described below.

ARCHED DIAL LANTERNS
In London the traditional lantern clock fell from fashion by about 1700. There followed a period when arched dial lantern clocks were made, the dial being shaped similarly to the arched brass dial of a longcase clock of the time, though much smaller. Many of these were small travelling alarm clocks, which retained the verge pendulum for ease of carrying (Plates 17, 18). A few survive with original carrying boxes, but most either never had them or have long lost them. These were often single-handers, but also exist as two-handers, especially the later ones. In the provinces meanwhile, the traditional shape of lantern clock continued, though mostly now with anchor escapement.

In terms of size, a normal lantern clock stood between fourteen and fifteen inches (38–40cms) high, including its top finial. Chapter rings on early ones might be six inches (15cms) in diameter, but slowly grew larger. Some exist about ten inches high (25.5cms), but true miniatures stand only six inches (15cms) or so high. Arched dial versions were usually of standard size (15 inches/40cms), but miniature ones also occurred. About 1700 some were made with square dials, but these are uncommon. Lantern

17. *Miniature lantern clock of the arched dial type made about 1730 by Robert Cressener of London. These small clocks were travelling alarms and were usually, as here, non-striking. It is still a true lantern, with feet and finials. Height 9in (23cms), dial height 6¼in (16cms). The alarm time is here set to 12.15, done by setting the tail of the hand to the required time. Diamond half-hour markers are typical of this period.*

18. *Side view of the travelling alarm clock (Plate 17). The hanging hoop can be seen, as can one of the spurs and the pendulum bob of the original verge escapement. The alarmwork is inside the backplate. The side door is removed for this photograph, as is the rope for the alarm.*

clocks with square or arched dials can easily be distinguished from other clocks (such as hooded clocks with the same dial shape and size) by the fact that they have finials and feet, and almost always hung from the wall by a hoop and two spurs, the latter fitted into the back feet or onto the backplate (see Plate 15).

The traditional lantern clock occasionally continued to be produced in some provincial areas into the middle years of the eighteenth century. More often by that time, they appeared in arched dial form. They seem to have lingered longest in more conservative areas, such as Suffolk, where examples occur as late as the 1770s, long after the type was extinct elsewhere.

TURKISH MARKET LANTERNS

A certain type of lantern clock was made at an unusually late period in London, and that was the arched dial type with verge pendulum, made for the Turkish market. These were usually two-handers, retained the short pendulum for ease of transport, and had numbers on the dial of a pseudo-Turkish nature. They were made roughly between about 1730 and 1770, later than other types in London, but were of a specialised nature, and were usually made by a few clockmakers who had a specialist trading connection with the Middle East. Rarely were Turkish market lantern clocks made outside London.

19. Full-size, two-handed arched dial lantern clock, made about 1770 for the Turkish market by George Prior of London. The hands are original, but the hour hand tip is broken. The acorn finial is not original, but is from a bracket clock. Note the Turkish numerals.

SPRING-DRIVEN LANTERNS

A great many lantern clocks were scrapped over the centuries, as being obsolete, or inefficient, or simply a nuisance to wind each day. Many were taken in part-exchange by clockmakers, who would scrap them for their metal values, especially the brass, as this was always an expensive material, and could be melted down and re-cast. Those which survive today often do so because they were discarded in a loft with other lumber, and have come to light in recent years. However, towards the end of the nineteenth century there was something of a revival of interest in antiquarian items as curiosities, and at that time a good many lantern clocks were given a new lease of life by being converted to spring clocks.

Such conversion involved the removal of the entire movement and the fitting instead of a spring-driven one, usually of the double-fusee type (Plate 20). This means that with such a fusee lantern clock we have a frame and external 'case', if we can call it that, which might date from the late seventeenth century, with a movement dating from the late nineteenth.

Such converted clocks have been 'spoiled' for the serious or purist collector, and have been shunned until recent times. On the other hand, it was often only the fact of such conversion which

20. Side view of the HP lantern clock (see Plate 9), showing typical double fusee late nineteenth-century bracket clock movement. Note straight movement pillars, thin, plain arbors, chain drive and upside-down pendulum regulation for easy adjustment within confined space. The clock was converted to spring drive more than two hundred years after it was made, and is spoiled for a purist, but still a collectable item.

saved these clocks from being melted down and destroyed completely, and today there is renewed interest in them. In terms of genuineness or value they do not compare with an unconverted clock. Yet there are some once-superb lantern clocks by fine makers, which are preserved today in their external form at least (see Plate 9).

These conversions had fusee movements fitted to make them available for what was seen as a more convenient use on a mantelpiece or table top, and of course they are key-wound and of eight-day duration. With some, the movements were specially made of such a size and shape that they could be fitted inside the lantern clock housing without spoiling the external appearance, and this often meant that the movements were made to wind from the back, which avoided cutting winding holes through the beautiful engraving on the dial. More often, however, front-wind movements were fitted, sometimes taken from a bracket clock or even a single-fusee wall clock, and these were sometimes squeezed into the lantern clock 'case' as well as could be managed, even if this meant cutting severely through an engraved dial centre or alarm disc, or both (Plate 9).

Anyone who buys a spring-wound lantern clock knows full well that there were no such things originally, as all are later conversions. Of course, there are modern ones built with spring drive as reproductions, so it is possible to buy a lantern clock which *was* built with a spring movement, but these were made new within the last century as modern copies of an older type of clock (Plate 114).

Some lantern clocks were housed in long wooden cases, though few survive today in that state. The wooden case was first and foremost a protective box built tall enough to allow the weight(s) the required drop. *The* wooden-cased clock was of course the longcase clock itself, and whilst in some respects the lantern clock can be seen to have developed into a certain type of thirty hour longcase clock, both eight-day and thirty-hour longcases originated long before the lantern clock expired. It is the origin of longcase clocks which we will examine next.

4 LONGCASE CLOCKS WITH BRASS DIALS

The longcase clock became possible with the introduction of the pendulum to London in 1658 by Ahasuerus Fromanteel, who had collaborated with Christiaan Huygens of the Netherlands, the man who had perfected the application of a pendulum to clockwork. It was Fromanteel who made the first pendulum clocks in England, as his announcements of that year proclaim. The main benefit of the pendulum was the greater accuracy of timekeeping which it offered. Therefore it now became worthwhile to make clocks of longer duration than had previously been the case. His clocks ran for a week, a month, or even a year, but he also made clocks of one-day duration. These were the permutations on offer. The customer could choose, and would pay the price accordingly.

So the first longcase clocks might be thirty-hour or eight-day types (or, of course, longer duration if desired, these being simply extensions of the basic eight-day system). The point is that one-day and eight-day clocks were available from the same moment by choice, and neither is older than the other. However, while this was true in principle, the reality was that clocks of eight-day or longer duration were the main category called for – presumably to take full advantage of this newly-available facility. After all, those who were content with a one-day clock had the lantern clock available to them, as it had been for many years, so in fact the London longcase clock was seldom of thirty-hour duration, either at this particular moment or at any other time.

In the short period before the anchor escapement appeared (about 1670), longcase clocks were made mostly by Fromanteel and a mere handful of other London makers, using, of course, the verge escapement and bob pendulum. It was not until the arrival of the anchor escapement that longcase clock production really got into full swing. After some experimenting with pendulums of extreme length, whereby the rating nut was in the very base of the case and the clock would beat 1¼ seconds or occasionally 1⅛ seconds, the standard one-second pendulum (39.13 inches, 103cms in length) was soon established, and was used till the end of longcase clockmaking.

Virtually all longcase clocks struck the hours on a bell. Those which chimed the quarter-hours or played tunes were in a special category of their own, which we shall consider later, but by and large the great majority of British clocks strike hours and nothing but the hours.

COUNTWHEEL STRIKING
The hourly striking of a lantern clock had been controlled by what is known as a countwheel (sometimes called a locking wheel), a

disc which turned during striking to allow an arm (called a detent) to drop into a notch at ever-increasing distances along the circumference. This was the earliest form of strike control (Figure 8) and its use passed on from lantern clocks to longcase clocks. Owners are sometimes puzzled as to when this system was used and when a later system, known as rack striking, was selected instead. In principle this is very simple.

Fig. 8 Countwheel or locking plate striking

The arm known as a detent slips into the next notch in the circumference after each strike. During striking it is prevented from locking off into the next notch by the wheel rim.

Numbers on the drawing indicate each hour. These numbers do not appear on countwheels on clocks except for a very few early examples.

For one o'clock the detent remains in the slot.

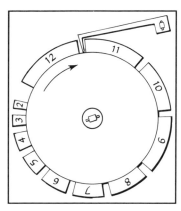

The thirty-hour longcase clock kept the countwheel form, positioned outside the backplate or at the back on a posted movement, throughout its entire period of manufacture. Therefore, countwheel striking is normal on all thirty-hour clocks of whatever age from the beginnings to the end of longcase clock making, and it is always positioned at the back of the movement – sometimes called outside countwheel because it lies outside the movement proper (Plate 21). Just occasionally, and it is unusual, a thirty-hour longcase might have been constructed with the alternative system (rack striking), and this was only done where the clock was to have repeating work, since the rack system allowed repeating and the countwheel did not.

Repeating was achieved by a pull-cord, whereby the owner might trigger off the hour strike for a second time, or, indeed, as many times as he might wish. It could be used by a servant to summon the family to meals, if they happened not to have heard the hour strike the first time. Or it could be used in the bedroom if a cord were run up through the floor, so that those stirring in bed might sound off the nearest hour as a time check, without the trouble of striking a light or going downstairs to look at the clock. We have little written evidence as to why the owner would want to repeat his clock, and these are simply two of the known reasons why some clocks were purposely fitted (at extra cost) with repeat

21. Thirty-hour movement of c1690 showing posted frame construction (iron posts) and countwheel for striking, which was always positioned at the back on thirty-hour work. Maker John Knibb, Oxford.

facility. In identifying clocks, however, it is enough to know that thirty-hour longcases always had countwheel striking, unless specifically built with rack strike for repeating purposes.

The earliest eight-day clocks also had countwheel striking, and normally they too had the countwheel positioned outside the back-plate *ie.* an outside countwheel. Within a very few years an alternative was to position the countwheel *inside* the plates beside the mainwheel, and this is known as inside countwheel striking. Inside countwheel strike is found only on clocks of eight-day duration or longer.

RACK STRIKING

Rack striking, sometimes called rack repeating striking, was invented at some time in the 1670s, but was not immediately adopted into widespread use, and countwheel striking continued in use on many eight-day clocks for some considerable years ahead, usually in its second form of inside countwheel. We already know that outside countwheel striking continued unchanged in thirty-hour clocks, but here we are speaking only of eight-day ones (and longer duration, of course).

Exactly when rack striking took over totally from countwheel on eight-day clocks is a factor which varies in different areas. In London, most eight-day clocks had rack striking by about 1720, and it became the standard form thereafter. In the provinces this was very different. Some areas, indeed most areas, followed the London principle. In Northern England, especially the North-West, the inside countwheel system was retained on eight-day clocks for much longer by many, though not all, clockmakers. Here the countwheel is found frequently into the middle of the eighteenth century, and, by a good proportion of clockmakers, into the third and even fourth quarter of the eighteenth century, and even, on unusual occasions, into the early nineteenth century.

The reasons why some clockmakers preferred to keep the older system are not known, but two explanations are likely. The rack system (Figure 9) involves the use of a small spring, which sooner or later is almost certain to fail from metal fatigue, whereas the countwheel system had no in-built design flaw, so was probably thought of as being more reliable. One other possible reason is that a clock with countwheel striking can be run without striking if so required (*eg.* by removing the strike weight, or simply by not winding the strike train), and this is something that cannot be done safely with most rack-striking clocks. In other words, the countwheel system gave the option of silent running, and by the same token was more customer-proof, in that a strike train inadvertently allowed to run down would not cause the clock to fail.

The presence of countwheel striking on an eight-day clock can be an indicator towards its period as long as it is borne in mind that its use was normal much later in the North-West and occasionally elsewhere than in the South. Hence it is not a very reliable feature on clocks in areas outside London or coming under London influence.

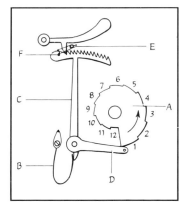

Fig. 9 Rack striking/rack repeating striking

The stepped cam, known as the snail (A), turns once in twelve hours. The rack spring (B) pushes the rack (C) sufficiently far to the left to allow the appropriate hour to be struck, that hour being determined by the point on the snail on which the rack tail (D) comes to rest. During striking the gathering pallet (E) claws back one more tooth of the rack at each successive blow, coming to rest against the stop pin (F) after completing the required hour.

DIAL STYLES

It is a relatively simple matter to assess the age of a longcase clock to within ten years by means of its dial style. Certainly the movement and case are important too, as is the question of ensuring that all three actually began life together. Of all the types of British-made clock, longcases are the easiest for the novice to understand and to date. Once the longcase dial is understood, then some other types of clock are so very similar in styling that they too are easy to assess – principally bracket clocks, hook-and-spike clocks and hooded clocks.

For this reason I shall devote the most space to longcase clock styles. To understand the age of the clock and its quality involves examining one by one the dozen or so separate features visible on the dial. Any one such feature taken in isolation may not pin down the clock to a precise period, and obviously some leeway has to be allowed in dating any feature anyway. But, when taken together, this composition of stylistic features proves highly accurate. The final assessment of age must be based on the *newest* feature of style. To take an example, if we have a clock with dotted minutes, a feature which we know did not begin till about 1770, then even if all other features on that dial suggested a date of about 1740, it would be unwise to conclude that this clock was unique in having a very early use of dotted minute feature. More likely, the position would be that the clock dated from post-1770 and happened to have some archaic features still in use by that particular clockmaker.

In practice, there is seldom such a discrepancy between features, and it will usually turn out that, while the style of any one feature of a clock may cover a span as wide as perhaps thirty years, if a list of all relevant features were to be drawn up, then they would usually match together quite surprisingly closely as to period. If they do not, then the reason will probably either be that you have misunderstood one feature, or that the clock is one made up from scrap parts, which are pieces from widely different periods which would never be seen together on a genuine clock.

The beginner should take these stylistic points one at a time. Seen in isolation, each is quite easy to understand. Having read about that one feature, one should then check it against as many illustrations as possible, so that not only will it become assimilated into the memory, but its reliability as a dating aid can be checked for accuracy. Those who write books are not infallible, and if you are observant enough you might be able to catch the author out.

An expert can glance at a clock dial across a room and tell its age instantly, just as a child can tell the period of a motor car of the 1950s from one of the 1970s or 1990s without ever having consciously learned to do so. A novice cannot assess the age of a clock by an overall glance, and it is folly to try to do so until this skill has been acquired. To begin with, he must take each dial feature in isolation, until he knows them off by heart one by one.

Eventually he will learn which combinations of features to expect together and which are impossible, and the latter will eliminate visually most made-up clocks as the fakes that they are. When using most of the stylistic features, it is important to bear in mind that there are differences when considering thirty-hour clocks as opposed to eight-day examples, and there are differences between provincial work and that of London makers. What will be reliable for one category may be quite misleading if mistakenly applied to the other. I have tried to make such distinctions apparent in the text.

London was *the* prime centre of clockmaking. It was the capital of the land and was the place where the largest and wealthiest population was gathered. Standards of clockmaking in London were high, and it was here that most advances in timekeeping first originated and developed. The great bulk of output of all clocks in Britain in the seventeenth century originated in London, and London output probably still exceeded that throughout the rest of Britain until about the middle of the eighteenth century.

This centralisation of the trade during what was almost the first century of British longcase clock making has a bearing on our study of the subject in two ways. Firstly, it means that London clocks are for the most part a category of their own, requiring separate consideration from provincial clocks. Those features applying to London clocks may not necessarily apply to provincial examples, and in general the London 'fashion' in styling was something from which few makers there would deviate. So London styling in its particular period was generally far more rigidly adhered to than any provincial style was in its own area and period.

It follows on from this that a study of provincial styles and features will occupy more space than that of London work. The reason is not because provincial work is more important, either in general or in my own particular viewpoint, but because it is far more varied.

DIAL SIZE

In London, which was where the great majority of clocks were made before about 1700, the thirty-hour longcase was never popular, for reasons suggested above, and most of the following comments on London clocks relate to eight-day examples only. Dials were small to begin with, being square in shape and having a size of ten inches (25.5cms) (Plate 6), or even occasionally less. Very soon dial size progressed to eleven inches (28cms) (Plate 22), and by the start of the new century the twelve-inch (30.5cms) dial had become normal (Plate 23).

A brass dial was constructed from several parts, each one cast in brass and finished according to its function. Those parts which

22. Eight-day dial, eleven inches square (28cms), from a longcase clock of c1695 by John Williamson of Leeds, showing many early characteristics: engraving between spandrels (corner pieces), engraved centre boss, ringed winding holes, signature below chapter ring, original hour hand (minute hand a later replacement), cherub head spandrels of the early type, arrowhead half-hour markers. A high quality dial.

23. Twelve-inch eight-day dial (30.5cms), c1765 by James Sandiford of Manchester, showing matted centre with scroll engraving, the pattern worked around the winding holes.

would be on show in the completed clock were highly finished by filing, polishing, burnishing, engraving, and even gilding. Those which would not show were often left with hardly any finishing work at all, sometimes even raw from the casting with traces of casting 'rag' remaining.

The dial consisted of the dial sheet itself; corner-pieces known as spandrels, each attached from behind by a screw (in country work by a rivet); the main chapter ring carrying all the numbers, usually attached by feet at the back pinned behind the dial sheet (on some country work by rivets); and often a subsidiary chapter ring for a seconds dial or perhaps other features too (calendar work, tune selection, etc.).

SOLID/CARTWHEEL DIALS

The earliest dials were London-made for London clocks, and London dials were cast in a solid sheet form. Early provincial dials followed the London principle, at least at first, but by the early eighteenth century provincial dials in Northern England were usually cast in a cartwheel form (see Plate 24). Quite why this was done is not known, but suggestions include the following. The casting itself may have been easier to form without faults, distortions and blow-holes if done in the cartwheel manner. The tendency for the dial to buckle and distort during the working of the matting process may have been much less with the cartwheel type, which helped absorb expansion under pressure, or during planishing (hammering). The surface of the dial sheet (and other visible parts) was planished to harden, filed to remove hammer-

24. *Twelve-inch dial (30.5cms), from an eight-day clock of the early eighteenth century, by Parkinson of Richmond (Yorks.), with its spandrels and chapter rings removed. Crude matting to centre zone, primitive herringbone type border engraving, ringing to winding holes, seconds and calendar holes. 'Cartwheel' type of dial sheet, the apertures showing much casting rag left unfinished, as was usual. Hammering marks left unworked on the spokes, as these did not show. Crack in lower right corner. The holes are for the chapter ring feet.*

25. *Close-up of the back of a part of the Parkinson dial. Dial backs were usually left unfinished, ie. not filed up or burnished. The rough nature of the cast brass shows well, with many pits, flaws and imperfections showing, as well as jagged edges left raw from the casting. Most pre-1800 brass dials look similar in texture, very different from the smooth surface of rolled brass, which was often used in later reproductions, fakes and marriages.*

marks, and ground smooth with polishing stones and compounds to produce a smooth and fine surface free of flaws, as this both improved the appearance and provided a good surface on which to work at either engraving or matting, or both. The unseen back of the dial (and other parts too) might well show signs of hammering produced when correcting any distortion but would otherwise be left unfinished and un-filed with all its pitting, sand marks, casting rag and blow-holes left just as they occurred (see Plate 25).

Whatever the reasons for employing the cartwheel method as opposed to the solid sheet method of dial construction, it can be a helpful feature of identification to know that dials from London and the South were usually solid, and dials from the North were usually of cartwheel type after about 1720.

ARCHED DIALS

Early dials were square in shape. The arched dial first appeared towards the end of the seventeenth century. At first the arch was shallow, forming less than a semi-circle. After a few years of this 'experimental' shallow arch, the full arch dial took over, by about 1715 in London, and within a very few years the arch dial of twelve-inch width (30.3cms) had become the standard London eight-day dial (see Plate 26). After this time, the square dial was used only occasionally in London, and often for clocks of a special purpose. For all London eight-day clocks the arched dial was the norm, right until the end of brass dial longcase clocks, which in London was about 1810.

In the provinces, things were more complicated, because eight-day and thirty-hour clocks ran side by side, and the two types need to be considered separately. The thirty-hour provincial longcase began with a ten-inch (25.5cms) square dial, though occasionally nine-inch (23cms) and exceptionally eight-inch (20cms) examples are met with in the earliest period. In the North, larger dials appeared sooner, and eleven-inch (28cms) and even twelve-inch (30.5cms) dials were common before 1700 (see Plate 22). Some Northern thirty-hour dials had reached thirteen inches (33cms) by the 1750s (see Plate 42), though brass dials seldom exceeded this size, especially on thirty-hour clocks. Southern regions tended to keep the smaller-sized dials for longer, and it is not unusual to find the ten-inch dial (25.5cms) as late as the 1790s (eg Plate 38). The general trend in the South and North, was always towards dial size increasing as time went by, though Southern brass dials seldom exceeded twelve inches (30.5cms) in width.

This progression in size occurred sooner in eight-day clocks than in thirty-hour examples in most areas, especially in the North. The brass dial died from fashion by the end of the eighteenth century, when it was replaced almost entirely by the white dial (see Chapter 5).

26. Dial of a twelve-inch, (30.5cms) eight-day longcase clock, c1720, by John Hindmore of London. Interesting use of the herringbone border engraving on an arched dial and sunburst feature in the arch, giving an overall more flamboyant appearance than the average London dial of the day.

SINGLE-SHEET DIALS

The dial, as we have seen, consisted of a dial sheet, a separate brass ring for numbers, known as a chapter ring, and separate cast brass corner pieces, called spandrels. About 1760, occasional examples are found of dials made from a single sheet of brass with no attached features and with all the information engraved onto this single sheet. This is known as a one-piece brass dial, or a single-sheet dial, and was met with increasingly towards the end of the brass dial period. By 1800 this too was replaced by the white dial, except in certain traditional areas (*eg* the South-West, and parts of Scotland), where occasional examples of this occur as late as the 1840s. The one-piece dial was also used for special clocks such as Regulators (Plate 12), on which it may occur well outside its usual period.

RINGED WINDING HOLES

Ringed winding holes on eight-day brass dial clocks can be a helpful indicator of period, but this is a feature which may easily be misunderstood, and you need to take care when considering this aspect. The ringing itself was a decorative border formed from two or several turned circles, and was positioned around each winding hole (see Plates 6, 22). Its purpose was probably to

27. Fine eight-day longcase dial of about 1710-20 by John Parker of Dublin, a dial full of character and interest, with much herringbone engraving.

76

prevent marking of the dial plate by careless insertion of the winding key, but it slowly became as much a decoration as a function. When a clock had a seconds dial (as most did), and when it had a *circular* calendar box above the numeral VI (as some did between about 1690 and about 1740), each of these two features might also be given the same decorative ringed treatment to match in with the winding holes. So the ringing of seconds and calendar features went with ringing of winding holes, and would not be expected on a clock which did not have ringed winding holes.

The earliest dials, from 1658 to about 1690, did not have ringed holes. The practice of ringing started from about 1690, and continued in London, where the great majority of these early clocks were made, until about 1730, only occurring later sporadically, until the practice fizzled out about 1740 and plain holes again became the norm. In the provinces, this practice began with the earliest clocks (see Plate 22), very few being before about 1690 anyway, and continued in regular use till about 1740 or a little later (see Plate 27). Not every single clockmaker ringed his winding holes, but most did in the main period mentioned. The number of those not using this method increased as the period progressed, so that few continued this practice after about 1730–40.

In the provinces, however, and especially in the North and North-West of England and in Scotland (though only sporadically there), some clockmakers carried on with the ringing principle after 1740, this being a whim of the individual maker (*eg.* Plate 33). Sometimes it was the same type of ringing as in the earlier period, but sometimes it was a more simplified form, in the shape of a single ring or a shallow double ring. The bolder type of ringing, as found on earlier clocks, was more likely to be performed on a dial with a matted centre, which in the North would often have considerable engraving into the matting (in other words, not on a *plain* matted centre). On those with a polished ground and engraved design to the centre, the ringing might be simply an extension of the engraved design into circular terminals, instead of the deeply-grooved earlier form, and so this engraved circling might not be regarded as 'ringing' in the earlier sense (Plate 33). In much of Southern England, where the dial centre of plain matting followed the London principle, the ringing principle was often dropped completely after about 1740, as it was in London.

The above comments relate to eight-day clocks or those of longer duration, of course. Thirty-hour clocks did not wind with a key, hence the concept of ringed winding holes seems impossible, yet some thirty-hour clocks did have them! There were two ways in which this might happen.

DUMMY WINDERS

A few thirty-hour clocks had what we now call dummy winding

holes, which were two holes positioned in the dial in a similar place to the winding holes on eight-day clocks (*eg.* Plates 28, 29), to give the superficial impression of an eight-day dial. This eight-day appearance was increased if such a clock had winding squares within the holes, and some did. Of course, the winding squares were purely visual, usually being square shanks attached to the dial on sprigs, or sometimes screwed into the movement frontplate. They did not actually wind, but were there to complete this eight-day look, and sometimes accomplished this so successfully that a clock can be mistaken for an eight-day at first sight. The practice of dummy winding holes (and squares too, though these were always fewer in number) was indulged mostly in North-Western England. Where a thirty-hour clock had such dummy winding holes, the maker might have opted to have them ringed or he might not; both forms are found, though the ringed

28. *Eleven-inch dial (28cms) of a thirty-hour longcase clock of about 1740 by William Reynolds of Wigton, Cumberland. Note the penny moon dial, ringed 'dummy' winding holes, and plain corners without spandrels, the latter a feature often used by Quaker clockmakers, but occasionally (as here) by non-Quakers.*

form is perhaps the commoner of the two alternatives.

Some thirty-hour clocks had ringed winding 'holes', which were not actually cut through as holes, but were just ringed decorative features, usually placed somewhere in the general area of where true winding holes would be on an eight-day clock. These are sometimes found on dials which have what would (without the ring turns) otherwise be the type with a plain matted centre, and the reason is probably not so much to give a true 'eight-day' effect, but just to decorate this over-plain centre. Such plain centres were not popular in the North as a general rule, with the exception of a few makers in certain towns whose eight-day work was of that formal nature associated with the London dial style. Clearly those makers were simulating the London style (if not in fact buying-in London-made dials) for the purpose of following the fashion of the stylish capital.

Ringed treatment of dial centres on thirty-hour clocks is usually more a regional feature than a help in assessing age. Ringed winding holes on eight-day clocks, on the other hand, are a very helpful dating feature. If this business of ringing sounds too confusing by far for the novice, the best thing is to ignore it altogether, and to use other, simpler stylistic features in dating.

29. Dial from a thirty-hour longcase c1770, by Christopher Caygill of Askrigg, Yorks. Note floral engraving around dummy winding holes. Painted landscape in the arch.

HERRINGBONE ENGRAVING

Herringbone edging, sometimes known as wheatear edging or bordering, is a manner of finishing a dialsheet in such a way as to give a decorative border running around the dial extremity outside the corner spandrels. Strictly speaking, the herringbone pattern is a slightly different design to wheatear, though the two terms are used indiscriminately. In reality there are several

30. Twelve-inch (30.5cms) dial from an eight-day longcase clock of about 1720-30, by Gabriel Smith of Nantwich. Penny moon in the arch, much use of herringbone engraving, and bold engraving characteristic of this fine maker.

variations in the manner of performing this engraved border, each engraver who used this system having his own preferred variant.

The important point about herringbone banding is that it was used over a relatively short period of time, and therefore can be a useful dating aid. In London, where this theme originated, it appeared on some (but by no means all) longcase clocks from the last few years of the seventeenth century, was at its most popular

31. Superbly engraved eight-day dial of a longcase clock by Randolph Bagnall of Talk-on-the-Hill, Staffordshire, dating from the 1720s or 1730s. Penny moon in the arch.

there from about 1700 to 1725 (Plate 26), but lingered a little after that in occasional use. In the provinces, this pattern came into fashion a little later, perhaps around 1700, and lasted till as late as the 1740s with some makers. In the provinces, however, its use was perhaps less popular than in London (Plate 30).

It follows from its period of use that herringboning was a feature mostly of square dials, at least initially. Sometimes it is found on arch dials too (Plates 30, 31), and then it is usually seen on early examples of the arched dial, thus the manner of its execution may vary. With square dials it runs right round the dial edge. With arched dials it might also run right round the dial edge (Plate 30), but sometimes the engraver on these early arched dials regarded the arch itself as a separate section, and so took the pattern completely round the square, then completely round the arch too, thus making an engraved border which appears to separate the arch from the square (Plates 26, 31). This divided manner is almost always a sign of a very early (for the region) arch dial example.

This design was sometimes used on bracket clock dials too, but perhaps less commonly than on longcase dials. Of course, not all dials, longcase or bracket, used this feature, but when they did it forms a very helpful dating aid. A few makers in the provinces might use a small section of herringbone engraving for decorative effect long outside the period of its more general fashion – in very limited form as a dial centre decoration for instance, to edge the dial centre, or as a rim around a penny moon feature. When used in this manner it may occur much later, in, for example, the 1760s even, though again as a general rule this sort of extra herringbone decoration will still fall within its main provincial period, *ie*. 1710 to 1740.

Engraving was used on some early dials, principally in the late seventeenth and early eighteenth centuries, to fill the otherwise blank area between the spandrels on the edge of the dial sheet on square dial clocks. Often, clocks of this age will have the maker's name along the lower edge of the dial, and an engraved design of vaguely floral nature would balance this feature on the other three dial edges. Engraving between the spandrels is found mostly between about 1690 and 1710, and can be a helpful dating feature (see Plates 6, 22). Of course, not all clocks of this period will have this feature, but many do.

SPANDRELS

Spandrel is the name given to a cornerpiece fitted to most brass dial clocks, not only of the longcase type, but also bracket clocks and any other clock of the composite dial type. Provided the clock has the original spandrels, their pattern can be a most helpful indicator of the clock's age. Spandrels were cast in brass, any rough casting 'rag' was filed clean, and the spandrel was attached to each corner of the dial by a screw from the back. Just occasionally they attached from the front by a single screw positioned so as to be concealed by the pattern. A very few top makers used two screws fitted from behind. On some provincial work the spandrels were riveted into place instead.

On some early London clocks the spandrels were gilded, and occasionally the gilding remains today, or traces of it. Otherwise the spandrels were lacquered against tarnishing like the rest of the dial. Lacquer which has gone off may remain on parts of spandrels and can sometimes be mistaken for worn gilding. The great majority at all periods were not gilded, just lacquered. Sometimes one sees spandrels painted with a sort of gold paint, which is usually some restorer's misunderstanding of what gilding was, but this is an instance of inaccurate restoration, and the gold paint should be removed. Today, spandrels are polished and lacquered before re-fixing, but original gilding should not be polished off, and it may take an expert restorer to recognise this.

Mercurial gilding, sometimes called fire gilding, involved

rubbing the surface of the object (the spandrel, for instance) with a mixture of mercury and gold powder, and then heating it to leave a coating of pure gold, which was then burnished. The inhalation of the toxic fumes given off in the process was injurious to health, and the process is no longer used.

Spandrel patterns were very few in number, and their styles kept changing as time progressed. This was partly because, as

32. *Dial of eight-day clock by Joseph Butterworth of Cawthorne, Yorks. from the 1730s, showing unusually large month calendar and elaborate spandrels.*

dials grew gradually larger over the years, the older spandrels would not fit the wider curve of the chapter ring, so that new styles kept appearing to suit the larger dial styles. One pattern of design seldom remained fashionable for more than about thirty years. At any one period, barely more than three or four patterns

33. *Twelve-inch eight-day dial c1760 by Thomas Clare of Warrington, Lancs., with the unusual feature for that date of two spandrels by the seconds dial.*

34. *Thirty-hour brass dial clock with single hand, made about 1720-30 by Edmund Bullock of Ellesmere, Shropshire, and numbered 208. The dial is 9½in square (24cms).*

were popular (for each appropriate dial size, that is), and so, in all, something like thirty patterns of spandrel would account for the great majority of clocks met with today.

It is not possible to show here every known pattern; for that one should refer to a book such as *Grandfather Clocks and their Cases*, which shows an example of each type. Several variations usually

35. Brass dial from an eight-day clock of about 1750, by John Coates of Tetbury, Gloucestershire, with a rocking Father Time in the arch and spandrels showing two eagles holding an urn. The hour hand has lost some of its loops.

exist based on the same basic theme. A pattern based on a cherub head (see Plate 22), for example, occurs in perhaps fifteen different forms, and to learn to distinguish the period factor from a spandrel you need to memorise the distinctly different types even of those based on the same theme.

The illustrations show some of the more common patterns. More variety tends to be seen in provincial spandrels than in London ones, where the diversity of patterns was relatively limited. This may be on account of the fact that once London dials reached the twelve-inch size (30.5cms), they remained static. Some spandrel patterns were almost exclusively provincial, such as the Four Seasons pattern for example, where each cornerpiece shows a figure symbolising the season, and these were hardly ever seen on London dials.

Some of the major themes are summarised very briefly as follows, the measurement representing the approximate length between the widest extremities. Periods given are only approximate.

> Early London cherub head (3 inch, 7.5cms) 1660–1680.
> Early London cherub head (4 inch, 10cms) 1670–1710.
> Twin cherubs with crown (5 inch, 12.5cms) 1690–1730.
> Twin cherubs with crossed maces (5 inch, 12.5cms) 1695–1740.
> Male mask head (5 inch, 12.5cms) 1700–1735.
> Female head (6 inch or 7 inch, 15cms or 18cms) 1715–1760.
> Two eagles holding urn (6 inch, 15cms) 1730–65 (see Plate 35).
> Four Seasons (5 inch, 12.5cms) 1740–60.
> Large (Lancashire type) cherub head (7 inch, 18cms) 1750–80 (provincial).
> Cockleshell (5 inch, 12.5cms) 1750–70.
> Question mark (7 inch, 18cms) 1755–85 (provincial).
> Scrollwork (many patterns and sizes) 1760–90.

These names are those I have invented for spandrels in an attempt at categorising them, albeit vaguely. Any clock enthusiast will know what is meant by these names, but with some of these types there can be many variations of that theme. Provincial clocks, in instances where they employ a pattern which was also used in London, may well employ them later than in London, and the above dates are only a guide, not definitive limits.

Clocks with arched dials often had spandrels in the arch, often a pair at each side of some central feature (Plates 26, 30, 31), such as a nameplate (see Plate 36). By far the commonest arch spandrels were those which centre on a dolphin, and these might be found over a wide period, c1710 to 1780 (Plate 35). Arch spandrels are not always a 'match' to the corner patterns, as, for example, with the dolphin type, as there are no corner patterns based on dolphins.

Not all clocks have spandrels in the corners. A few have finely engraved flowers or some similar design instead, of the nature of the engraved corners found later on single-sheet dials. Some

36. *Twelve-inch dial (30.5cms) from an eight-day longcase clock of about 1730, by Robert Henderson of Scarborough, this example clearly bearing the name of the first owner, R. Temple. Typical dial layout and original hands.*

Quaker clock-makers left their corners plain, *ie.* without spandrels or engraving (see Plate 28). A few, including some Quakers, engraved verses in the corners. Some country makers drilled cup-and-ring patterns as a corner design, these being cheaper than spandrels and easier to do than engraving. Engraved pattern corners might be of any period. Cup-and-ring turns, plain corners, and verses are usually pre-1750.

SIGNATURES

The earliest longcase dials were usually signed on the dial sheet itself *underneath* the chapter ring (see Plate 22), a practice which ceased by about 1700 in London and perhaps a little later elsewhere. In this early period, also, the signature often included the word 'Fecit', being Latin for 'made it' (see Plate 32). By the end of the second quarter of the eighteenth century, this word had dropped from London use, though provincial makers sometimes used it at a later date, but even there it was very seldom used after mid-century. In keeping with this Latinisation of the signature, the maker's name itself was also often Latinised, as was the name of the town. For instance, a clock of the second half of the seventeenth century by John Fromanteel might well be signed (below the chapter ring) 'Johannes Fromanteel Londinii Fecit', whereas that same maker, if he had been working a century later, would probably have signed it 'John Fromanteel, London'.

A few makers might opt to sign their names using English forms: 'Jno. Williamson at Leeds' is an example (Plate 22). A few used 'in' or 'of' and a very few used 'de', as, for instance, 'Thomas Ogden de Halifax'.

Towards the end of the seventeenth century, the signature moved in position, usually *onto* the chapter ring itself, where it was often positioned in the lower space between V and VI and VII (see Plates 6, 27). This position was used by some clockmakers, especially on square dial clocks, right to the end of brass-dial clockmaking. On arched dials there was more choice of position available, and these were often signed on a circular plate in the arch, or sometimes a plate or plain zone in the dial centre itself (see Plates 35, 36). Moon dials were very often signed round the arch rim above the moon feature (see Plates 45, 47). The variability of the position of the signature is little help in dating a clock after about 1750, because of the numerous options available.

Abbreviations in first names take a little getting used to. Jno. was commonly used as a short form for John (Plate 22), and as I and J were interchangeable in early lettering, this could well appear as Ino. or In., until about 1800 (see Plates 26, 27). For instance, Ino Hindmor is John Hindmor.

Engraved lettering styles take a little practice to read, especially early ones. In particular the letter w is often engraved rather like a modern n, and is commonly misread. So what might at first sight look like Nencastle is Newcastle. To complicate matters, there was no such thing as fixed spelling in the past, so a variety of what we would think of as eccentric spellings are met with. Some letters were used interchangeably at times – so a name might be spelt Lawson or Lauson, and, because of unfamiliarity with old lettering styles, it is often misread as Lanson. Several times a year I am asked if I can help trace a maker called Lanson, when it is merely a misreading of one of the numerous clockmakers called Lawson.

DIAL CENTRES

The style of longcase dial centres can be a very helpful dating factor, once the stylistic trends are understood, though these may seem complex to a beginner. For this purpose it helps to see longcase clocks as having two distinct origins – the thirty-hour version deriving from the lantern clock, and the eight-day having its own quite separate origin. Lantern clocks, as already mentioned, had a polished dial centre onto which was worked an engraved design, often of tulips, but sometimes of other entwined flowers and leafy sprays. Early thirty-hour longcase clocks almost always began with a continuation in style of the contemporary clock principle, that is, of flowers (often tulips) engraved onto a polished background.

Thirty-hour longcases were mostly provincial, though there were a few London-made ones, especially in the earliest period. The engraved centre concept persisted in thirty-hour longcases until roughly the second quarter of the eighteenth century – both in London and provincial examples.

The eight-day dial centre began in a very different and distinctive style, with what is usually known as a matted centre, having a sandpaper-like finish (see Plate 26). The idea was that it avoided the reflections of a polished/engraved centre, and made it easier to read time on the *two* hands. Early eight-day longcase clocks had an entirely plain centre, matted all over. Towards the end of the seventeenth century, a little decorative engraved scrollwork was often added around the lip of the calendar box, and about this same time, as we have seen, ringed decorative edging was introduced around the winding holes (see Plate 22), and also sometimes around the seconds centre and, in those cases where it was circular rather than square, around the calendar box. The ringing is thought to have been intended to disguise knocks occasioned by careless use of the winding key. Ringed winding holes fell from fashion in London by about 1720, but some provincial regions kept a simplified form of ringing for much longer, especially the North-West.

On London eight-day dials, where a formal effect was usually intended, the dial centres might remain undecorated right to the end of brass dial longcases. Seldom was there more than a hint of engraving (see Plate 26). Provincial dials in some areas followed

37. Thirty-hour single-handed clock of about 1710-20, by Walter Archer of Stow-on-the-Wold, a small dial only nine inches (23cms) square, with flowers engraved in dial centre and lozenge-shaped half-hour markers.

the London principle, but might allow themselves a little more decorative effect in the engraving. This applied principally in the South, where the London fashion always held greater sway.

In the Northern provinces, the second quarter of the eighteenth century saw considerable deviation from the London theme, in that some clockmakers might use engraving to decorate much of the dial centre, still onto a matted background (see Plate 30), though the engraving could be so lavish as to leave little undecorated area. This happened particularly in Lancashire and the North-West. After about 1750 some provincial makers decided that the engraved designs looked better against a polished background and did away with matting altogether, in other words, they returned to the old principle used on lantern clock dials, though by this time the engraved patterns were very different – most being scrolled and entwining patterns of leaves and branches, often working the design around the essential features such as the winding holes (*eg.* Plate 40).

Just to complicate things, some thirty-hour dials after about 1720 copied the same principle for the dial centre as the eight-day clock of the period – that is, to use a matted ground (Plate 38). After about 1760, some thirty-hour dials used the polished-ground principle with leafy-scroll engraving, just like many eight-days of that type (see Plate 29).

Puzzling as this might sound to a beginner, there is nonetheless a very strong dial centre styling on all clocks, which with experience will enable a dial to be dated by the style of its centre alone. The beginner needs to look at as many dials as possible to try to learn and memorise this treatment of dial centres.

38. Ten-inch dial (25.5cms) of a single-handed thirty-hour longcase clock of about 1750, by Thomas Pinfold of Banbury. Note crude matting and tulip and windmill engraving.

CHAPTER RINGS

Most brass dials have a numbers ring, which is a separately cast brass disc onto which the numbers for hours and minutes were engraved. The engraved information was filled with black wax, and the chapter ring, as it is known, was silvered over its surface so that the numbers stood out clearly in black against a silver background. Today, many chapter rings show no sign of silvering, as this has been polished away by house-proud owners to reveal the brass surface. Most restorers can re-silver a dial, and this is regarded as normal restoration. The silver itself is applied as a paste of silver chloride, followed by a clear lacquer, without which it would tarnish rapidly. In the past it was normal for all engraved areas to be silvered, with the exception of engraving onto a matted ground, as matting will not take silvering.

Numbers are only one of several features which are engraved onto most chapter rings. A knowledge of the style of numbering and of the other chapter ring information enables a clock's age to be assessed quite closely from scrutinising the chapter ring alone, although of course there are numerous other factors which offer additional evidence.

The earliest two-handed dials had very small minute numbers marked at every fifth unit and positioned *within* the double engraved line, known as the minute band (*eg.* Plate 6). Roman hour numerals occupied most of the chapter ring width. At this time the minute numbers themselves often had characteristic early

39. *Typical eight-day brass dial, thirteen inches (33cms) square, dating from the 1760s and made by Thomas Richardson of Weaverham.*

shapes – for instance the curl-tailed 7, the curl-tailed 1 and the flat-topped 8. Before the end of the seventeenth century, minute numbers moved to be positioned *outside* the minute band (Plate 22, for example), in which position they remained ever after. As the eighteenth century progressed, the minute numbers grew gradually larger in relation to those of the hours (see Plate 23). After about 1770 many (and after about 1780 almost all) dials had minutes marked by dots (see Plate 42), a style which was probably copied from the dotted minute style of the earliest white dials (see Plate 45).

With single-sheet brass dials, there was no separate chapter ring as such, but the stylistic trend in numbering and minute marking often runs similar to those with chapter rings. One exception found mostly on single-sheet dials towards the turn of the eighteenth/nineteenth centuries, is a single line with the minutes marked through by short dash lines (as an example, see Plate 49 in next chapter).

HALF AND QUARTER MARKERS

A single-handed clock, of course, had no minutes marked at all, but simply Roman hour numerals (Plate 34). Instead of minutes, the inner chapter ring edge was marked off in quarter-hour units, to give quick legibility of time to the closest quarter-hour. The half-hour position was usually marked by a device such as a fleur-de-lis, which stood out boldly between hour numerals.

However, many two-handed dials also carried the same markings as a single-handed clock, especially in the early period. This is believed to have been for the benefit of those not yet accustomed to what was then the relatively new system of two-handed time reading, whereas all were used to the single hand, which was as easy to read as the single shadow of a sundial. Until about 1740, it was normal for two-handed chapter rings to also feature the inner quarter-hour units and the half-hour marker (fleur-de-lis, *etc.*). After that date these items slowly began to be dropped, the quarter-hour divisions usually disappearing first, while the half-hour marker was retained until about 1760 by some makers. Certain London makers, in attempting to lead fashion, did this earlier than provincial makers, who were sometimes loath to let the half-hour marker drop.

HALF-QUARTER MARKERS

Many early brass dials had another indicator marked on them, which showed the 'half-quarters'. Its purpose was to assist those still not yet accustomed to the two-handed system. With single-handed clocks, time was measured in quarter-hours (the band on the inner chapter ring edge just discussed above). It must have been difficult for those new to clocks to think in terms of minutes, while quarter-hours were more straightforward. As a transitional means of measuring, some clockmakers indicated those points on the dial which marked half of a quarter-hour. Of course, the minute hand registered quarters already – when it pointed to 15, 30, *etc*. But some clockmakers positioned a marker, such as a star, asterisk or other engraved device, at such points on the dial which divided a quarter into two – *ie.* at 7½ minutes past the hour, then also at 22½ minutes past, and at 22½ minutes to the hour and 7½ minutes to (see Plates 27, 30). These were known as 'half-quarters'. London clockmakers indicated these between about 1690 and 1730, provincial makers from about 1690 to perhaps 1740 or even 1750. Not every clockmaker did this, but most did, and since its use was confined to a limited period, a half-quarter marker can be a helpful indication towards period.

CALENDAR STYLES

Most longcase clocks had a calendar feature to indicate the date by a number. Early ones would often show this through an opening, normally square but occasionally round (see Plates 6, 22). To show the date in this way the clock needed an extra gear wheel, and by about 1730 an alternative method was devised, which did not require this extra wheel and so was simpler and cheaper to make. This is known as a 'mouth' calendar (see Plate 32), and occurred occasionally on eight-day brass dial clocks but more often on thirty-hour examples, where there was greater concern to keep the price low. The mouth was sometimes almost a half circle, but more often was a narrow band, through which a whole section of the calendar disc showed, the day in question usually being indicated by a pointer or 'pip' by its topmost point. Thirty-hour clocks often used this mouth type of calendar from about mid-century to the end of the brass dial period. Most eight-day examples would use the square box system throughout this time, though after about 1780 a few late brass dials used a pointer instead. The two types, square box or mouth, are more often an indicator between eight-day and thirty-hour clocks than a guide to period.

Another type of calendar indication appeared on some clocks, almost always eight-day examples, as it was costly to apply to a thirty-hour. This was what is known as a centre calendar, whereby a third hand based on the dial centre rotated round a series of numbers on the chapter ring. The calendar hand was usually of quite different style and metal from the main two hands, in order to avoid confusion – with brass dials having blued steel hands this would mean the centre calendar hand would usually be of brass for contrast. The centre calendar was used only occasionally, and only by some makers, not every maker. It was fashionable in the North-West in particular, though it could conceivably occur anywhere. It was used only after about 1760, and continued as a possible option until the end of brass dial longcases (indeed it also ran into the white dial period). So a centre calendar is certainly a helpful indication of period.

Some arched dial clocks showed a calendar indicator in the arch area (see Plates 30, 31). This was fashionable mainly in the early period of arched dials, from about 1700 to 1730, and usually a pointer travelled round a small circular chapter ring, though occasionally a cut-out box system might be used. Sometimes the box system was used in a modified form, whereby a triangular space was cut and the disc behind might show not only the calendar number but the month too, and even the day of the week as well, with occasionally a figure representing an ancient god – such as Saturn showing for Saturday. This type of calendar *could* occur at any time, but in practice was popular only during the early years of the arched dial, roughly 1700 to 1730.

MOON DIALS

The calendars referred to so far are those which show the day of the month, but some clocks also had a lunar calendar, usually known as a moon dial. These show the moon's phases by means of a circular moon face passing behind a shaped shield, so that the section which shows does actually represent the shape of the moon as visible in the night sky: *eg.* a crescent moon, full moon, and so on. As well as the moon phases (*ie.* its shape), a moon dial will also show the lunar date. The lunar month is consistently one of 29½ days, the full moon being on the fifteenth lunar date. Once a moon dial is set to position from a printed calendar or diary, the lunar phase and date will remain accurate for the year, requiring none of the long/short resetting of normal day-of-the-month calendar.

A moon dial was used if one were planning a night-time journey at a period when there was little, if any, street lighting, and was more often necessary in country areas. Not all clocks had moon dials, as of course these involved more work in the making and added to the price. Even today a clock with a moon dial is more valuable than a similar one without. The commonest form of moon dial was that which filled the arch of an arched dial clock, and is known as a rolling moon (see Plate 42).

On a few moon dials, usually of the rolling moon type, a further band of information was made available, being a tidal dial, which would show the times of High Water. Normally this would be for the particular port (*eg.* Hull or Bristol), and would involve a series of numbers additional to the 1–29½ lunar date, being calibrated I to XII (see Plates 40 and 41). In Plate 40, for example, the moon dial (read from the pointer above the arch) shows the 27th lunar date with High Water just before III (3 o'clock). As the moon's age and the tide times were consistent with each other, both readings could be read from a single pointer.

A tidal dial could not show precise high tide times (*ie.* the turn of the tide), as this varies by unequal amounts daily. High Water is an average reading, which can be shown by regular daily time indications, and shows that there is an adequate water level to set sail. An occasional tidal dial may show readings for several named ports at once, though these are unusual. Some tidal dials have an adjustable pointer so that the clock can be set to read High Water

40. *Eight-day longcase clock of about 1760 showing moon phases and high tide times, being clock no.518, made by Archibald Strachan of Tanfield, County Durham. High quality work. Width twelve inches (30.5cms). The moon dial shows the 27th lunar date with high water at just before III (3 o'clock).*

41. Dial of an eight-day longcase clock of about 1780, by John Baker of Hull, with rolling moon and tidal dial. Here the moon dial has two pointers, the centre one reading the 6th lunar day, and the second, adjustable one indicating high water at X (10 o'clock). Arabic numerals were normally used for the lunar date; Roman for the tidal times. Fine engraving, and original blued steel hands of non-matching type, here with the traditional straight minute-hand.

for any port of the owner's choice in addition to the port of manufacture of the clock.

SECONDS DIALS

A seconds dial was normal on most eight-day clocks (*eg.* Plate 22) On thirty-hour clocks it was seldom fitted, for the practical reason that the wheel behind the seconds dial position just below XII, on a thirty-hour clock, turned anticlockwise. Just occasionally, one does see an anti-clockwise-turning seconds dial, but this must have seemed unworkmanlike to most clockmakers, and was seldom done. A few clockmakers would sometimes fit a seconds dial to a thirty-hour clock by building an extra wheel in the going train to reverse direction. Such a clock would have four wheels rather than three, and would have the additional advantage of having less 'slop' on the hands than with the normal three-wheeler, so it is often regarded as a sign of higher quality.

An early eight-day clock would usually have a seconds dial marked with numerals reading 5, 10, 15, 30, *etc.* together with a track marking off each second, and this track on early dials would run around the *inner* edge of the seconds chapter ring (see Plates 6, 22). By about the middle of the eighteenth century, the method of numbering gradually altered to marking every 10th second (10, 20, 30, 40 *etc.*) and along with that change often came a change of position for the seconds track, to place it around the *outer* edge of the seconds chapter ring (see Plate 42). Just occasionally, very late brass dials might mark the numbering 20, 40, 60.

The reasons for this change were probably merely to save the amount of engraving work involved, and later dials generally have a lot less engraving work than earlier ones overall. One cannot pin down a date as to when this change took place, as different clockmakers would vary considerably. It would be fair to say that, by about 1760, most clockmakers would adopt the later system, and before about 1740 most would adopt the early system.

This principle applied even with those clocks which had no seconds chapter ring as such (Plate 42), but which instead had the seconds information engraved onto the dial plate itself, or perhaps on a recessed plate. Later brass dials of the type having dotted minutes would more than likely also have dotted seconds rather than a track, and at this late period these would probably have the 10, 20, 30 numbering method instead of numbering in fives.

CENTRE SECONDS

One alternative method of showing seconds was to have a centre seconds hand, along the same principle as the centre calendar. Just occasionally *both* are found on the same clock, though this means that four hands show from the centre, leading not only to confusion of time reading, but also to possible fouling of one hand against another.

On any clock, the seconds hand can be seen to recoil a little at each beat. This is the normal action caused by the anchor escapement, which is sometimes known as a recoil escapement. Some clocks were made to show seconds from the centre, as just described, and the long central seconds hand would have exaggerated this recoil action. For that reason, a centre seconds clock was usually built with a deadbeat escapement (see Figure 6), being a variation of the anchor which did *not* cause recoil. Centre seconds hands are unusual before about 1760, and might occur until the end of the period. They were popular for a time in the North-West, but for several reasons never became widely popular, although they do crop up here and there at random too. Their limited popularity does mean that the centre-seconds feature may be of assistance in dating a clock, but like all other dating aids, needs to be used alongside other indicators.

HANDS TYPES

The hands of a longcase clock can also be of assistance in dating, provided they are the original hands. Because of breakage, a great many clocks have had one or more hands replaced over the years, the minute hand being the more fragile and the one most used when re-setting the time. Experience is needed to recognise original hands from replacements. This is not quite as difficult as might first seem to be the case, because a replacement hand, fitted

42. *Thirteen-inch (33cms) eight-day clock with moonwork, made about 1780 by John Blaylock of Longtown, and showing especially fine engraving. The non-matching hands in blued steel are original and typical of the period, the minute hand now being of serpentine form. The moon dial indicates the 23rd lunar day.*

some time in the past, was often chosen without proper regard to its correct style. This means that most replacement hands are of a totally different era and style from the damaged originals, and so stand out very obviously as incorrect.

Brass dial clocks had steel hands, heated till they turned a dark blue in colour (see Plate 42), at which point the colour was fixed by lacquering or rubbing with oil. Throughout the brass dial period these hands were made so that the hour hand was visibly quite different in shape from the minute hand, what we usually call 'non-matching'. The reason was so that there could be no possible confusion as to which was the hour hand and which was for minutes. It must be remembered that at this time people were not familiar with clocks from birth, as we are today.

Matching hands first appear about 1790, just as the brass dial clock was becoming extinct in favour of the new japanned dial. It is possible to come across matching hands, in steel still, on a late brass dial clock, but more usually matching hands were made for painted dial clocks, and almost all brass dial clocks would have hands of non-matching type. A glance at some of the illustrations will show some typical hands patterns. Generally, the hour hand on early clocks was large and very ornately pierced, then filed clean and chamfered along all its surface edges. Simpler versions with fewer piercings and more open fretting developed after about 1760. Early minute hands were mostly straight pointers with a little shaping or piercing towards the centre to provide strength (*eg.* Plate 6). The piercing increased with time, so that by about 1760 many minute hands have piercing reaching one-third or more along the stem (see Plate 39). About 1770 a serpentine pattern minute hand evolved, and this was used until the end of the period by most makers (Plate 42).

Just occasionally an individualistic clockmaker might use brass for his hands. Very few did this, and to give strength these hands were usually heavier in profile than the steel ones they resembled – of non-matching pattern of course. The two Thomas Listers of Halifax, father and son, used brass hands, but it is doubtful if more than a dozen makers used the material for hands on brass dial clocks – and these were mostly in the Lancashire/Yorkshire Pennines area. Hands of brass in matching pattern are very different, and these were used on almost all white dial clocks after about 1820 (see Plate 50). It is quite common to see such matching brass hands used as incorrect replacements on brass dial clocks, and there should be no danger of mistaking these for the originals.

SINGLE-HANDERS

Thirty-hour longcase clocks were made at all periods between about 1660 and 1870. Some of these were single-handed clocks. In the period before about 1740, probably most of these would in fact have been single-handers (see Plates 34, 37). By 1760–70 the majority were two-handed (Plate 29). At any time, the clockmaker would make what the customer wanted, and either type was available on request. So while it is true that most single-handed thirty-hour clocks may date before 1760, by no means all pre-1760 clocks are single-handers, and at all times there were exceptions. In the North of England, the single-handed clock was never as popular as at the same period in the South, and here the two-hander came into more widespread use sooner. It is very difficult, therefore, and sometimes misleading, to attempt to date a thirty-hour clock by the number of hands, and it is best to stick to more helpful guidelines.

While the option was open for the thirty-hour clock to have a single hand or two, that same option was not available on eight-day clocks, which were *always* two-handed. In fact, single-handed eight-day clocks *do* exist, but these are very rare, and it is doubtful if more than half a dozen have been recorded in the entire published history of horology. Sometimes one does see a two-handed eight-day clock with a single-handed chapter ring, and these are alterations probably made by fitting an eight-day movement onto a clock which originally had a thirty-hour one.

POSTED AND PLATED MOVEMENTS

So far we have said little about movements, which in longcase clocks were of two basic types. These were the posted movement and the plate movement. They are very different from each other, easily recognised without any knowledge of engineering or horological technicalities, and can prove of assistance in dating and establishing the region of origin of a clock.

The posted movement is sometimes known as a birdcage movement. Its origin was in the style of the lantern clock movement (see Figure 4), in that it had four corner posts supporting a top and bottom plate. Its wheels were pivoted between upright crossbars, and its use was confined to thirty-hour clocks only (see Plate 21). The posted movement was never used for clocks of eight-day or longer duration. Once seen, the posted movement cannot be mistaken for any other kind. Some had turned and shaped corner posts just like a lantern clock, made in brass. Others had square upright corner posts (or rectangular even) in brass, or they could also be in iron. Generally speaking, those with turned (rounded) posts will be earlier than those with square ones.

Eight-day clocks, and those of longer duration, always had the plated forms of movement from their very beginnings right to the end of longcase clock making, so the plate construction is not an indicator of age. This type had a back and front plate of brass, and pillars running horizontally to hold them apart. The wheels were pivoted directly into the front and back plates. Usually the pillars were hammered into the backplate and pinned by taper pins at

43. Frontplate of the eight-day movement by Samuel Deacon of Barton, with the dial removed (and some of the wheelwork) in order to show his serial number (1250) and the year of making (1806), both neatly engraved. The two bolts protruding below are the seatboard bolts, the left being original, the right a replacement. Any engraving on a frontplate is unusual, especially a date. A typical plated movement.

the front to hold the frontplate in position, which kept the wheels locked into place (see Plates 43, 44).

Some early clocks, principally London ones, had latches instead of pins, little swivel catches which slotted into place very easily during assembly. The pin system replaced latches on most clocks by about 1730, after which latches would be very unusual, although the very occasional eccentric maker might have used them later.

Posted movements originated in the South of England, which of course was largely the region of the lantern clock from which the movement derived. Northern clocks were seldom of the posted type, though a few eccentric makers here and there in the North did use that form of frame. In the North, most thirty-hour clocks at all periods were built on the plate form, just like an eight-day always was (at all times and in all areas).

Some thirty-hour clocks in the South were also of plate form, even at early periods, and gradually those makers there who used the posted form turned to the plated construction. By the mid-eighteenth century the posted movement was falling from favour with most makers, and by the 1780s the majority of thirty-hour clocks even in the South were of plated construction. A few makers here and there, principally in more rural areas, such as Suffolk, continued to use the posted form long after the plated movement had taken over elsewhere, and these can even be found as late as the 1820s, though by this time they are most unusual.

So the posted movement can be an indicator towards age and region. It is not a pointer towards quality. Some collectors take a greater delight in a 'birdcage' movement than in a plated one, but this is only because they see them less often, especially if they live in the North. If anything, the plated form is probably the sturdier and stronger of the two, which is more than likely the reason that the latter form ultimately replaced the former entirely.

44. Typical early nineteenth-century eight-day longcase movement attached to its seatboard and showing the falseplate positioned between dial and movement.

MOVEMENT PILLARS

Some collectors set great store by the number of pillars in a movement (ie. in plated movements only), but this is a topic much misunderstood. Very early clocks (principally, of course, in London) had a greater number of pillars in order to hold the plates sturdily when assembled. Later it was found that four pillars did this task quite adequately, and that more than four were not needed. So, on the earliest London longcase plated movements, six pillars are sometimes found. By about 1700 this number had generally reduced to five, and five pillars remained standard practice on London clocks thereafter. On clocks of *longer* than eight-day duration, which would be carrying far heavier weights, more than five might still be employed, just to ensure strength and rigidity.

In the provinces, as we know, longcase clocks began a little later than in London, so it is very unusual to find six pillars on a provincial clock. Here, early clocks often tend to have five pillars, but by about 1720 it was well known that four were quite enough, and so the great majority of provincial clocks after 1720 will be found to have four pillars, as this became standard practice. Some provincial makers either came from London, or were trained there, or bought-in their movements from London, and these makers would keep the standard London practice of having five pillars instead of four. It follows, from sheer considerations of geography, that this was most likely to happen in the South.

It is incorrect to assume that a five-pillar clock is in any way necessarily better than a four-pillar one. Earlier clocks were generally better made than later ones, and, as early clocks are more likely to have five pillars than later ones are, it may well be that an early, five-pillar clock is better made than a later four-pillar one. This, however, is not because of the five-against-four pillar factor, but because the earlier makers tended to put more skill, time, and show into their movements; it is the clock's age making the quality factor, not simply the number of its pillars.

Longcase clocks with brass dials had a long run of popularity covering the period from roughly 1660 to 1800. Long before the end of that period however a new type of dial had appeared on the scene known as a white dial, and it is these we will examine next.

5 Longcase Clocks with White Dials

ENAMEL DIALS

Some clocks and many watches were made with white dials. These are often known as enamel dials, sometimes correctly so but more often erroneously. True enamel was a vitreous compound fused under heat in a kiln onto a metal surface, usually copper. It worked successfully for small areas such as a watch dial. With larger surfaces, such as clock dials, it was less suitable. Some French clockmakers got round this problem by having clock dials using small individual plaques for each number. Some English bracket clock dials were made of enamel, but because of the problem of using this technique on large surfaces, these would often have only a part of the dial enamelled – perhaps the circular dial centre – or might be made up from more than one enamelled piece. A few longcase dials were attempted in true enamel, usually made in smaller individual sections. These are seldom met with, and were largely of an experimental nature. Apart from the problems in making them, they were very fragile to use in general, being liable to crack on the surface.

JAPANNED DIALS

About 1770 a new method was found of making dials, longcase dials in particular, of the normal size required, in such a way that they looked like true enamel dials but were stronger, and probably cheaper too. This process was called japanning, and such dials may be known as japanned dials, though originally the term 'white dial' was used. Today they are sometimes called by either of these names, or may often be referred to as painted dials. Japanning produced a hard-baked white ground surface onto which decoration was painted in oils and then varnished over (*eg.* Plates 45, 46). From the very beginning, these dials were made by specialists, as it was quite outside the scope of the clockmaker himself to make them.

With the traditional brass dial longcase clock, the maker had always had the option of making his own dials, or of buying his dial or parts of dials (such as the engraved chapter ring) from a specialist. With the new dials, however, he had no choice, and this presented certain problems. Most important of these was the factor as to just how the dial joined to the movement, as there was a chance that the dial feet might meet the movement at some awkward place, for example, where they might foul against a wheel. With brass dials he had been able to position his dial feet to suit his movement layout, but the feet of white dials came ready-fixed, and to attempt to have moved them would have broken the japanned surface.

45. *Twelve-inch (30.5cms) dial of an eight-day clock c1780-90 by John Smith of Pittenweem, Scotland's most famous clockmaker. The dial is by James Wilson of Birmingham, with typical flower corners of the period. The original hands of blued steel are of the same style as on a contemporary brass dial clock.*

46. *Eight-day white dial clock by Rogers of Leominster, c1780-90, the dial supplied by James Wilson of Birmingham. Gold corners of this nature were one form of the earliest white dials. The original hands are of blued steel and are typical of the period. Twelve-inch dial (30.5cms).*

As it happened, the makers of the new white dials were very well aware of this potential impediment to sales, and when they first offered their new white dials for sale, they also offered with each dial a backing plate of iron, known as a falseplate. This enabled the dial feet to fit into the falseplate instead of the movement frontplate. The feet of the falseplate could be fixed in position by the clockmaker himself, which gave him the very same choice of location as he had with the traditional brass dial (see Plate 44).

Of course, this difficulty only arose anyway if we assume that the clockmaker made his movement first and then hoped to fix a dial to it. If he selected the dial *first*, then he could build his movement in such a way that the dial feet would not foul inconveniently, simply by positioning his wheels and gearwork thoughtfully. The falseplate option was probably for the benefit of those clockmakers who were resistant to changing their movement layout. So the result was that many early white dials had accompanying falseplates, though not all did.

THE FIRST WHITE DIALMAKERS

The first people we know about who manufactured japanned clock dials were two partners, Osborne and Wilson of Birmingham. They advertised their 'white clock dials in imitation of enamel' in September of 1772. They may not have been the very first to make japanned dials, for occasionally we come across examples that may well be a little earlier, but these are usually un-named dials, so that it is very difficult to be able to date them precisely. Osborne and Wilson took the opportunity of imprinting their names into the falseplates of their dials, as did almost all the dialmakers who succeeded them. For that reason we can identify and date many white dials from the facts known about the dialmakers. Some dials have the name of the dialmaker on the back, as well as, or instead of, on the falseplate. Where a dialmaker's name can be seen, this provides a most helpful secondary means of dating in addition to the name of the clockmaker himself (see page 222). Often such a name is only apparent when the dial is removed, and many dials go unidentified because the name, whilst present, is concealed from view.

The great majority of dialmakers were based in Birmingham, and the names and working dates of most of them are recorded in my book *White Dial Clocks*. The partnership of Osborne and Wilson was shortlived, for they went their separate ways in late 1777, after which each stamped his own falseplates with only his own name. This means that if a dial is seen which was made by this partnership, it must date between 1772 and 1777, and clearly this must tally with the period of the clockmaker, whose name appears on the dial front. If not, then something is very wrong. In this way, falseplates and a knowledge of the dialmaking system are excellent indicators towards establishing whether a clock is genuine or much altered, or even an outright fake.

Once the japanned dial system is understood, it is obvious that falseplates were made and sold *only* with these new japanned dials. If a brass dial clock has a falseplate, then something is clearly amiss. If the dialmaker's name appears on such a falseplate, it is often very obvious that the period known for the dialmaker clashes with that known for the clockmaker (*ie.* the name on the brass dial). This is evidence that dial and movement do not belong together but have been married together at a later date, perhaps by someone making up a clock from spare parts (see Chapter 11). It might, alternatively, be evidence that a brass dial has been fitted to replace the original white dial, something which was quite often done around the end of last century, when brass dials were considered 'better' than painted ones. But brass dial clocks were not made originally with falseplate fittings. A clock which is made-up from non-original parts is known as a 'marriage' or a 'married' clock, which is precisely what brass dial clocks are if they have a falseplate (for further details on 'married' clocks, see Chapter 11).

THE BRASS DIAL DECLINES

For all practical purposes we can regard white dials as beginning about 1772, but few would be met with from the very first period, and the majority seen today will date from after 1780. Such was their popularity over the brass dial, however, that by about 1790 most longcase clocks had white dials. The virtues were seen as residing in such factors as, for instance, that the dials would never tarnish or need re-polishing or re-silvering, and that they were much more clearly legible from across the room. Additionally, they had more colour about them in the form of the decorative treatment, which was often of flowers at this transitional period (*eg.* Plates 45, 47, 54). By the end of the eighteenth century, the brass dial was old-fashioned, and was extinct in normal domestic clocks, except in a few traditionally-minded areas, where they lingered in the form of single-sheet dials. Such areas were few, but included parts of the West Country and parts of Scotland, and occasionally London, though there the late brass dial would more often appear at this late date (after 1800) on clocks of a specialised type, such as Regulators. It is not uncommon to see clocks from Devonshire made as late as the 1840s still using the single-sheet brass dial, which was by then long outmoded in most parts.

CENTRALISED MANUFACTURE

It happens that, for the collector or enthusiast, this centralised manufacture of white dials in one area (Birmingham principally) means that dial styles were not the random hotch-potch of features they might have been if they had originated in several widely-separated areas. On the contrary, there is a very definite and easily-learned sequence of dial styles, which makes recognition of period very easy. As new dialmakers came on the scene, they copied the kind of styles which their rivals were already successfully marketing.

So distinctive are the styles of white dials that, with a little practice, it is possible to establish the age from a distance of twenty yards. This stylistic development was unknown before 1974, when it was pointed out in my book, *The White Dial Clock*, but today it is well understood by most clock enthusiasts. Overall dial patterns fall into three very convenient periods: 1770–1800, 1800–1830, 1830–1870. This latter date saw the end of longcase clock making in Britain, though imported longcase clocks were still sold after this time, principally with German movements.

FEATURES OF WHITE DIALS

First Period Dials progress in style in two different aspects, both of which have considerable bearing on the immediate impact of the dial. The first consideration was that of the numbering itself. In Period One (1770–1800; see Plates 45–7, 54), hours were marked by Roman numerals (I, II, III, *etc.*) and the minutes were shown by dots, every fifth minute being numbered in Arabic numerals (5, 10, 15, *etc.*). This appears to be the unfailing numbering system used throughout Period One and at no other period. This numbering pattern is instantly recognisable, and I think I am correct in saying that I don't recall ever seeing any other form of numbering on white dials in this first period, with the exception of the beginnings of a change of style sometimes found in the last five years (roughly 1795–1800).

47. Square dial of about 1790, by George Hewitt of Marlborough, showing moon dial below XII.

Second Period At the end of Period One, an experiment begins in using Arabic numbers for hours, and this was to become a feature of many dials in Period Two (1800–1830; see Plates 48, 49, 91). A few dials occur in the last five years of the eighteenth century, which keep the dotted minutes with five-minute numerals as well as Arabic hours (Plate 48) – principally late dials by James Wilson, one of the original partners mentioned earlier and who was at this time trying an innovative numbering style, which was soon to catch on. Arabic hour numerals, however, are most often found between 1800 and about 1820. Dialmakers seem to have had difficulty in finding a happy method of lettering these numbers, because if, like Roman numerals, they were lettered concentric to the centre, they would have been upside down at the hours of 4 to 8. Some dialmakers therefore positioned their Arabic hours upright, and some used what we now call 'tumbling numbers', by which we mean that numbers from 4 to 8 inclusive swing round to appear visibly upright. With 'tumbling number' dials the hours from 9 to 12 and 1 to 3 inclusive are set with their bases to the dial centre and those from 4 to 8 inclusive have their tops pointing to the centre (Plates 48, 91).

Arabic numerals fell from favour within twenty years of their appearance, perhaps because of this awkwardness as to which

48. Twelve-inch dial (30.5cms) from the clock by Samuel Deacon of Barton, dated 1806. The dial is by James Wilson with double Arabic numbers (hours and minutes). The decoration is in gold on to a solid blue ground, an unusual treatment.

49. Dial of an eight-day clock (twelve inches, 30.5cms) of about 1810 by James Bath of Cirencester. The flowers in the centre are unusual for this period.

angle to position them. By about 1820, most dialmakers had gone back to using Roman numerals for hours. However, this poses no problem in identification, because by this time the minutes had also undergone a change of numbering style.

Very shortly after the introduction of Arabic hours, the minutes cease to be marked by dots. Instead, a solid circle (or two circles) runs round the minute track, and each minute position is indicated by a crossbar, producing either dash minutes (if a single line; *eg.* Plate 49) or banded minutes (if a double line), this latter form being the same principle as had long been used on brass dials (*eg.* Plate 39). At this time the minute numbering itself also changes, and often only the quarter-hour minutes are numbered (15, 30, 45, 60; *eg.* Plate 49). Where the other minute numerals had formerly been (*ie.* at 5, 10, 20, 25, *etc.*), there now appears an asterisk or similar marker. This quarter-hour minute marking might appear with Arabic hours or the new-form Roman hours. Now, however, the minute numbers are much smaller than earlier, so that the Roman hours take up a larger proportion of the available space and are usually larger than before. Very soon the asterisks cease to appear, as do the quarter-hour minute numbers,

50. *Twelve-inch (30.5cms) white dial of thirty-hour clock of about 1825, by John Wilson of Nuneaton, showing decoration and numbering typical of the period. Original brass hands.*

51. *Dial of about 1830 from a clock by Richards of Uttoxeter, fourteen inches wide (38cms). Classical landscape in arch and shell corners were popular themes of the time.*

and we are then fully into Period Three (Plate 50).

Third Period Period Three starts about 1830, but by the late 1820s there are signs of this last style, which ended with the termination of British clockmaking around 1870. Here the hours are marked by full Roman numerals, and the minutes, though spaced round within a minute band, have no numbers at all (Plates 50, 51). By this time the population at large was well enough accustomed to reading clock dials that they could understand that, when the hands pointed to V after II, it was twenty-five minutes past two, even though no minute numerals were written on the dial to say so.

Because of this quite easily-recognised system of numbering, it is possible to identify a dial period by the numbering alone. But other features on these dials also offer a guide to dating, too. In particular, the painted decoration of the corners and arch area usually give very helpful clues to period. With a round dial, there was no corner or arched decoration, and therefore numbering is *all* there is to go on, although in Period One some round dials may have an occasional flower spray or a bird in the centre, just as in non-round dials from that time. For square dials, the corner paintings are ample evidence, but if the dial has an arch, then that is an added bonus in terms of decorative identification.

PAINTING STYLES

In the first period, white dials begin by being largely of the ground colour with just a little restrained decoration. This ground is usually white or near-white, sometimes with a distinct blue or pale green tint to it. For our purpose we regard all these shades as being white. In each corner (and perhaps the arch too) there might be gold scrollwork, resembling somewhat in paint the brass corner spandrels on a brass dial clock (see Plate 46). This goldwork was raised up above the dial surface by gesso, then painted over with gold. If in worn condition, such dials show the gesso through as being of a creamy buff colour, with gold left at the edges. This is just one form of early corner decoration. It may be found at any time within Period One, but mostly at the earlier part of it; very seldom was this style used after 1800.

However, that was not the only decoration used in Period One. More often the corners were decorated with a flower or a small spray of two or three flowers (see Plates 45, 47, 54). These were often roses or carnations or sometimes strawberries, the latter being especially favoured. In 1974 I coined the term 'strawberry corners' to describe this style, and that term is now in widespread use. Most of these flowers have a pink colouring to them. Sometimes other colours appear as well or instead, but the overall effect of most Period One dials is one of pink corners. Most have a dot-dash border of gold-surfaced gesso beading to enclose the corner decoration (see Plates 45, 47), though a few do not. In the arch of dials of this period there is often an oval or circular centre plaque, again edged in gold beading, with gold scrollwork at each side. This panel might contain a vignette scene, maybe a landscape, but more often a classical scene of a shepherdess or a young lady in a garden or perhaps a representation of a classical goddess. Occasionally it might have a portrait, or a bird (see Plates 45, 54), or a maker's name or a spray of flowers. On a moon dial, the moon itself would fill the arch area.

The term 'strawberry corner' is often used to refer to any pink-cornered Period One dial, whether having strawberries or not.

Dials from this period sometimes have a flower or two in the dial centre (roughly between X and II), or maybe a bird or two. This restrained type of centre painting seldom appears after this time, though a much heavier and bolder type just occasionally might (see Plate 50).

In Period Two the corner paintings, just like the numbering system, were going through a period of experiment, and so were more likely to vary than was the case with the decorations of Periods One or Three. A common theme was to have fans in the corners, radiating lines based on the corners, with divided coloured sections. The fans were often gold-coloured or included gold blades in them, but all kind of colours are possible, including sometimes strong and bright colours, much bolder than earlier periods. Seashells were popular in this period, and many of the corners now held patterns based on geometrical shapes rather than natural objects (Plate 49). Occasionally, portraits might fill the corners, or small painted scenes of subjects which went happily in fours – the four seasons, four virtues, four continents, though these fourfold subjects more often occur in the following period. In general, the dials of Period Two show a larger amount of coloured area, the decoration filling completely, or going well towards filling, the corner sections (see Plate 49). In the arch the vignette type of central panel still appeared sometimes, though often it was larger in size now. Sometimes a large central fan pattern echoed the corners (Plate 48), or a basket of fruit or flowers. On some dials now, the whole arch might be filled with a painted scene such as a landscape, a feature which appeared more often towards the beginning of Period Three and well into that period (see Plate 50).

Occasionally in this period the whole of the dial centre might be painted with a solid scene, such as a romanticised garden scene of a large country mansion. With moon dial versions the two 'humps', which usually carry maps of the two hemispheres, might also be painted with solid landscape or other scenes. The effect of this type of dial is to have the whole dial coloured with just a white band for numbers (usually at this time being Arabic hours). A few Scottish dials of Period Three, principally round dials, produce a similar effect but use gold rather than coloured paints.

52. *Eight-day white dial clock of the Third Period, about 1840, by D. W. Laird of Leith, Scotland. The dial is an unusual size, at 12½in (31cms), and shows typical romantic landscapes of many Victorian dials, though here the artistry is better than in many. Original matching hands in brass.*

CHEAPER DIALS

Many dials of Period Three were more cheaply made in an attempt to beat competition. Their artwork was often cruder, the representations of human figures betraying this poor artistry more than landscapes. Many corner paintings now look as if they were painted by children, often being as crude as fairground paintings (see Plate 53). Colours were often brighter, garish at times. Some dials, especially Scottish dials, had silver leaf behind the colours, which gave a bright and iridescent effect. At this time it was possible to buy a dial for one-third of the price of a Period One dial half a century earlier, which may indicate the falling of standards.

53. Poor quality late white dial of about 1860, showing the Garden of Eden and the Four Continents. John Waite of Bradford.

On most dials of this period the arch is filled by a complete painted scene, often a landscape, and so is each corner (see Plate 52). Victorian landscapes with romanticised ruins and castles were popular. So were the Four Continents, Four Countries (England, Ireland, Scotland, Wales), and Four Seasons. Country sports, such as shooting, coursing, foxhunting, with associated animals, often on their own, were common – stags, rabbits, squirrels, pheasants. Each corner painting now took up so much space on the dial that the four corners actually joined together to leave a white central circle for numbers. With the arch included, this meant that five separate oil-paintings joined into one colourful border (see Plate 52). A few are well-painted, but many are very poor, including often biblical scenes (see Plate 53), which were also popular at this time.

DIAL SIZE

Dial size can be one indicator towards period in white dial dating. In general terms, as we have seen, dials increased in size as time went by, but it is not quite as simple as that. Thirty-hour dials tended to remain a little smaller than eight-day ones, largely because the thirty-hour clock was more often destined for a smaller room and lower ceiling, and small dials suited small cases best. In the South there was a general tendency for dials to be smaller than their Northern contemporaries. A few early thirty-hour dials were 10 inches square (25.5cms) and a few 11 inches (28cms). Rarely would such small dials be of the arched shape and rarely eight-day. Twelve inches wide (30.5cms) is the standard small size white dial, square or arched, for either duration (*eg.* Plates 45, 50). By the end of the century some had reached 13 inches (33cms), even 14 inches (38cms). These larger dials came sooner in the North, and many Southern dials did not increase beyond the 12-inch level (30.5cms). A few late Northern dials were 15 inches wide (40cms).

HANDS

The hands of a longcase clock can be of assistance in dating, where it can be established that these are original. Period One hands began in exactly the same style as on contemporary brass dial clocks, usually with multi-pierced hour hand and non-matching minute hand, of the straight type early on and of the serpentine a little later in this period (Plate 46). However, towards the end of the eighteenth century 'matching' hands had arrived, where the hour and minute hand were each of the same pattern but of different lengths and proportions (*eg.* Plate 54). These were initially of blued steel, just as non-matching hands had been earlier. However, brass began to be used for hands about 1795, initially of the simple matching type with diamond-shaped tips. Brass hands were considered better originally, and cost a little more than steel. By about 1820, however, almost all longcases had gone over to matching-pattern brass hands, and these were now machine-stamped and for the most part of lower quality.

It has long been the tendency of collectors to regard the white dial as an inferior type to the brass one which preceded it. In recent years this attitude is changing, as we acquire a greater understanding of the situation. As far as we can judge from original prices, it would seem that white dials were in fact more costly than contemporary brass dials, whereas until recently it has always been assumed that the reverse was true.

MADE IN BIRMINGHAM?

One factor which may have had a bearing on attitudes is that occasionally the word 'Birmingham' was glimpsed on falseplates, and writers of the past assumed that this meant that the clock was 'made in Birmingham' and therefore had in some way been mass-produced. Even in recent years, some books write about the 'Birmingham movement', when what they have failed to recognise is that it was the *dial* that originated in Birmingham. A Birmingham dial is certainly not evidence of a mass-produced movement. We have only to look at the work of one or two makers who had their own eccentric working methods to see that they made the same unusual movements for white dials as they had made for brass ones.

By about 1810 it was true that part-made movements could be bought-in by clockmakers with just the finishing left to do, although this was not a practice adopted widely until about 1840. While some painted or white dial clocks will be found to have mass-produced movements, it is not correct to think that these may be recognised by the presence of a Birmingham dial.

Just occasionally one comes across a wooden movement on an English japanned-dial longcase clock, almost always thirty-hour in duration. These are imported German movements, sometimes fitted originally to an English dial, and date from about 1860 or a little later. Occasionally one also comes across these with wooden dials, painted in what might be thought of as vaguely the English style. These are examples of German-made clocks and dials, which were sometimes hung on wall-brackets or sometimes housed in an English long case (see Chapter 9). Dating these follows the same pattern as for japanned dials.

WITH OR WITHOUT FALSEPLATES?

The question as to which clocks had falseplates and which did not is rather complicated. Thirty-hour clocks in general did not have falseplates, but the dials fitted directly to the movement. The reason behind this may have been that the thirty-hour dial usually had only three dial feet rather than four, hence only three points of contact with the movement frontplate. Moreover, as the thirty-hour frontplate carried fewer wheel arbors anyway, the chances of a dial foot being so positioned as to foul the wheelwork were much less than with an eight-day clock. Just occasionally a thirty-hour clock may have a falseplate, but this occurs principally in instances where the clockmaker chose to use an eight-day dial, such as might apply when he wanted to have dummy winding-holes to stimulate eight-day appearance.

With eight-day white dial clocks, some examples have false-plates and some have direct fitting. It is difficult to pin down when or why these two different options applied. In general, in the earlier period, *ie.* from about 1770 to about 1790, the majority have falseplates, though a considerable number do not. From about 1790 to about 1830, an even larger percentage have falseplates (see Plate 44). After about 1830 more dials have direct fitting without a falseplate. In this later period (*ie.* after about 1830), movements were increasingly assembled by the clockmaker rather than actually made by him, and this may well be why fewer falseplates appear at this time, since standardised layouts would take standardised dial feet positions.

It is not possible, however, to regard the presence or absence of a falseplate as being in itself a dating feature, nor to draw any firm conclusions as to whether the presence of a falseplate would generally indicate a hand-made movement, or whether the absence of one would indicate a bought-in one. The business is far more complicated than that, and to draw any such conclusions would be more misleading than helpful. The dialmaker's name, when it can be established, is certainly a vital aid to dating (see page 222), but the presence or absence of a falseplate is not, and a beginner is likely to get bogged down in complications in trying to pursue that line of thought.

SCOTTISH-MADE DIALS

Birmingham was the main centre of white dial making from the very beginning, and remained so at all periods. The great majority of white dials which are seen to have a dialmaker's name will be found to originate in Birmingham. However, it was not the only dialmaking centre. The first makers of japanned dials in Scotland were Dallaway and Son of Edinburgh, and they are believed to have made these dials from about 1790, or perhaps a little earlier (see Plate 54). The partnership of father and son began in 1793, and the son had learned his japanning practice in Birmingham.

54. Dial of an eight-day clock (thirteen inches, 33cms) of about 1790, by Walter Scott of Lauder, a Scottish-made dial by Dallaway of Edinburgh, showing typical crazing. Original hands of unusual pattern.

Early Scottish-made dials follow the general style of the English ones of the same period in regard to the decorative features. The quality of the work, however, is usually inferior to that of the best English dials of the day, both in terms of the decoration and the quality of the japanning itself. This means that today we find that the condition of many early Scottish-made dials is not as good as on a contemporary English-made one. For example, all these dials tend to be subject in greater or lesser degree to crazing of the surface, but early Scottish-made dials usually are more prone to this than the English equivalents (see Plate 54). After about 1800, and increasingly as time went by, the quality often fell off even lower (though this applied in England too), and some late Scottish-made dials suffer very badly from serious crazing and surface shrinking.

Scottish-made dials seem to have been slow to overtake the lead the English-made dials had achieved in Scotland, so that many early Scottish white dial clocks have English dials (often by Wilson or Osborne *eg.* Plate 45). At all periods English dials continue to have been used by Scottish clockmakers, sometimes instead of Scottish-made ones and sometimes alongside them. In England these dials were available as round, square or arched shape. Even though English dials were used by some Scottish makers, the square dial seems to have been uncommon in Scotland, where the great majority of japanned dials at all periods were arched. The implication is that the square dial form was not popular with Scottish clockmakers or their customers.

SCOTTISH FALSEPLATES

Some Scottish-made dials had falseplates on the same principle as the English equivalents, particularly in the earlier period (before about 1810). In general, however, the falseplate was less often used in Scottish-made dials than with English ones, and after about 1820 it is unusual to come across them. The names of dialmakers are less often found on the backs of Scottish-made dials than on English-made ones, but lettering such as 'Finest Fancy' may be seen, indicating the style/quality of the dial rather than its maker. Some earlier-period Scottish-made dials are of thinner iron than English ones, some being almost flexible. With experience, one can often recognise a dial as being of Scottish make even if unnamed, on account of the lesser quality.

Popular though it was from its inception, the longcase was not the only form of household clock. Clocks driven by weights were always of a more robust and reliable nature than spring clocks, and it is these other types of weight-driven clock we shall look at next.

6 OTHER WEIGHT-DRIVEN CLOCKS

Longcase clocks of both eight-day and thirty-hour type flourished in increasing numbers as time went by. In the country at large, however, it was 1700 before these clocks began to be well-known items, this slow provincial start being largely accounted for by the fact that in many counties clockmakers were only just beginning to set up in the trade at that time. By now the lantern clock was already losing ground to the thirty-hour longcase, and in London, by that time, the battle had already been lost.

HOOK-AND-SPIKE CLOCKS

In the provinces, some lantern clock production continued, especially in more southerly counties, but it was a dying breed. An alternative form began to develop about this time, which in some ways represented a half-way house between the lantern and the full longcase thirty-hour. This type is known as the hook-and-spike wall clock. In essence, it was a smaller thirty-hour longcase which in fact had no case, but was made with the hoop and spurs with which the lantern clock had always been equipped, and which could thus be hung from any convenient wall hook, exactly as the lantern clock had done (Plate 56). Many were made in the post-framed tradition, but often using a larger proportion of iron

55. Dial of mid-eighteenth century hook-and-spike wall clock in very dirty condition. Nine-inch dial (23cms). Typical Oxfordshire Quaker work, perhaps by John Simms of Chipping Norton: monogram I.S. and dated 1760.

56. Movement of the hook-and-spike wall clock in Plate 55. Basically a thirty-hour birdcage clock, but with the hook and spikes integral.

than the lantern clock, whereby they could be offered at a cheaper price. Iron was only one-tenth of the price of brass. The hook-and-spike clock usually represented a cheaper and humbler version of the lantern clock, displaying a greater amount of blacksmithing work. Not all were made in posted form, but plate-framed examples are uncommon in the earlier period. These clocks were made from about 1700, and continued throughout the brass-dial period. Occasional examples do exist in white dial form, but these are uncommon, as by that time other forms of clock had largely superseded them.

Earlier examples of hook-and-spike wall clocks often had small dials, less than 6 inches (15cms) square on occasion. Size increased a little as time progressed, as with longcase dials, but these clocks would always tend to have dials considerably smaller than the longcase clock of the same period. Later dials might be as much as 9 or 10 inches (23–25.5cms), but no more (Plate 55).

These clocks were more often made in the South of England than in the North, since they replaced lantern clocks, which had also been largely a southern product. Like lantern clocks, they quite often had alarmwork, and alarm versions might well have no striking train, since it was not usually thought advisable to have a clock which was intended for use in the bedroom to strike all night long. Another name sometimes applied to these clocks is that of kitchen alarm clocks or hanging alarms. Occasionally the term pantry clock is used, as it was often assumed that any clock of humbler form was made for the servants' quarters.

These clocks are not commonplace nowadays. Being simple and sometimes primitive in appearance (made that way deliberately, to keep the price low), they were more often discarded and scrapped than might be the case with finer clocks. So their survival rate today probably does not give a true reflection of their popularity two hundred years ago. In the nineteenth century the imported hanging alarm clocks from Germany, known as post-man's alarms, replaced this type totally (see Plate 121).

Hook-and-spike clocks could be hung on the wall like a lantern clock. However, the option was available to use such a clock as a form of posted-movement longcase clock, by fitting it into a wooden case. Some were undoubtedly cased that way from new, and in other instances it might be that owners would buy the clock first and save to buy a case for it a few years later. When they *are* found in cases, they are very often hung from a hook in the backboard (just as they would from a wall hook), instead of having the normal seatboard arrangement found in most longcase clocks.

In essence, then, most hook-and-spike clocks are smaller versions of the thirty-hour brass dial longcase. A few, however, show in their styling transitional features which illustrate their link with lantern clocks, amounting almost at times to a hybrid form between the two. One hybrid form is shown in Plates 57 and

58, a weight-driven clock by John Sanderson of Wigton, which is essentially a square-dial lantern clock with a larger dial size.

57. Twelve-inch dial (30.5cms) of a thirty-hour posted movement clock by John Sanderson of Wigton, Cumberland, dating from c1720, a clockmaker with a highly individual style. A dial full of interest and character.

58. Posted movement, of lantern clock type, of the clock by John Sanderson in Plate 57. These clocks could be hung on wall brackets, like a lantern clock, or housed in a case as a longcase clock. Made with anchor escapement and long pendulum.

HOODED CLOCKS

The hooded clock was in some ways an alternative of the hook-and-spike clock. Instead of having hoop and spurs for wall-hanging, the hooded clock solved the problem of wall-mounting by enclosing the clock movement in a protective box, which itself hung on the wall (Plate 60). So what might, in principle, be an almost identical dial and movement as that of a hook-and-spike, was sometimes housed in a hood instead. Again the hooded clock, so-called because it resembles a longcase hood of simple type, was a humble clock for use in the kitchen, perhaps, or on the landing. These were often provided with alarmwork too, and, again, often had a greater proportion of blacksmith work (*ie.* ironwork) than other types of clock. Working in iron was more difficult and more time-consuming than with brass, but the country clockmaker often charged for his time lightly, while to work in costlier metals needed ready money.

In terms of styling, the dials of both hook-and-spike clocks and of hooded clocks follow very similar principles to those of thirty-hour longcase clocks (see Plates 55, 59). Certain differences are

59. Ten-inch dial (25.5cms) from a single-sheet dial hooded clock with birdcage movement, a timepiece only with alarmwork. Date about 1780-90. Maker William Gill of Hastings. The dial is in a very dirty condition.

60. The William Gill clock in its original pine hood, though the dial is a rather cramped fit. Here, the pendulum and weights are not assembled. One weight drives the going train, the other the alarm train. The clock has no strikework, as was the case with many alarm clocks.

often apparent, in that the very small dial size of many of these clocks meant that such fittings as spandrels were not readily available. For this reason, the clockmaker might improvise by using something readily and cheaply available for his dial corner decoration, often making do with a simple engraved pattern (*eg.* Plate 59). Even a clockmaker who was no great engraving artist could manage a few decorative twirls for the corners, or a decorative pattern of punch-marks or drill-marks. Some would engrave their corners very finely, but these were in the minority. For many makers, the low price market for these clocks would not justify the cost of making (or buying) cast brass spandrel sets.

These types of clock which had alarms would very often use the same alarm system that the lantern clock used, that is, they would have a central setting disc whereby the appropriate hour number on the disc was set against the tail of the hour hand to determine the alarm time (see Plate 59). Many of these clocks were single-handers for cheapness and simplicity of use. Some were two-handers, in which case the hour hand would have an extended tail just like a single-hander, and this extended tail on a *two-*

handed clock served no other purpose, so its presence indicates that such a clock originally had alarmwork.

By their very nature, both hook-and-spike clocks and hooded clocks are almost always thirty-hour running. Eight-day examples do exist in the form of a higher-quality gentleman's alarm, but these are rather an eccentric contradiction in terms. The brass dials from these two categories of clock often resemble miniature longcase dials, and hence many were used to make up fake 'grandmother' clocks. These are normally easy to recognise, most obviously by the fact that the dial decoration has been drilled right through to receive the two winding squares of a normal eight-day longcase movement, which of course would be of the standard size, while a genuine eight-day hooded clock would have tiny barrels, probably tiny plates, and dial decoration *not* pierced by later winding holes.

TAVERN CLOCKS

Another type of weight-driven wall clock was made in England – I don't think any example is recorded from Scotland, Wales or Ireland. This type is of eight-day duration and is often known as an Act of Parliament clock or, more correctly, a tavern clock. This was a wall clock of large size, commonly standing as high as 5 or even 6 feet (153–183cms), and with a very large dial, usually made of wooden boards and as much as 30 inches (80cms) in diameter (Plates 61, 62).

The Act after which these clocks are named was passed in 1797, and imposed a tax on watches and clocks. It was repealed shortly afterwards, as it almost destroyed the trade at a stroke. The argument was that this tax on individual owners created an increase in clocks for public display and hence the production of these clocks, which were made for such places as taverns, coaching-inns, and public buildings of all kinds. The over-large dial was legible at a considerable distance, and in a way this was an indoor equivalent of a church clock. This type of clock, however, was made as much as fifty years *before* the act after which popular tradition has named it, so tavern clock is really a more sensible term.

Many had their dials painted black with gold numbering, though some had white dials. The cases of many of these clocks were japanned (or lacquered, which is the alternative term for the same treatment) in gold and black to match the dial, though sometimes they were in other ground colours such as blue. The extra large hands usually had counterbalanced 'tails', to avoid drag from the sheer weight of the hands. Many had circular dials, but some earlier models had their dials of a square shape with clipped corners, known as a 'shield' shape (see Plate 61).

The movements of tavern clocks were of eight-day duration, and in principle were much like those of eight-day longcase clocks.

61. Act of Parliament or Tavern clock, made about 1755 by Matthew Worgan of Bristol, and of the type known as a shield dial. Note counter-balanced hands. Height about 5ft (152cms). Picture courtesy Strike One, Islington.

62. Tavern clock in black lacquer made about 1770 by Thomas Perkins of Evesham with typical 'ears' and counter-balanced hands. (60in, 153cms). Picture courtesy Strike One, Islington.

However, tavern clocks did not normally have strikework. This means that the movement wheels occupied only half the space as did those of a normal eight-day longcase, and for that reason the movement plates were made narrower, and tapered towards the top on most examples – these being known as A-plates from their general shape. Another difference from the longcase movement was that these clocks were required to run for eight days in a shorter drop than the longcase offered. To effect this, an extra wheel was usually designed into the train, giving a five-wheel train, against the normal four wheels of an eight-day longcase.

Tavern clocks must have suffered a very high destruction rate, by sheer virtue of having been in public rooms where wear and tear would be considerably higher than with a domestic clock. Some had their dials re-painted time and again, and sometimes

 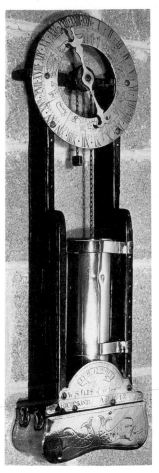

63. *Eight-day weight-driven wall clock (timepiece only), made about 1840 by Isaacs of London. This is the type of clock sometimes known as a Norfolk clock, although they were not necessarily made in Norfolk.*

64. *Water clock with 24-hour dial engraved with astrological symbols and lettered 'Tyme is swift. W.S. Iles of ye towne Richmond AD1642'. Made about 1920 to look antique, as they all were. There are no genuine antique water clocks. This is a weight-driven clock, where the water in the canister is the weight.*

the cases too. The wooden dial boards would be prone to expansion, shrinkage and warping in a much more vulnerable manner than the brass or japanned longcase dial. Those which became battered or shabby would often have been turned out for the garden bonfire. These factors make tavern clocks uncommon today, though of course they were never in any event as commonplace as domestic clocks.

Tavern clocks seem to have been more popular in London and the South of England than in the North, and few examples seem to survive by Northern makers. Of course, all the coaching-roads led to London, so that the distribution in coaching-inns would naturally be concentrated in the South-east.

NORFOLK CLOCKS

By about 1800, another type of weight-driven wall clock had appeared, which was a smaller version of the tavern clock with a total height of about four feet and a much smaller dial, often a japanned 'Birmingham' dial. The cases were sometimes of oak but more often of mahogany. Like their larger relations these were usually non-striking clocks. Some had circular brass dials of the single-sheet style, silvered over the surface. This was a type of clock popular in Norfolk, and they are often known as Norfolk Clocks, or sometimes Norwich clocks, even though they may not have been made in those parts.

Some Norfolk clocks were made with deadbeat escapement, or semi-deadbeats (the latter gave most of the advantages of the deadbeat but without the delicacy of the deadbeat escape wheel's teeth). These were probably used in banks, offices and public buildings. Most were timepieces, *ie.* they did not strike. These are not really commonplace clocks, probably because the advantage which they offered over the shorter-length-drop dial wall clock driven by spring power (see page 187) was only slight. In theory, the timekeeping of a Norfolk clock would be superior to that of a spring-driven one, especially if of a deadbeat or semi-deadbeat type, but it is doubtful whether we are talking in terms of more than a minute's variance in a week.

We have looked at clocks thus far which were driven by weights and controlled by the pendulum, and next we will examine just what kind of weights and what kind of pendulums these were.

7 Weights and Pendulums

Eight-day longcase clocks had two weights, which each weighed anywhere between 10lbs and 14lbs, occasionally a little more or a little less (see Plate 132). Often they were a matched pair, identical in pattern and weight, but where one was heavier than the other, the heavier was normally for the striking train (usually positioned on the left), which tended to need more power than the going train. Most pairs would have matched originally in pattern. The reason that many clocks today have odd weights is because one has at some time been replaced due to loss or mishap.

London clocks, and some better-quality provincial ones, had brass-cased weights, filled with lead until about 1780. Ordinary clocks mostly had them of lead, just occasionally cased in tin, but usually plain lead. Cast-iron weights (as seen in Plate 132) came into use in about 1770, around the same time as the white dial, and these may be found on either white dial or brass dial clocks. Seldom is it possible to be certain that the weights to a clock are original. A great many get mixed up or swapped in auction rooms, and have done so for generations. The question of the originality of its weights does not affect the value of a clock normally.

THIRTY-HOUR WEIGHTS

Thirty-hour clocks had a single weight, which would weigh anything from about 6lbs to 9lbs, made of lead before about 1770 and increasingly more frequently of cast iron thereafter. Sometimes weights are seen with the number of pounds weight cast into them – *eg.* 10 or 12 (see Plate 132). Scottish clocks seem more often to have this feature, and they also often have weights (of cast iron) which are flatter in outline than the otherwise cylindrical shape.

Most clocks have weights which are heavier than they actually require, and they would probably drive adequately with less. In fact, one collector I know removed the two original 12lb weights from an eight-day longcase and replaced them with two 6lb ones he had made, and reported that the clock ran perfectly well on those (though he kept the originals with the clock anyway). The reason for this may well be that modern oils are more efficient than old oils, and that household conditions today are less dusty than in the past. Perhaps the old clockmakers used weights which were heavier than required to ensure that the clock kept running despite an accumulation of dust and the drying-out of the oil, and also to compensate to some degree for wear by owners who did not have their clocks serviced regularly. With many eight-day clocks which have rack striking, there is always the danger that if the strikework should fail, the clock may well jam because

128

of the rack tail fouling on the snail. An over-heavy weight, especially on the strike side, would reduce the danger of this happening.

The situation sometimes arises that the weight or weights of a clock are missing, perhaps lost in some house-move, and the owner may need to know what weight his clock needs to drive it reliably and without damage. It used to be a regular practice that a dealer might hang on an exceptionally heavy weight to force a troublesome clock into action. This may well have been effective in the short term, but was destroying the clock, as it forced the wheels round. This practice was carried out as a cheap alternative to cleaning and bushing the clock, and represents the same solution as would putting a larger engine into a car because its brakes were jammed on! So how does an owner establish what weight his clock needs? It is really a matter of trial and error. One solution is to hang onto the lines a plastic bag filled with scrap lead or similar material which has first been weighed. Try an eight-day clock on, say, 10lbs, and increase the weight by 1lb a time until it runs without failing. This is always assuming, of course, that the clock has been serviced and bushed correctly first. Once the required weight has been established, then buy or make weights of that size. New weights can be bought from parts suppliers, or made by casting lead into a canister, though it is doubtful if you would find a pair of old weights for sale, especially of the set size needed.

PULLEYS

Eight-day clocks had two pulleys on which the weights hung (see Plate 132). If they are original, the two will match in pattern. Often the maker would have inscribed circles round them or added some decorative feature to the loop. Many clocks have non-matching pulleys today because one has had to be replaced in the past, through loss or damage. Replaced pulleys are not regarded as a detriment to a clock, though obviously an original matching pair would be seen as a plus point.

Thirty-hour pulleys were of two different types, made either for rope-drive or chain-drive. Rope pulleys have a smooth, rounded channel to carry the rope. Chain pulleys have a narrow central groove within the channel to allow the alternate chain links to ride smoothly. Most pulleys, thirty-hour or eight-day, are made of brass. Quite often, country thirty-hour clocks would have wooden pulleys, turned from a hard wood, and sometimes possessing considerable charm and decorative effect. Thirty-hour clocks also had a counterweight (in the loop of the rope or chain which did not carry the pulley), to keep the rope/chain taut and thus prevent it slipping. This was a circle of lead, and old ones usually show considerable wear where the chain may have bitten into it with years of friction.

ROPES AND CHAINS

If fitting a new rope or chain, it is important to fit the correct drive, *ie.* not to fit a chain into a rope-driven movement, or vice versa. If the correct drive is not fitted, then the clock will run down too quickly as it slips. Special rope can be bought from parts suppliers. So can special chain, though getting the correct linkage may be tricky. A new rope/chain must be of the right length, which is such that, when the clock is fully wound in its case, the free-hanging loop with its counterweight should be off the ground. Too long a rope/chain will mean the counterweight rests on the ground or on the bottom of the case, thus failing to keep the rope/chain under tension, and the clock will usually slip in the first few hours after winding, until the counterweight is off the ground and is actually putting tension on the drive.

Longcase clocks of longer duration than eight days might have very variable weights. Month clock weights could be anywhere between about 24lbs and 30lbs, even more. I once had a clock of six-month duration with each of its original lead weights of 60lbs weight. This required a two-handed crank winder instead of the usual one-handed crank.

Tavern clocks were usually timepieces, and had only one weight, which was attached to a pulley like a longcase weight. However, the weight itself was often shaped into a wide, square section block to keep its height shallow and therefore assist the duration of the clock within a relatively short drop. Some had the lower edge chisel-shaped to let the weight run into the shallow base of the case that little bit further. The weight would normally be akin to a longcase weight, perhaps 12lbs to 14lbs, but some variation may occur.

Hooded clock are often timepieces with alarmwork, and these, since they have no strikework to power, may well run on quite a light weight of about 3lbs to 5lbs. The alarm has its own separate weight, which is often very small and might weigh as little as 1lb or 2lbs. Again, considerable variation may be found.

Weights for lantern clocks are similar for the most part to those on thirty-hour longcases. Those lantern clocks which are time-pieces only will generally run on a lighter weight than strikers. Alarm trains on lantern clocks take a similar weight to those on a hooded clock.

PENDULUM RODS

The oldest longcase clocks generally had pendulums made from a wire rod. Attached to this at the base was a brass block holding a brass-fronted lead bob, regulated by a rating nut below the bob, which raised or lowered it on the brass block (see Figure 10). Some early bobs were brass-covered at the back as well as at the front. This principle was used for most longcase clocks right throughout their period of manufacture.

Some clocks, often those of higher quality, had a pendulum rod made as a strip of brass. This principle came in about 1710 but was used infrequently, perhaps because brass is subject to expansion and contraction from temperature change to a greater degree than iron, and perhaps also because such pendulums are prone to breakage if handled carelessly. Flat-strip pendulum rods were sometimes of iron instead of brass.

Wooden pendulum rods were sometimes used, since wood was less prone to expansion. These were more liable to damage than metal rods, and most will show some signs of repair today. Wooden rods appear infrequently, and mostly after about 1800. They seem to be more common on Scottish clocks than on English ones.

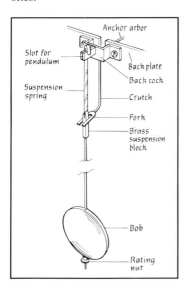

Fig. 10 Pendulum arrangement on anchor escapement longcase or bracket clock

PENDULUM BOBS

After about 1770, pendulum bobs were sometimes of cast iron (see Plate 132), usually painted black but sometimes with one or two gold circles painted on. On Scottish clocks, cast-iron bobs were sometimes japanned or painted in a colourful manner with flowers or fruit or patterns in the same sort of manner as the japanned dials, and they are mostly, if not entirely, found on white dial clocks.

By about 1830, some pendulum bobs of the cast-iron type had a stamped brass facing-piece, often with an embossed pattern to the front, and these are met with occasionally up to 1870.

Some special clocks had special pendulums which sought to overcome expansion, especially on precision timekeepers such as Regulators. The grid-iron pendulum was one such attempt, and involved using multiple-piece rods of alternate iron and brass in such a way that the expansion of the one metal counteracted against the expansion of the other. The same principle was sometimes applied with pendulums with multiple tubes used in the manner of a telescope (see Plate 12). A few clocks have pendulum bobs in the form of mercury-filled jars, again in an attempt at compensation for temperature change, but these are almost always limited to Regulators.

With verge pendulums, sometimes called bob pendulums, the rod itself was of iron wire, and the bob, usually pear-shaped, was of brass. It did not have the usual rating nut regulation of a longcase, but instead the bob was drilled through its centre and a wooden filler-piece inserted, which acted as a grip on a thread cut on the rod. The bob itself would be turned to gain or lose speed by lowering or raising it, and the wood filler-piece gave finer tuning than an internally-cut thread would have done.

It is seldom possible to be able to tell with certainty if a pendulum is original to the clock, though it is often possible to recognise one which is clearly of the wrong sort of age to match the clock, and so must be a replacement. The most one can say is that as long as the pendulum is of the right character and the correct sort of style and type for the clock, then it is not vitally important if it *is* a replacement. Sometimes one can feel confident that a pendulum is in fact original, though a novice will not have the experience to be able to do this. It is a matter not only of the right type and style, but of the correct fit of the brass block to the crutch with no signs of filing or alteration, and of the bob being the right size and shape and weight for the period – in short, things too time-consuming to go into in detail here, and in any event not of vital importance in a choice of a clock or in influencing its value.

Having considered the weight clocks themselves, let us now look at the kinds of cases they had and the types of wood they were made from.

8 CASEWORK

It is very difficult to generalise about clock casework, especially that of longcase clocks. The case was made by a separate craftsman from the clockmaker, usually the local joiner, carpenter or cabinet-maker. There *are* very general stylistic fashions, both in the woods used and in the styling of the cases themselves, but as each cabinet-maker had his own ideas as to just how the ideal case should look, there are probably as many variations in casework as there were men who made them.

Two very important factors determined the shape and perhaps also the styling of any longcase. The first was the dial size, which formed the nucleus around which the case had to be designed. The other factor was the height that the case was to stand, and that would often be determined by the customer, according to the height of his ceiling. Many clocks were custom-built, and so all cases had to some degree to have their styling based on the maximum height to which they might stand. To take an extreme example, an 11-inch-dial (28cms) thirty-hour clock may well look sleek and slender if standing 6ft 6inch (198cms) tall, but a 14-inch-dial (38cms) clock standing to the same height would look very stocky. Personal tastes, however, are such that what one person might regard as stocky, another might see as elegant, and the views we take today on such things may be very different from the way these clocks were seen at the time of their making. When these clocks were new, the buyer regarded them as being important and imposing pieces. A clock was normally the most costly single item ever bought for the household, and so it was felt natural that it should stand in a proud and dignified fashion. For many a married couple of the past a longcase clock was *the* major piece of furniture for the home, which was probably why these were often bought for them by parents as a wedding gift. With our smaller room sizes of today, the public tends to shy away from large clocks, so today's buyer may see the question of size from a totally different viewpoint from that of the first buyer.

Cottage clocks were always of a very different nature from those made for a grand mansion. Firstly, they had to be kept in the lower height ranges, but alongside this was the fact that they had to be in a lower price range, as well. It follows, then, that cottage clocks will be of humbler woods, and mansion clocks, where cost and height were far less restricted, will be of more costly woods, often of more elaborate styling, and often with brass ornaments on top (known as finials). By and large, it would be a contradiction in terms to expect to find a cottage clock in such a wood as mahogany, for this was a very expensive wood and its use was restricted by its cost to the wealthy, who did not live in cottages.

65. *Simple cottage-style case in fruitwood of the thirty-hour clock of c1750 by Thomas Pinfold of Banbury (see Plate 38). Height about 6ft 4in (192cms).*

66. *Eight-day mahogany longcase clock c1760 by Conyers Dunlop of London, with typical pagoda top. Height about 7ft 11in (242cms).*

EBONY CASES

The first longcase clocks had cases of ebony. These clocks were conceived in a Puritan atmosphere, where black not only represented sobriety, but was also thought to be the best framework in which to show off the beauty of the brass and silvered dial. These first clocks had tiny dials, and might have stood at a height which we would think of as cottage height, but they were very costly and so was ebony, which was used only in veneer form, applied onto a base which would be oak or maybe pine. There are very few clocks surviving today in ebony cases. Probably few were in fact made, and many cases of such great age perished long ago. It is said that, within the first few years of the introduction of the longcase clock (by Fromanteel), all available supplies of ebony had been used up. It is also said that many of the ebony cases housing such clocks are reconstructions made less than a hundred years ago and that they are far better made than the originals they replaced. Be that as it may, a case veneered in ebony is very unusual on a longcase clock (more are found on bracket clocks (see Plate 97), though even they are still unusual).

An alternative to ebony was to veneer a case in a fine, close-grain wood and polish it black in colour, so that it looked like ebony. This process was called 'ebonising', and produced an 'ebonised' case. Some black cases were ebonised onto pine, but many had a surface veneer of such a wood as pearwood, which took the polish more richly with a more realistic effect. Many bracket clocks were ebonised onto pearwood veneer; if strippped down to bare wood, pearwood is a nondescript and miserable colour.

The fashion for ebony or ebonised longcases faded away by about 1690 in London, and lasted perhaps another thirty years at most in the provinces. In bracket clocks, however, the ebonised case lasted until the 1780s, or occasionally even later (see Plates 92, 99).

ENGLISH WALNUT CASES

English walnut took over after the ebony period. This wood was used as veneer (see Plate 67), usually in the form of finely-matched pieces which could be set onto a base of pine or oak in patterns, which were restricted to the front of the case, principally the trunk door and base. Veneers were often matched into two, or four, or eight to make radiating patterns, and this was known as quartering (even if there were more than four). The term 'bookmatched' is used to indicate those veneers joined at the centre and thus giving a mirror image at each side. Bookmatching was used for the door and base, and sometimes for other areas, and could be in two pieces, or four, or more. In general use the two terms, quartered and bookmatched, mean the same thing, and they are often used interchangeably, and often, too, without regard to how many pieces actually form the pattern.

Another method of using walnut was to use oval or even circular slices of veneer and to set these out in patterns. Known as oystershells, these slices were usually cut from a branch at a shallow angle, and these oystershells could be of any wood. The woods most often used were those which produced rich figuring,

67. Case of the John Williamson clock, c1695 (see Plates 22 and 87), the ground of walnut veneer with panels of marquetry inlay of the fine scroll type known as seaweed or Arabesque marquetry, a type of marquetry usually used all over rather than in panels. Height 6ft 11in (211cms).

68. Primitive case of the Archer clock (see Plate 37) in elm. Note surface hinges to door ('H' hinges), lack of hood pillars, and holes in the hood sides to act as sound frets. Typical elm figuring on door.

69. Simple oak cottage case of the eight-day clock by Rogers of Leominster, c1780-90 (see Plate 46). A blind fret across the hood top is the only attempt at ornamentation. Height 6ft 9in (206cms).

such as laburnum, olive wood and walnut, often laid within a surround of walnut veneer. This patterned process using oyster-shell cuts is known as parquetry. Oystershell pieces were only one form of parquetry, which might otherwise be formed from different shaped cuts such as sunbursts or starbursts or all manner of patterns.

Walnut cases were usually made using the finest veneers for the clock front, often busily-patterned and highly-figured pieces or burr pieces full of rich grain and knots (see Plate 67). The sides of the cases would usually be of much plainer veneers, often set within lined panels of yellow stringing made of boxwood or holly. This type of walnut case was obviously very costly, and was used on London clocks and some finer provincial eight-day ones from as early as about 1680 until walnut fell from favour in London by about 1760, and perhaps even a little earlier in the provinces. This was clearly not a type of case to be found on a more humble cottage clock.

COTTAGE CLOCK CASES

On cottage clocks, walnut was sometimes used, but normally in solid form and of much plainer grain – the best cuts of the timber obviously being used for grander cases. Solid walnut was at the time no more costly than oak, so that many cottage clocks may have been cased in walnut. Walnut, however, was very prone to woodworm, and many such cases have been destroyed from beetle attack. Solid walnut might have been used for cottage clocks from about 1700 to perhaps 1800, though not many survive today. Other woods used for cottage longcases were elm (Plate 68), oak (Plate 69) and pine (see Plates 60, 70). These woods were sometimes painted on the surface when new. In fact, it is probably true to say that pine cases were always painted, and often it is only the paint which saved them from destruction by woodworm, damp and rot. Pine was the cheapest of all case timbers, a simple cottage case in pine being available new in the eighteenth century at less than ten shillings (£0.50), whereas an oak one was closer to one pound.

OAK CASES

Oak (see Plates 28, 71, 72, 86) was a readily available wood, and in its best form was riven or quarter-sawn, which involved taking cheese-shaped segments. When cut this way the flowery rays, known as medullary rays, showed off to best effect, but the real purpose of quarter-cutting was to retain the strength in the timber, as in this form it was less prone to warping. The best cuts of oak, and especially those with the most figuring, were usually used for the front of the case, principally for the door and base. This might mean the base had to be glued up from two or more pieces, but this was preferable (and more costly) than for a single straight-sawn plank to be used, which was more likely to twist or

137

split, or both. Oak which was straight-sawn (sometimes called slash-sawn) would be likely to show less, if any, figure, and this cut was normally used for those parts which were less evident, such as case sides and hood sides, which in any event were narrower panels and were thus less prone to warping. On

70. *Case of the eight-day clock by James Bath (see Plate 49) in white pine. Height 6ft 8in (204cms). Preserved in unusually good condition for pine.*

71. *Oak country case of the clock by Joseph Butterworth of Cawthorne (see Plate 32), from the 1730s. Height 6ft 6in (198cms).*

72. *Simple oak case of the Henderson of Scarborough clock (see Plate 36), c1730, showing many early features: attached hood pillars, glass hood side windows, half-round beading to door edge, long and narrow door. Height 7ft (213cms).*

73. *Oak case cross-banded in mahogany, housing the clock by Caygill of Askrigg (see Plate 29). The hood is of the break-arch style. A good case with considerable fretting and mahogany trim on, for example, the quarter-pillars. Height 7ft 3in (212cms).*

74. *Oak case trimmed with mahogany of the eight-day clock c1780 by John Blaylock of Longtown (see Plate 42). Height 7ft 10in (238cms).*

75. Thirty-hour white dial clock of about 1790 by Thomas Hargreaves of Settle, Yorks. Oak with mahogany trim. Height 7ft (213cms).

76. Eight-day brass dial clock with rolling moon by John Aspinwall of Liverpool c1780 showing the typical style of a Lancashire mahogany case of the period.

eighteenth-century cases the main door was very long and narrow, and such a shape was likely to warp if the oak used for the door was not quarter-cut.

Oak was often used for country clock cases, but it was by no means only used on those. Some very fine clocks of high quality were also made in oak – longcase clocks, that is, for oak was not used at all in bracket clocks. On many higher-grade oak clocks, the oak panels were cross-banded round the edge for decorative effect and also for strength, as a cross-banded door presented an end grain all the way round the panel, and this was more resilient to knocks than long grain, which might splinter. Cross-banding was normally in walnut veneer before roughly the middle of the eighteenth century, and in mahogany thereafter (see Plates 8, 73, 74, 90). Occasionally oak might have been cross-banded in oak, but that was unusual, for oak on English longcasework was seldom used as veneer.

EARLY MAHOGANY CASES

Mahogany came into use in England in the late seventeenth century, but was a rare and little-used wood until after about 1740, and most mahogany seen in longcase work will date after 1760. Early mahogany came from the West Indies, particularly the Spanish West Indies, and this wood is very dark and heavy, not usually very spectacular in the figure. It was mostly used in solid form, and is often known as Spanish mahogany, or Cuban mahogany. Cases of this wood are found from about 1735, but occur more usually between about 1745 and 1760 (see Plate 127). By the middle of the century, a paler mahogany was imported, and the best parts of this were chosen for their very rich figuring, some pieces having rich, flame-like splashing. This lighter-coloured wood came from Honduras or the Americas, and is sometimes known as Honduras mahogany or flame mahogany, the best-figured parts being termed crotch mahogany. This latter term signifies that part of the trunk where a large branch joined (the crotch), and where the rays when sawn were very lively and highly-figured.

The best-figured pieces of crotch mahogany were used on the most visible parts of the case – principally the door and base – and were always used as veneer. This was because it would have been very wasteful to have used the best parts of the tree in solid, when as veneer it could be made to spread much further, but also because the tensions and pressures within these twisted patterns may well have caused warping and splitting.

Any mahogany was shipped half way across the world before being sawn and used. It was a very strong and rich wood, immune to woodworm, and very durable. At the time it first appeared here, it is said that cabinet-makers complained that its hardness took the edges off their tools, but it soon became known as the King of Woods. Its strength made it possible for craftsmen to work it into all manner of shapes, to carve or veneer with it, and to use it in large boards or small. In short, it was a very versatile wood. Consequently, mahogany was usually used for clocks of an ornate, complex and highly-sophisticated nature – the kind of work where a craftsman could show off its potential. It was, therefore, often costly in work as well as in materials, and most eighteenth-century mahogany clocks were grand and tall affairs built for a gentleman's house, not a cottage (Plates 7, 66, 89, 127). A good mahogany case could cost ten times the price of an oak one, in the eighteenth century at least, for in nineteenth-century work we are talking of a different type of case.

LACQUER CASES AND LATER MAHOGANY CASES

Another kind of case was used for longcase work in the eighteenth century, and that was known as a lacquer case or a japanned case, sometimes today called a chinoiserie case. This was a style which began in London about the end of the seventeenth century, spreading into the provinces within ten years or so, and which was used until about 1770, when it fell out of favour against the more popular mahogany. Many provincial clocks were enclosed in lacquer cases, though a good number of these would have been made in London and bought by country clockmakers for special orders. Few, if any, rural or even provincial city cabinet-makers would have been skilled at japanning wood.

Some lacquered cases have a carcase of pine with the main feature parts (door and base) of oak, though others are entirely of oak. The exterior surface was coated with lacquers and gums to give a coloured ground, onto which were built up scenes of an oriental style in golds and sometimes multiple colours. These clocks are known by their ground colour; most had a ground in black, though blue and green grounds are not unusual, red or maroon is less common, and least common of all is a yellow ground. These cases were of a nature to match imported Oriental cabinets, and it was sometimes suggested that they were made in London, shipped to the Far East for lacquering, and then shipped back again, though as far as I know no documentary evidence has ever been produced to show that this was indeed the case, and it seems more likely the work was done here, in London.

While oak was the base wood on some London-made lacquered longcase clocks, it was not used as a case wood in London in its normal form. Today one sometimes sees a London clock in an oak case. Most such have been re-housed in non-original and obviously provincial cases. Others may be examples which were originally lacquered, but which have been stripped down to bare oak once the lacquer deteriorated beyond recovery, for lacquer does deteriorate with age, and is also prone to problems arising from heat, sunlight and damp, any of which may badly affect the

77. Round dial eight-day clock of about 1830-40 by Bryson of Edinburgh. This round-topped case style is known as a drumhead clock, and is peculiar to Scotland. The figuring on this mahogany case is exceptionally fine. Height 6ft 8in (200cms).

78. Eight-day longcase in mahogany, by P. Feren of Dundee, c1840. The bow door is a feature of many Scottish cases of this period. Height 6ft 11in (211cms).

surface with cracking and peeling.

As the eighteenth century progressed, oak was used increasingly less in isolation from other woods, except in very simple cottage cases. More often, and increasingly so as the century progressed, oak was decorated with mahogany trim (*eg.* Plates 73, 74, 90). By about 1820, it is uncommon to find any case made only of oak. By the 1840s, the great majority of clock cases are in mahogany veneer, often by now onto a pine carcase, though probably retaining solid form mahogany in the structural sections of the sides and hood sides. These Victorian mahogany cases are not in the same league as mahogany ones from the eighteenth century, though the fanciful use of veneers as patterns and banding and stringing work may be greater (Plate 78). 'Stringing' is the word used for inlaid lines, usually of white woods (holly or box), set in to divide up veneered panels. Some stringing is black, which might be ebony but is more likely to be some more common wood stained black for the purpose.

BRACKET CLOCK WOODS

The same woods and treatments were used in bracket clocks (see Chapter 9) as in longcases, to a large degree. Lacquer was perhaps less popular in bracket clocks than in longcases, provincially at least. By about 1760, mahogany was widely used in bracket clocks (see Plates 102, 103), and its use lasted until the mid-nineteenth century. Rosewood was used on bracket clocks as veneer mainly in the 1830s and 1840s, often on clocks which were inlaid with much white stringing (now yellow with age) or brass stringing (see Plate 106). Rosewood was also used on longcase clocks, though only sparingly, and principally as occasional cross-banding on parts of Victorian clocks, where more widespread mahogany banding was also used. In other words, the rosewood on such cases was intended for contrast with the mahogany. Ebonised bracket clocks (see Plates 92, 98, 99) were still produced into the 1770s and even later, then fell from fashion. However, ebonised versions were re-introduced with the imported clocks from Germany in the late nineteenth century, often by then with applied brass figures for contrasting ornamentation.

CASE STYLES

Styles of longcases are very difficult to summarise, and the best way for a beginner to learn about shapes of cases is to study as many clocks as possible, both as real examples and through the illustrations in books. The shape and proportion of a case will very often in itself be enough to assess its age, so that one could accomplish this, for example, from a line-drawing, if the latter were accurately balanced. But the vast variety of shapes are impossible to summarise in a few words, and the regional factors complicate this beyond description.

79. Case in red walnut and mahogany of the eight-day clock by Thomas Clare of Warrington (see Plate 33). Height 6ft 11in (211cms). This form of break-arch pediment is uncommon on a square dial. The gold-painted frieze is a glass panel.

80. Oak case of the John Smith of Pittenweem clock (see Plate 45) standing only 6ft 6in (198cms). The style is simple and in this instance daintily small. The shallow swan-necks are set low and have inset frets in pale wood, typical of the Edinburgh region at this time.

81. Oak-cased longcase clock, cross-banded in mahogany, from an eight-day clock (see Plate 48) by Samuel Deacon of Barton, Leicestershire. The case stands 7ft 4in (223cms) and is typical of late eighteenth-century styling. This clock was actually made in 1806. Here the swan-necks have unusual curl-pieces between them.

82. Mahogany eight-day longcase clock c1810-20 by Woolston Roberts of Derby. This distinctive style of pagoda-topped case was made in the Hull area, yet is original to the clock as delivery note on case confirms. Height 7ft 2in (219cms).

Cottage clocks often retained the square dial, and square dial clocks often had flat tops in order to keep total height low (Plates 65, 71, 72, 86). So a square dial flat-topped cottage clock may vary little from the late seventeenth century to the late eighteenth century in shape, though they grow gradually broader as dial sizes increase (see Plate 8). By the nineteenth century, the flat top was falling from favour, as swan-necks and occasionally other shaped pediments took over (see Plates 79, 80, 81), though by the 1820s the square dial itself was largely replaced by the arched form, even on thirty-hour clocks (Plates 80, 81).

Arched dial clocks were less likely to have flat-topped cases at any period – today many have, because their caddies and upper pediments have been removed to decrease height. By the third quarter of the eighteenth century, most arched dial clocks outside of London (and the area of London influence in the south-east) had swan-neck pediments, and the swan-neck became the most popular style of all – though there are many varying shapes, proportions and styles of the basic swan-neck concept (see Plates 80, 81, 89).

In London, the pagoda top was the most fashionable regular style in use after about 1750 (see Plate 66). Today, many London clocks have had their hoods cut short because of their excessive height, and a large number of clocks with a rounded top (a dome with a shoulder at each side, sometimes called a break-arch top) were once pagoda tops, but have had the pagoda removed. The swan-neck was never a popular style in London, to the extent that a London clock with a swan-neck pediment would be sufficiently unusual to call for close inspection to make certain of the originality of the clock to its case.

In the late seventeenth and eighteenth centuries, the doors of longcase clocks were long, and filled the whole of the long trunk area, with just a framework being left around them (see Plates 5, 67, 68, 71, 72, 83, 86). By the end of the eighteenth century, many doors were now only three-quarter length, though the trunks still remained long (see Plates 66, 77, 78). The spare space below the trunk door was often filled by a panel, and this three-quarter-door style with a panel below it was popular from roughly 1800 to about 1830–40, by which time trunks in general had shortened to produce what we now call a short-door clock. In simple terms, the progression from long to short door is very much the history of longcase styles. A very simple pointer such as that, and a knowledge of which woods were used at which periods, may alone be enough to guide a novice in the direction of the period of the clock – assuming it is a clock in its *original* case. On the other hand, a novice cannot distinguish what is meant by a long or a short door until he has seen a number of examples of each, and has compared them.

83. *Simple oak case of the William Reynolds clock (see Plate 28) with typical shaped doortop, here in Cupid bow shape. Height 7ft (213cms).*

84. *Handsome mahogany case of the clock by Laird of Leith, c1840 (see Plate 52), standing 7ft (213cms). The door does not now run the full length of the trunk (known as a three-quarter length door), yet the case retains the slender elegant proportions of many late eighteenth-century examples. It is the original case for the clock.*

85. *Oak case with mahogany cross-banding, from the eight-day clock c1830 by Richards of Uttoxeter (see Plate 51). Note shorter door now with panel beneath. Height 7ft 2in (219cms).*

LENTICLE GLASS

Some early longcase clocks had a circular window in the lower area of the trunk door (see Plates 5, 67). This is known as a lenticle glass, and as the glass itself was sometimes of the bottle-glass nature, it is sometimes known as a bull's eye glass or a bull's eye window. From about 1680 to perhaps 1710, this lenticle was popular in London clocks, and from about 1680 to 1740, in provincial ones, so that such a feature is an indicator of period. The purpose of this window is not really known, but it was probably just to show the glint of the pendulum as it caught the light in swinging. The window was positioned in front of the pendulum bob – and one that does not line up with the pendulum bob may well be an indicator of a swapped case.

HOOD SIDE WINDOWS

About the same period as the lenticle glass, many longcase clocks had glass side windows in the hood, through which the movement could be seen (see Plates 66, 67, 72, 87). It may have been simply an observation window to allow the curious to view the wheels turning in this, the first of machines, or it may perhaps have been a means of establishing at a glance that the clock was in need of winding, since the extent of the gutline on the barrel can easily be seen. As these glass side windows also occur on thirty-hour clocks, the implication is that this was probably simply for observation. London clocks tend to have these side windows from about 1680 to 1720 or 1730, after which time some had pierced frets backed with coloured cloth, while others retained the glass window principle. Provincial clocks in the South of England followed the London influence in this respect. In other parts of the provinces, glass side windows fall from use by about the middle of the eighteenth century, and in the North especially they would be unusual in the later eighteenth century, though in parts of Scotland, such as Edinburgh, the London fashion was followed. So hood side windows *can* be a dating aid. Not all clocks had them, but those which did would tend to be London- (or Edinburgh-) influenced, or pre-1750, or both. The presence of such windows was always more likely on eight-day clocks than on thirty-hours.

INTEGRAL HOOD PILLARS

Some early longcases from London and elsewhere had hood pillars of the barley sugar-twist style (see Plate 86), which consist in fact of three-quarter pillars attached to the hood door and quarter-pillars at the back of the hood. Barley sugar pillars were popular from about 1680 to about 1700 in London, and until about 1730 in the provinces. Not all clocks had them, but, when they did, they tend to fall in these periods.

When barley sugar pillars fell from use, plain turned pillars

86. *Primitive oak country case of the Bullock of Ellesmere clock, c1725 (see Plate 34). There is no door to the hood, which slides forward. Height 6ft 10in (208cms).*

87. *Detail of the hood of the John Williamson clock (see Plates 22 and 67), c1695. There is no opening door to the hood, as it rises upwards for winding. The convex mould below the hood is typical of the period, as are the glass side windows and the caddy top.*

replaced them, fitted along the same principles, *ie.* attached to the hood door, and we term these integral pillars (see Plates 5, 87). These remained popular in the South, especially on cottage clocks, until as late as the end of the eighteenth century. Not all clocks had them, but a good number did. In the North, however, integral pillars were less popular, and most clocks had separate, free-standing pillars after about 1730, even on simple cottage clocks. So integral pillars can also be an aid to dating, as long as this regional factor is taken into account.

A longcase hood slides into place on top of the top-of-trunk moulding, and on most early clocks this mould was of convex shape (*eg.* Plate 87), rather like a quarter of a circle. The convex mould was normal on most longcases until about 1700 in London and perhaps 1720 or 1730 elsewhere. After that time the mould reversed in direction to being concave (Plates 5, 73, 83, *etc.*), though on some Northern clocks it might be half-and-half, *ie.* an ogee mould. So a convex mould below the hood is very often a sign of an early clock. Occasionally late throwbacks are met with – some Dublin cases, for example, use the old-fashioned convex mould as late as the 1760s.

RISING/SLIDING HOODS

The earliest longcase clocks had hoods with a fixed front glass area with no opening door. Access for winding with a key or for setting the hands to the correct time was obtained by lifting up the hood, which ran on grooves at each side of its back part, onto wooden protruding tongues on the backboard. Once raised, the hood would latch into place by means of a trigger catch on the backboard. This method of access was known as a rising hood (see Plate 87).

Rising hoods were normal on most longcase clocks in the earliest periods, and probably all would have had this system until about 1695, and a great many until about 1710. The later method was to make the hood slide forward for removal, and sliding hoods had a hinged door which swung open for all normal access such as winding. After about 1720, all longcase clocks had sliding hoods and opening doors, with the possible exception that an occasional country casemaker may have made a sliding hood with a fixed (non-opening) glass window (Plate 86).

While the earliest hoods were of the lift-up type *originally*, almost all of them were later converted to slide forward, occasionally keeping the fixed glass feature but more often having a swinging door cut in them for easy winding access. Such a conversion is known as an original lift-up hood, converted to sliding. This was normal practice, and such a conversion is in no way seen as detrimental. The way to establish whether a hood was originally of the lifting type is to examine the back of the inner sides of the hood for a groove, and the backboard top for signs of a runner (though the latter have sometimes been planed off in converting to forward slide). There will also probably be signs on the upper right-hand of the backboard where a locking catch once was fastened, and also signs on the inside of the frame of the trunk door at the top, where a 'spoon' catch once held the hood in position.

Today, some collectors and dealers will re-convert a hood which was once lifting, and is now sliding, back to lifting again – in other words, back to its originally-conceived form. Most, however, do not do this, as there is no doubt that a sliding hood is far more convenient in use, and will operate with a much lower ceiling height.

BASES

The bases of longcase clocks, too, can be an identification aid, but are a rather variable factor. Many clocks have been cut short in the base, either to remove rot or to reduce height, and so the shape may not be as made. In very general terms, the base of a longcase (the lower section below the trunk and including its feet) will be square or shallower than square on Southern clocks (see Plate 5), square or taller than square on Northern ones (see Plate 71). Where the base carries a raised panel as a feature, or stringing/banding lines are evident, then the panel/stringing outline will also follow this pattern, *ie.* square or taller than square in the North (Plate 41), square or shallower than square in the South (Plate 66). This trend applies more to quality eight-day clocks than to cottage cases, as in the latter instances a country joiner may well have followed his own practice regardless of general trends.

It follows from the above that, because of simple commonsense rules of joinery, the direction of the wood grain will run horizontal on Southern clocks and vertical on Northern ones. In other words, the joiner would line up the grain in the longest direction allowed by the space available. These pointers concerning the bases of clocks are not infallible, and in fact are less reliable than some of the other ones mentioned above. There were always local joiners who may have worked in a manner contrary to others.

These casework pointers are only a general guide, and must not be taken as absolute rules. However, it is always possible to examine a clock case with these indicators in mind and arrive at a conclusion as to its age, and even, with experience, its region of manufacture. Ascribing a clock to a region is a far more difficult skill to learn than identifying its age, and few people can do this. The only way to accomplish it is through studying actual clocks and, perhaps even more importantly, photographs in books, as the latter have dates ascribed to them, as well as regions and other salient points. However, if using reference books, *do* use modern ones – we have learned more about clocks in the last twenty years than in the previous hundred, and there is little point in studying antiques through books which are themselves antiques. Some old clock books contain more wrong clocks than right ones. Old books are a pleasure to own, but their informative content may be outdated and inadequate.

CARVED CASES

One style of longcase not yet mentioned is the carved case, an area of great interest and often great confusion. Those cases which are carved usually have the carving on the door and base panels, and often too around the hood door, the door frame and the base perimeter. Almost all of these cases are made of oak, and the majority were stained after carving to a very dark brown, almost black colour, with the type of coloured varnish which obscures the grain – the same sort of varnish stain often used for floorboards outside the edge of a carpet square (see Plate 88).

The nature of the carving varies enormously, as does the quality. It may involve a vine with leaves or some kind of climbing plant; it could consist of stylised figures such as a Roman soldier, eagles, sea monsters, Adam and Eve; or it might just be formed into patterns positioned in such a way as to fill the shapes available. Sometimes a date is incorporated into the carving, often an impossibly early date (such as 1637), from a period when longcase clocks did not even exist.

These cases are normally genuine old cases, often original to the clock itself, and the majority will date from about 1750 to about 1800, and almost all will contain brass dial clocks. It is a relatively easy matter to decide from experience whether the case is a genuine old one of the time of the clock, but what is less easy to determine is whether the carving is original or was done much later. Many of the clocks carved in this way are Northern ones, principally from the Lancashire/Yorkshire Pennines, where this sort of carved case seems to have been especially popular. There may well have been a local fashion for this kind of carved case in the third quarter of the eighteenth century, and it could be that some of these carved cases are entirely original both in the making and the carving.

However, examination will show that the great majority were carved later, perhaps a hundred years later than the clock's manufacture (and that of its case). At the end of the nineteenth century there was a fashion for heavily-carved 'black' furniture in a revival of Gothic taste, and many of these carved cases were carved and stained black at that time to match in with other items in that trend. Northern cases, being often of thick oak, would lend themselves better to this carving, whereas Southern cases were often of much thinner timbers, and would not. Many owners persuade themselves that their clock, with its carving, is original and as made. The great majority who do so delude themselves. Many carved themes are typical of the Art Nouveau style,

88. Thirty-hour brass dial longcase clock, by Thomas Lister senior of Halifax, c1760, standing 7ft 3in (212cms). An example of a heavily-carved case, stained dark. Note gilded wooden flambeau finials.

89. Eight-day clock of highly complex nature, by Thomas Lister junior of Halifax, in its original mahogany case of the grander but heavier Liverpool style: brickwork base, pierced trunk columns, double hood pillars, glass panels below the swan-necks. Height 8ft 6in (259cms). About 1780.

particularly popular being entwined flowers and leaf sprays. Mahogany cross-banding on many of these cases, carved through and blackened over to the point where the mahogany can no longer show, is a sure sign that the case was not meant to be carved or blackened.

SIGNED CASES

Clock cases were rarely signed by the craftsmen who made them. A very few cabinet-makers did leave a trade label pasted inside their cases, though many were no doubt peeled off over the years. Casemakers' labels tend to survive haphazardly here and there, though in Lincolnshire at least three casemakers regularly pasted a label on the backboard of their cases, with the result that in that county these are less scarce than elsewhere.

A few cabinet-makers used a name-punch, and would punch in an impressed mark of their name, usually in some inconspicuous area such as inside the case door or perhaps along a door edge, and it is surprising how such a punch-mark is easily overlooked. A few, and they are *very* few, casemakers lettered their names on the clock front, on, for example the frieze above the hood, and I have seen at least two different Cheshire cabinet-makers using this method in the eighteenth century.

The label of a cabinet-maker or clock case maker is sufficiently unusual on a clock to be of special interest, especially in the eighteenth century. I came across one a year or two ago on a mahogany longcase clock by John Drinkwater of Liverpool, being a printed label with engravings of cabinets and clock cases and lettered with the name of John Orme, cabinet-maker of Liverpool, and dated 1771 – an original date on a label being extremely unusual.

It always pays to examine every part of a clock case, especially a longcase, even in hidden parts such as inside the backboard or on the back of it. Just occasionally one will find the original delivery instructions there, on a faded and torn slip of paper, or even an original receipt of hand-written instructions from the clockmaker. I doubt if I have come across a dozen in my twenty-five years as a clock dealer, but they are exciting things to find, and the chances of a novice finding them are just as great as for an expert.

CASEMAKERS

A correspondent once sent me photographs of a hand-written signature of the casemaker which he found during removal of the trunk quarter-column of his clock, which had come loose and which he was in the process of re-glueing. The name, place of origin, and date were neatly written in ink on the bare wood, in a spot where nobody was ever likely to see it again once the quarter-pillar had been glued into place, and it was only by chance that it was found.

While joiners and carpenters were the makers of many simple country cases, those of higher quality were made by the more expert woodworkers known as cabinet-makers. While we know quite a number of these from their advertisements of the past, seldom did they label their products, and so, though we know their names, we cannot recognise their work. Cabinet-makers normally made all manner of furniture as well as clock cases, but there were a few specialists who made nothing but clock cases, or so they claimed.

An advertisement typical of many was placed in the *Ipswich Journal* in 1812: 'To Clockmakers. George Goodwin (from London), Clock Case Maker, Thoro'fare, Woodbridge. Respectfully begs . . . acquaints them (*ie.* clockmakers) and the public in general, he has constantly on sale at the lowest prices, a neat and elegant variety of highly-finished clock cases, of the most fashionable shapes . . . Cases made to order on the shortest notice.'

From this advertisement alone, we see the varying options open, namely, that a clockmaker could select from a cabinet-maker's range or have one made to his own requirements, but also that these options were available to the general public too. This suggests that some clocks were sold ready-cased by the clock-maker as complete units, but that in other instances the clock was sold loose, and subsequently housed in a case bought by the first owner. Sometimes an owner may well have bought a new case to re-house his old clock in the newest fashion – hence some clocks appearing in later cases!

FINIALS

A feature of many clocks, especially longcases, were the fancy brass fittings often used to trim the hood pediment, known as finials (see Plates 7, 51, 66, 81, 88, 90, 91). Many clocks had these, particularly those with shaped hood-tops, and they would be disposed according to the layout of the hood pediment. Flat-topped hoods, as found on many cottage clocks, would be less likely to have them, since much of the purpose in a flat hood-top was to keep down the height factor for low ceilings. But a typical swan-neck hood, for example, would almost always have a central finial, normally a sphere topped by either a spire or an eagle with outspread wings (see Plate 81). Some swan-necked pediments carried three finials, the central one and another at each side (see Plate 127). Many clocks have lost their finials, though empty holes will usually make it obvious where they had them.

Even though the clock may have been designed to have finials and have been fitted with them when new, subsequent owners often removed them, for all manner of reasons. Height reduction was one, over-fussiness was another. Brass finials were based on a hollow sphere, and these both corroded from the inside and were polished away from the outside until the spheres ultimately

90. Oak case trimmed with mahogany and shell inlays, and with elaborate finials, of the longcase clock by John Baker of Hull (see Plate 4). Height 7ft 8in (234cms).

91. Oak-cased eight-day clock c1810 by Vurley of Wisbeach. Typical mahogany cross-banding, shell inlay and finial. Height 6ft 6in (198cms).

collapsed. Eagle finials in brass went through a particular period of unpopularity in Britain during two world wars with Germany, for, in the First World War in particular, the eagle was seen as a symbol of the enemy, and was regarded here as being very unpatriotic by some clock owners.

Finials were often in brass, in which instance the casemaker would have had to buy them in from the brassfounder. In the eighteenth century, good quality ones of cast brass could cost about 8s. 0d. (£0.40) a set, but by the 1840s cheaper ones could be bought for as little as 1s. 6d. (£0.7½) a set. Because of the cost of brass finials and no doubt the delay in sending away for them, many casemakers opted to make their own by turning them in wood and usually gilding over the surface. These were usually of spire type and usually of soft wood, and many became worm-eaten and were discarded. They were gesso covered to provide a smooth surface and then gilded onto the gesso, sometimes only on the front areas.

PATERAE
On the end of each of the two swan-necks many clocks have a circular brass disc (see Plates 80, 81, 91). These are known as paterae, and again the original brass ones often wore right through from polishing. Some paterae were made in wood as turned roundels, for the reasons explained above, and some casemakers chose to have carved flowerheads instead, especially in north-west England.

CAPS AND BASES
Hood pillars on many clocks had brass capitals and bases (eg. Plate 66). Here, too, some casemakers, especially with cottage clocks, chose to make their capitals of turned wood, probably because it was not only cheaper but quicker. Wooden caps and bases were originally gilded but often have worn down to a 'brown' wood colour over the years. Some owners would re-paint them in gold, which made them look rather gaudy.

BRACKET CLOCK FINIALS
With bracket clocks, the carrying handle would serve as a sort of top decoration on early examples (see Plate 92). By the late eighteenth century, however, bracket clocks too had finials on top of the cases, often a ball or spire type, but by early nineteenth century a pineapple was a favourite theme (see Plate 106). Throughout the eighteenth century many bracket clocks had four corner finials (with the carrying handle still at the top centre). These corner finials might be of spire pattern but many were of 'flambeau' style, ie. a torch with a burning flame, though urns, acorns and pineapples are known. Bracket clock finials would tend to be brass not wood.

HOOD LOCK

On London longcases, and on some provincial ones based on the London pattern, the hood door would fasten with a lock and key. This was not a system favoured by most casemakers. Many were content to let the hood door stay closed by friction, and a small knob was usually fitted to pull it open. Some cases had a bolt trigger set behind the top-of-trunk moulding, which was pushed up by reaching up inside the case via the main door to lock into a large staple-like fitting on the lower inner hood door frame. The effect was not only to lock the hood door, but also to lock the hood itself in place to prevent it working forward and slipping off. So it was a door-lock and hood safety-catch all in one, and this system was used on many London clocks and on some, mainly earlier, provincial ones, often in addition to the key lock.

Instead of the staple, many clocks had an L-shaped fitting of brass or iron protruding inside the case from the inside of the hood door. A pivoted wooden latch swung to sit in this half-staple for the same purpose, *ie.* holding both the door shut and the hood in place. On many clocks both the bolt and staple, or latch and hook, have long ago been lost, and many owners puzzle over a narrow slot in the lower hood mask, which now fulfils no apparent purpose. The position was usually at about the seven o'clock area in the lower section of the mask surrounding the dial.

PATINA

The patina of a clock case is a surface glaze built up over generations by polishing with wax, so that a glassy film covers the surface. It is a mistake to over-clean a case, though sometimes a crustiness in the finish can be gently eased down by more waxing with a coarse cloth. If the patinated surface is broken, lighter wood will show through from beneath, and this can be both unsightly and impossible to deal with other than by stripping down more of the surface. Patina tends to grow ever darker, as dirt is one ingredient which is rubbed in during the waxing process.

The surface of a clock was treated in some way when new to seal in the colour. A hard wood such as mahogany may have had a coat or several coats of shellac; oak was usually varnished. The patina is therefore a build-up of dirt and wax on top of an original sealant of some sort. If the surface is scraped down to the bare wood, it will be in effect a new surface, its colour will be artificially light, and its appeal as an antique will be greatly reduced. It is far better for the inexperienced to leave well alone than to risk spoiling a case finish by amateurish attempts at cleaning. If the polish has perished (usually showing signs of crazing), it will need the attention of an expert restorer.

Having looked in detail at weight-driven clocks and their cases, we next turn our attention to the other totally different nature of domestic clock, that driven by springs.

9 SPRING-DRIVEN CLOCKS

The fusee clocks powered by springs had certain in-built disadvantages compared with those powered by weights. A spring was something which a clockmaker could not make for himself, but was obliged to buy from a specialist spring-maker. By their very nature, springs are liable to failure, but the main problem with a spring is that it pulls strongly when fully-wound, but increasingly weakly as it runs down, as well as being subject to variation through temperature change. The fusee gear (see Figure 11) was used by British clockmakers in an attempt to compensate for the spring's loss of power in running down. Even so, the spring-driven clock was less accurate than one driven by weights, and was more fragile and expensive. Its only advantage was that it could be carried from room to room, such as to the

Fig. 11 The fusee, shown here connected to the spring barrel by gutline (some have chain)

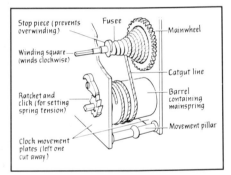

When fully wound the spring has its strongest power and is obliged to pull against the narrow end of the fusee cone. When almost run down the then weaker spring power pulls against the less-resistant (wider) end of the fusee. In this way the fusee gear attempts to compensate for loss of spring power during running.

bedroom at night, if so wished. For these reasons, the spring-driven clock was bought only by the wealthy, and was for the most part made in an ornate style to appeal to such wealthy customers.

BRACKET CLOCKS

The spring-driven clock was made for use on a table or mantel, or sometimes on a wall-mounted bracket. Today such clocks are known as bracket clocks, even though most of them never had a bracket originally, and even though many of those which once did have a bracket, have long ago lost it.

Bracket clocks were first made with the introduction of the pendulum (1658), and continued to be produced until the end of

British native clockmaking, in about 1860. About the middle of the eighteenth century, a wall-mounted type of spring clock began to appear, known as a cartel clock. Towards the end of the eighteenth century, the first round dial wall clocks appeared, usually known as English Dial Clocks (Plates 122, 123), and these were made in increasing numbers as the nineteenth century progressed.

92. Ebonised bracket clock, c1690, by Henry Jones of London. Height 15 inches (40cms).

93. Walnut bracket clock, c1725, by Barnaby Dammant of Colchester, showing mock pendulum feature below XII. Verge escapement.

By the middle of the nineteenth century, imported versions began to appear of bracket clocks and dial clocks, mainly from Germany and America respectively. These sold here for much lower prices, and while they were also of much lower quality, they were still serviceable clocks, and found a huge market here.

The average bracket clock stands eighteen to twenty inches high excluding the carrying handle, which adds a further two inches if raised. With square dial examples, naturally, the height is lower, and in comparing heights it is obvious that one can only compare examples with the same dial shape, as any square dial example (see Plate 92) is likely to be at least 3 inches lower than a similar arched one (see Plate 93).

DIALS

The arched dial was introduced about 1700, and in the period 1700 to 1725 those clocks with arched dials often have a shallow arch, *ie.* less than a semi-circle (Plate 93). Occasionally a square dial example may occur after 1700, and in the second quarter of the nineteenth century the square dial was re-introduced, from which time on they are not uncommon.

Round dials (see Plate 105) are found from about 1760, some of brass but after about 1790 increasingly in the white (japanned) dial form, until by about 1820 the majority are white round dials. Unlike longcase clocks, however, the brass dial never fell completely from fashion, and brass dial examples, usually of the single-sheet type, may be found right until the end of native clockmaking about 1860 (see Plate 103). The brass dial was re-introduced in composite dial form in many imported bracket clocks made after about 1860, mostly German, and in these the style of the dial was based on early eighteenth century principles. With a little practice these can be recognised as being very different from those they imitate in quality of materials, quality of engraving, and in having a mixture of stylistic features from widely different periods, such as could never be found together on any one clock in its period. Most imported examples lack any 'clockmaker's' name on the dial, or if they bear a name at all it is frequently one of a large department store or chain store retailer.

HANDS

Hands on bracket clocks follow broadly the same stylistic development as on longcase clocks until the latter part of the eighteenth century, with the exception that there are no single-handed bracket clocks. Early examples were made in 'non-matching' principle in steel (see Plates 92, 93), blued for clarity of time reading. About 1790 matching-pattern hands first appear, most commonly in steel, and these continue until the end of native clockmaking about 1860 (see Plate 105). Matching hands in brass were sometimes used on bracket clocks, again after about 1790, though brass hands were far less often used on bracket clocks than steel ones. After the middle of the nineteenth century, imported bracket clocks often copied older styles in hands as well as in the dials, though some had contemporary (German pattern) hands of Gothic nature such as trident design or battleaxe styling, as found on imported wall dial clocks (as an example of Gothic styling, though present on a different type of clock, and one of British make, see Plate 109).

SUBSIDIARY DIALS

Moon dials do occur on bracket clocks, though far less often than on longcases. Those bracket clocks which do have a moon dial almost always have it in the form of a rolling moon in the arch (see Plate 101), though occasionally the penny moon type is found, also in the arch area. Moon dials on any clock were largely a provincial feature, and as the great majority of bracket clocks met with at any time before the mid-nineteenth century were London-made, this explains why relatively few bracket clocks have moon features. As with longcase clocks, some moon dials also incorporate a tidal dial to show high water, but only a small proportion of moon dials have high-water indications, which means they are very uncommon on bracket clocks.

Calendars appear on the majority of brass dial bracket clocks, mostly in the form of a square box aperture above the VI numeral (see Plate 96), or occasionally a circular aperture. On a few clocks this feature appears under the XII numeral. On arched dial examples, the calendar feature was often positioned in the arch area. Japanned (white) dials seldom have a calendar, though occasionally those with arched dials may do so. Round white dials hardly ever show calendar features. The presence or absence of a calendar feature is not in itself a dating guide.

Seconds dials do not occur on bracket clocks except in very rare circumstances, since a bracket clock does not have a long enough pendulum to beat once a second. A maker who went to the considerable trouble of showing seconds on a bracket clock is likely to have been a very exceptional maker, or to have gone to those lengths because he was making a very special clock. Hence a seconds dial is likely to be an indication of exceptional quality.

CHIMING MUSIC

Chiming of the quarter hours is found on some bracket clocks. This was a costly extra feature, and may indicate a high-quality clock. The simplest form of chiming is what is known as 'ting-tang' chiming, and this is normally on two bells, chiming 'ting-tang' once at quarter past, twice at half past, and so on. Ting-tang chimes can usually be operated on a clock with the normal two trains. More complex chiming, such as would chime on six or even eight bells or more, would normally require so much extra power that it would be driven by a third train. Thus the presence of three winding holes in the dial is an instant recognition sign for quarter-chiming work (or, of course, music). After the mid-nineteenth century, imported clocks from Germany often have ting-tang quarter-chiming, and these are commonplace. English-made examples are quite uncommon, though not exactly rare.

Grande sonnerie chiming (more strictly called striking) is a system whereby the last hour is struck after every quarter-hour chime. This is a highly-complex system requiring a massive reserve of power, and was limited mainly to the work of a number of prestigious makers of the seventeenth century. It is a rare feature, highly valued amongst collectors, but unless it has a silencing switch, such a clock can be an irritation to live with.

Musical bracket clocks play a tune, often a choice of several tunes, on any number of bells from four to twenty-eight, or even more. Some have a tune selection lever, whereby the owner can select which tune he wants. Others change automatically each day, thus playing a different tune for each day of the week, often being a hymn for Sundays. It is possible for such a clock to play its music every hour, but most will play every third or fourth hour only, which is enough for most owners. Musical clocks are often very large, partly because the movements need to be bulky, but often also because they were costly and important items made in an ostentatious style.

REPEATING AND PULL-REPEATING

Many bracket clocks, both normal hourly striking, quarter-chiming and musical, will have a repeating facility in the form of a cord, which can be pulled to repeat the strike, chime or music at will. This is known as repeating work, and is a normal feature of many such clocks. On some the repeating cord has been removed deliberately, since if it is abused, *eg.* by children, it can cause damage to the clock.

A quite different repeating system is known as pull-repeating (see Plate 94). The principle behind this is that it does not draw power from the main striking or chiming train. Instead, the pulling of the repeat cord loads power into a spring-loaded drum, allowing the chime to play once the cord is released (see Plate 95).

94. Backplate of the Rimbault clock (see Plate 98), c1770, showing exuberant engraving and verge pendulum. The pull-quarter-repeat mechanism (on a single bell) is seen upper left.

95. Backplate of the John Bushman clock (see Plate 97), showing pulleys for pull-wind alarm and pull-repeating. Note fine engraving.

Pull-repeating can be found on any clock, even a timepiece (*ie.* one which has no strikework). Pull-repeating can be on as few as two bells, when it would perform as a ting-tang pull-repeater, but it is more often on four or six bells.

When discussing the number of bells on chiming or musical clocks, the strike bell itself is not included. So that an eight-bell quarter-chiming clock would have eight bells plus the ninth bell for the strikework, known for short as 8 + 1.

Some bracket clocks have additional sub-dials for features not usually found on other kinds of clock. A strike/silent lever (see Plates 96, 98) is often present, especially with multiple-bell clocks. A fast-slow adjustment lever is also found on some bracket clocks (see Plate 96). The timekeeping is regulated by adjusting the pendulum rating nut, as with a longcase clock, but as bracket clocks are more prone to irregularity of timekeeping than longcases, it was often thought convenient to include a fast/slow switch on the dial, for convenience of fine tuning without moving the clock.

96. Dial of twin train bracket clock, c1720, by John Gerrard of London, and showing mock pendulum feature below XII. The sub-dials are for fast/slow regulation (top left) and strike/silent option.

DURATION

Bracket clocks were always of eight-day duration. Month-running examples are known, but are exceptionally rare, partly because of the problem of storing power in the strike train, but no doubt mainly on account of the aggravated problems of spring drive increasing with longer duration.

WOODS

The very first bracket clocks were conceived in a Puritan age, and their cases were made in ebony, a rare and very costly wood (see Plate 97). It was thought that black showed off the beauty of the dial best, and would suit any other furnishings. Within a very few years ebony supplies were inadequate, and instead cases were ebonised, which means that they were polished in black (see Plate 92). Other fine-grain woods were used, often pearwood, which

97. *Ebony bracket clock, c1700, by John Bushman of London, standing 15in (40cms) including handle. Pull-quarter-repeating on six bells, and pull-wind alarmwork.* Courtesy M. Williamson.

98. Double fusee bracket clock with verge escapement, in ebonised case with brass caryatid corners, by Stephen Rimbault of London, c1770 (see Plate 94). Note strike/ silent option on sub-dial and mock pendulum below XII. Height 20in (52cms).

99. Ebonised bracket clock with brass inlay in the lancet style, c1815, maker John Davidson of London. Striking with pull-wind alarm, set by the central disc. Height 14in (38cms).

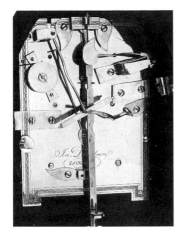

100. Signed backplate of the John Davidson clock, showing engraved border, pull-wind alarm pulley, alarm hammer. Bell removed for photograph.

101. Twin-train bracket clock in red walnut, by Thomas Moss of Frodsham, with rolling moon, late eighteenth century. Silvered brass dial, finely engraved. Height 15in (40cms).

when ebonised would closely resemble true ebony. The ebonised fashion lasted well into the late eighteenth century (Plate 98), and, with brass inlay, into the nineteenth (see Plate 99).

Walnut became fashionable for bracket clocks by about 1690 and remained popular into the middle of the eighteenth century (Plates 93, 101). Some clocks were made with marquetry cases, but this style was never as popular in bracket clocks as in longcases. By the 1740s mahogany came into use, and after about 1770 was the most popular of all woods for these clocks (Plates 102, 103). From about 1700 lacquer cases came into fashion, and many early eighteenth-century clocks were cased in this style, principally in black ground colours, although blue, green, red and even yellow are known. Lacquer fell from fashion by about 1770. About 1810 rosewood became popular, and remained so until the late 1840s (see Plate 106). Oak was not a wood normally used on English bracket clocks, except as a basewood onto which veneers might be laid. This was probably because it was regarded as too humble a wood for such a costly item as a bracket clock. However, when imported clocks appeared in the mid-nineteenth century, their cases were often of oak, and an oak-cased bracket clock is almost certain to be an imported one of the late nineteenth or early

102. Mahogany bracket clock by Strigel of London, c1760. A twin fusee clock with fast/slow regulation in the arch. Height 20in (52cms).

twentieth centuries. Some imported clocks were in beech, either in its natural colour or ebonised, and some were in walnut, but a walnut of a very different quality and character to that on an early English walnut clock of the early eighteenth century (see Plate 120).

STYLES

Basket top

Case styles follow certain well-defined trends, and are very helpful in dating. The early square dial clocks often have a caddy top, not unlike that on a contemporary longcase hood, and being a flat-topped caddy with rounded shoulders (see Plate 92). This shape on a bracket clock is normally called a basket top. The folding carrying handle is attached to the basket top. The basket can be simply of wood, but often has a pierced brass mount based on the handle fixing-points. With some examples, the pierced brasswork can form the entire basket top, and some even have double basket tops.

Inverted bell top

By about 1700 the arched dial came into fashion, and the basket top then became extenuated into a taller form, whereby the round-shouldered caddy had an upper section on top with concave sides (see Plates 93, 98). This form is usually known as an inverted bell top, a style which remained popular well into the 1770s. A far more sensible term for these two basic styles (basket top and inverted bell top) would be 'caddy top' and 'double caddy top', but terminology in bracket clocks is somewhat antiquated, and often confusing to a beginner.

Broken-arch top
The next principal development in style comes in towards the later eighteenth century, most often with round dial clocks, and in these the case top is a continuing dome, or a dome with small shoulders at each side (see Plates 103, 104). This is usually known as a broken-arch top, or sometimes a break-arch top. Earlier examples in this style retain the carrying handle (see Plate 103), but after about 1800 the carrying handle feature falls out of fashion (see Plate 104). Instead, post-1800 examples may have a plain domed top or occasionally a raised concave block to take a ball

103. Mahogany bracket clock with verge escapement and double fusee, made c1800 by Richard Ward of Winchester. The silvered brass dial has separate discs for time, strike/silent and fast/slow regulation. Height 15in (40cms).

104. Small timepiece bracket clock in mahogany with brass inlay, early nineteenth century. Unsigned. Dial of enamel. Height 10in (25.5cms). Courtesy R. Sewell.

105. *Typical lancet-style bracket clock, c1810, in mahogany with twin-train movement and anchor escapement. Height 17in (45cms).*

finial (sometimes three blocks for three finials). A few break-arch top examples are ebonised, but most are in mahogany, some later ones in rosewood.

Dome top
The balloon clock is one development of the dome top, and appears mainly around the turn of the century. Balloon clocks are usually in mahogany with some paler inlays, often of satinwood, but occasional examples may be entirely in satinwood. English balloon clocks stand full size normally, *ie.* about 20 inches (52cms). French-made balloon clocks, which date from the end of the nineteenth century, are much smaller, about half this height.

Lancet top
The lancet top (Plate 105) is another style found around the end of the eighteenth century, but more usually into the early nineteenth. Again, these are mostly in mahogany, but occasionally are ebonised. Many have brass inlay work.

Chamfer top
By about 1820 the chamfer top style became popular, with a shallow-sloping roof-like top, usually having a centre flat and a top finial, such as a pineapple (see Plates 106, 107). These were made into the 1840s. These were the basic stylistic shapes, but

106. Timepiece bracket clock in rosewood, c1820, by James Smith of London, with typical fish-scale side grilles. The dial is of the japanned type. Height 15in (40cms).

after about 1830 all manner of variations are found, especially after about 1830, when Victorian exuberance added all kind of scroll-work and carved details.

107. Chamfer top bracket clock by W.C. Bartle of Northampton, late nineteenth century in the style of the early nineteenth century. Height 19in (52cms). Timepiece only. Courtesy R. Sewell.

NAMES AND MAKERS

Most bracket clocks display the name of the maker on the dial, in the same way as do longcase clocks. Until about the middle of the eighteenth century the maker's name was also usually engraved on the backplate of the clock as well, often within a finely-engraved panel of decoration. In the third quarter of the eighteenth century that backplate engraving gradually reduced in extent, sometimes down to a mere engraved border pattern, and so when the name appears on the backplate at this time, it often stands as almost the only engraved detail there. In the last quarter of the century many makers ceased to engrave their names on the backplates, so that after the end of the century it is only occasionally that a backplate is signed (see Plate 108). Sometimes the year of making would also appear on the backplate, but that is uncommon at any period (Plate 108).

108. Backplate of double fusee bracket clock by Gerrans of Wortley, showing typical restrained engraving of this later period, and dated 1819.

The great majority of bracket clocks will be seen to bear the names of London makers, as this type of spring-driven clock was always a speciality product. At all times until the end of English native clockmaking, London was the centre of bracket clock making. There are very many provincial makers by whom no example of a bracket clock has ever come to light, and from this we can deduce that a great many provincial makers never attempted to make this type of clock. When we do see a bracket clock by a provincial maker, the question arises as to whether he really did make it, or bought it ready-made from London with his name engraved on it. This is a very difficult aspect even for the experienced to ascertain. The decision in the end is determined by an examination of features of the clock which are unusual and particularly different from typical London work – shapes of plates, pillars, hammer, engraving styles, *etc.* Those clockmakers from provincial areas who did make their own bracket clocks, and especially those in the earlier periods (say before 1760), were often makers of unusual skill and abilities. Final assessment depends much more on the actual qualities evident in the clock, than on the name on the dial.

After about 1760, it is much more likely that a provincial bracket clock would have been supplied by London specialists. Such spring-clock makers as Thwaites & Reed and Handley & Moore supplied not only many provincial makers, but also many London-based makers who themselves saw fit to buy-in this type of clock rather than actually make it. Usually they would leave their name or initials and/or serial number on the movement frontplate.

ESCAPEMENTS

The verge escapement was used in bracket clocks from the very earliest times (about 1660), and continued in use, despite the invention of the anchor escapement with its superior timekeeping properties, until about 1800 (see Plate 94). The reason was that the verge was less fussy about level surfaces and was more suitable for a clock which might well be moved from room to room in use. After 1800, the anchor escapement was used in most bracket clocks. Occasionally the pinwheel was used, which was a type of anchor escapement.

Very many verge pendulums were later converted to anchor, so that many bracket clocks survive today which were built as verge movement but were converted to anchor later. Some restorers today like to convert these back to verge again, while others prefer to leave an old alteration, as part of the clock's progression through history; it all depends on which point of view you take.

Many verge bracket clocks had a small slot in the dial below XII, which displayed what is called a mock pendulum, this being a small circular disc which swung to and fro with the pendulum swing (see Plates 93, 96). Not every bracket clock had this, but a high proportion of them did until about 1760, after which it gradually fell from fashion. The mock pendulum was not used on anchor escapement clocks.

QUALITY AND SCARCITY FACTORS

Quality is a difficult factor for the novice to attempt to evaluate. A great deal depends on experience, and even quite modest bracket clocks tend to be well-made, so that there is not the availability of poor examples to compare with as there is, for instance, with longcase clocks. Higher quality tends to go hand in hand with greater age. Factors that are highly prized include very small size, and, with complex clocks such as musical ones, very large size; clocks with signed backplates as well as dials; dated clocks; 'coloured' clocks (*ie.* coloured woods) as opposed to black; special names; unusual features; pull-repeating, especially if on more than two bells; original verge escapements; quarter-chimes; music; automated figures; moon dials; and the original bracket on which the clock stood.

Scarcity may not equate with higher value. For instance, a bracket clock of the late seventeenth century by a provincial maker is a very rare item, but may fail to reach the price of a clock of the same age and quality by a well-known London maker, although it may be many times rarer. Quite a number of bracket clocks, often of highly complex nature, were made for the Turkish market, and may easily be recognised by their pseudo-Turkish numerals. These are uncommon, though not as uncommon as the novice might imagine, yet they are not valued nearly so highly as the English equivalent. Beware of once-Turkish clocks with a replaced chapter ring, done to make them appear English, a much more common practice than is sometimes realised.

SKELETON CLOCKS

The skeleton clock (see Plate 109) was a type of bracket clock, but one which had no external case. Instead, the front and back plates of the movement were shaped into any one of a variety of

109. Simple skeleton clock of single fusee type with passing strike, made c1860-70 by T. & E. Rhodes of Kendal. Gothic hands and battleaxe hammer. Height 14in (38cms).

interesting patterns, and were pierced through, so that all the clock wheels and gearing was visible. When new, a glass dome covered the clock to keep out dust, but today many stand open to the elements, the dome having been broken long ago. Simple skeleton clocks are usually timepieces only, but many have what is known as passing strike, a form of striking seldom found on any other type of clock. A single blow is triggered as the clock hand passes the hour, thus giving a strike of one, regardless of which hour it actually is. Of course, two-train examples have full strikework in the same manner as any bracket clock. Three-train examples usually have quarter-chiming on multiple bells. Three-train skeleton clocks are often very large, and many are shaped into outlines, such as a cathedral, often based on an actual building, such as York Minster.

Skeleton clocks mostly date between about 1840 and 1890. Some have the name of a maker, but many are unsigned. Many were produced by specialist makers in London and retailed in jewellers' shops in the country at large. Normal size would be about 15 to 18 inches in height (40cms to 48cms), excluding any base/dome. Small examples are sometimes found as little as perhaps half that. Large examples may be twice that size, these often being of the three-train type. Value-points in skeleton clocks include examples of extreme size, *ie.* very small or very large; complex mechanics (occasionally including helical gears); prestigious names; and rare or individualistic plate patterns.

FRENCH CLOCKS

English bracket clocks had certain disadvantages. They were large, and they were costly. By the beginning of Victoria's reign (1837), the standard escapement was the anchor, which meant they were no longer portable in the way the verge escapement examples had been, and even verge models had needed some sort of level surface on which to stand. So, by and large, they were set down in one place and remained there, perhaps on a mantel shelf or a table top. By the middle of the nineteenth century, the French carriage clock was widely available (Plates 110, 111, 112). This was small, readily portable, would run happily regardless of level surfaces, and was not expensive. Indeed, many were supplied with a leather-covered carrying case (see Plate 110), so that they could be used on a journey or in a hotel, and these could be packed into travelling luggage and would still be running on arrival at the destination. The carriage clock was ideal as a bedside clock or a travelling clock.

The balance wheel escapements of these clocks were not as accurate for the most part as the anchor of the English bracket clock, but would suffice for most purposes. The carriage clock found a gap in the English clock market, and very soon they were imported into Britain in their thousands. Many were simple timepieces, but some had strikework, alarmwork, and even quarter-chiming or grand sonnerie striking. Many were made expressly for the English market, and some are lettered with the name of retailers in England (*eg.* Plate 111), although they were not made here. Most examples date from the period between 1870 and 1920, but manufacture continued long after this date, and examples are still made today.

110. *French carriage clock in its original leather-covered carrying case, the dial shutter removed ready for bedside use. Late nineteenth century. Height 5in (12.5cms), including case.*

111. *An ordinary carriage clock removed from its travelling case, c1900. Height 4½in (12cms).*

Carriage clocks were not really bracket clocks, but they did take over a certain section of the market formerly dominated by the bracket clock. The French, however, excelled in the small movement which we know as the drum movement, being circular in outline. Some drum movements were regulated by a pendulum, but many had balance-wheel control, as in a carriage clock. The drum movement had the great advantage that it could be fitted into a great variety of cases. Some were set into wooden cases which were miniature in size but often based on the late eighteenth-century English designs – such as the lancet style (Plate 113) and the balloon style. Many examples exist of wooden-cased clocks which stand only about 10 inches (25.5cms) high, often in mahogany with inlays of fans, shells, *etc.* in satinwood, resembling smaller versions of mahogany-cased English bracket clocks. These were made around 1900, but resemble English clocks of a

112. French carriage clock, late nineteenth century, of a more ornate design.
Height 6in (15cms), including handle.

hundred years' earlier (Plate 113), or more in the case styles. Some were lettered with English retailers' names, but most were unsigned. Most were balance-wheel-controlled, and were, and still are, highly popular, having been imported into England in vast quantities between about 1870 and 1920.

113. French mahogany mantel clock with drum movement. Late nineteenth century, in style of English late eighteenth century. Height 9in (23cms).

114. Lantern clock in the English style of the seventeenth century, but French made in the late nineteenth century, with carriage clock movement. Height 10in (25.5cms). An old 'reproduction' clock.

French clocks had concentrated since the late eighteenth century on ornate cases. The interchangeable nature of the drum movement (and dial) meant that it was capable of being housed in a variety of cases. By the time we see great numbers of French clocks imported into England, we also find a great range of cases, both in materials and styles, yet often with the same type of drum movement. Some cases were of brass or ormolu, some of base metals, some of bronze, but porcelain cases also appeared, or those

115. French novelty clock in the form of a ship's stern. The helmsman rocks at the wheel as the pendulum swings below decks. Late nineteenth century.

made of marble or alabaster (see Plates 116, 118). All these are very un-English in nature and tend to be instantly recognisable as French, although any of them might be found lettered with the name of an English retailer. Some retailers would try to give the impression that they had a French 'branch', so that one might find an imported French clock lettered on the dial 'Z. Barraclough, Leeds and Paris', when in fact Barraclough was a Leeds retailer selling French clocks.

The true maker of a French clock can often be discovered not from the dial, but from an inspection of the movement backplate, where on many the presence of the imprint 'Made in France' betrays not only its country of origin but the fact that it was obviously made for the English market. The name of a French

116. French novelty night clock in alabaster and brass, late nineteenth century. Height 9½in (24cms). A candle throws light from inside the globe, which rotates against a fixed pointer to show hours and quarters.

117. A French-made clock of the type known as a portico clock, as it stands on four corner columns like a portico. This one is in buhl work, being a red tortoiseshell background inlaid with brass. Middle to late nineteenth century.

maker, and town, will sometimes be engraved on it, but in other instances there is no apparent trademark. In fact, the trademark is sometimes the engraved pattern of the arrow mark which indicates direction of winding or direction of hands turning. An arrow might have varying numbers of feathers in its tail, or a trail of dots after it, and in some of these instances the arrow itself is the trademark. To check on the maker, one needs to look at the book by Charles Allix entitled *Carriage Clocks*.

GERMAN CLOCKS

It was not only the French who spotted this gap in the English market for cheaper and smaller bracket clocks than the English-made ones. The Germans, too, aimed at this market from about

118. French novelty clock, late nineteenth century, in alabaster with a swinging cherub pendulum. The glass cover is removed for the photograph. Height 9in (23cms). **Courtesy R. Sewell.**

1850 to the 1920s, and even later (see Plates 119, 120, 121). Many German-made bracket clocks adopted in a way the same principle as the French ones, in that the cases were based on English styles of a century or more earlier, but the Germans often made the dial in the same style as English dials, that is, of brass with brass chapter ring, spandrels, etc. German cases were made of oak or walnut (see Plate 120), or sometimes were ebonised (*ie.* polished black), the latter often with attached brass fitments in the manner of some late eighteenth-century English examples. For the most part, German clocks were smaller than the English ones they imitated, although occasional ones were very large, in closer imitation of the grander English ones.

German clocks often included quarter-hour chimes on gongs rather than bells, and many were lettered on the dial for a choice of chime, such as Whittington, Westminster or Cambridge chimes.

119. Late nineteenth-century Vienna Regulator, a double-weighter, hence striking hours. Similar clocks were also made in Germany to copy the Vienna clock style. Height 4ft (120cms).

120. Late nineteenth-century German novelty bracket clock, in walnut case with a carved figure on top. The second train is not for strikework, but to wind the automated figure, who raises his arm and chews on what appear to be plums in a dish. Height 20in (51cms).

This very fact once more illustrates that they were purpose-made for the English market. Where names appear on the dials (see Plate 120), again these are the names of English retailers, but most dials are in fact un-named. Some were built with fusees, but most were built without. Some had skeleton plates, which were cheaper as they used less brass. On most the backplate carries a trademark such as WHSch., for Winterhalder & Hoffmeyer, Schwarzwald, or the Junghans mark. Most of the marks can be checked in a book such as *Clock Types* by E.J.Tyler.

In the late nineteenth century there was a fashion for what we now call novelty clocks, and both French and German makers catered for this market. Many included moving figures, turning lighthouses, moving steam-hammers, steering helmsmen, and an endless variety of eye-catching features (*eg.* Plates 115, 116, 118, 120).

121. Thirty-hour German wall clock, mid-nineteenth century, of the type known as a Postman's Alarm (not all had alarms), or a Wag-on-the-Wall clock. This one was retailed here by Faller & Hummel of Portsea. Mahogany with brass inlay. Pendulum removed in picture. Courtesy R. Sewell.

CARTEL CLOCKS

It is a little surprising that, while spring-driven table clocks were made from the time of the arrival of the pendulum invention into England, it was almost a century before spring-driven wall clocks appeared (see Plate 122). This may have been on account of the fact that a bracket clock, when supplied with a wall bracket, was in fact a wall clock. The first true spring wall clocks, those which could not be put down on a level surface but had to hang from a wall hook, were cartel clocks, and these first appeared in England in the second quarter of the eighteenth century, from about the 1740s.

Weight-driven wall clocks had long been made in the form of hook-and-spike clocks and hooded clocks (see Chapter 6), all of which developed from the original lantern clock form. But these earlier weight-driven wall clocks were of thirty-hour duration, and were almost always of a simple and humble nature. The cartel clock was a much grander version, made for the more sumptuous settings of the salon, and, like all English spring clocks, of eight-day duration. The dials were circular and about the same size as a bracket clock dial – about 7 inches (17cms) in diameter. They were made as timepieces only *ie.* non-striking, and in effect were the same thing as a timepiece bracket clock with circular dial. The verge escapement was used, as it was in bracket clocks, since it did not call for exactness in levelling which the anchor required.

The cases were of wood, ornately carved and gilded, and much resembled the rococo wall mirrors of the day. Sprays of flowers, fruit, cherubs, spread eagles often combined to form a case which might be as tall as 3 feet (90cms) and as wide as 20 inches (50cms). About the same time the cartel clock appeared in France too, but French examples had metal cases, and cannot be confused for English.

Cartel clocks seem not to have been widely popular if we can judge by the numbers which survive today, for they are uncommon and are very much an acquired taste.

122. Spring-driven English wall dial clock, with silvered brass dial and verge escapement, c1770 by Hedge of Colchester.

ENGLISH DIAL CLOCKS

About the same time as the cartel clock first appeared, we find the first examples of what are usually today called English Dial clocks (see Plates 122, 123). The very early ones were made with circular wooden dials, often black-painted and lettered in gold, with a large diameter of about 16 inches (42cms). These were made for use in public buildings such as taverns and coaching-inns, where a large dial meant easy legibility and the delicate cartel clock would have been totally out of place. The tavern clock proper (sometimes today called an Act of Parliament clock; see Chapter 6) originated about this same time, but was weight-driven. So that the wooden spring-dial clock, sometimes called a black dial clock, was an alternative form of tavern clock. These are rare today, perhaps because they were never as popular originally as the weight-driven version, which would be more accurate and more reliable in running, but perhaps also because they would tend to suffer a high destruction rate.

The movements of these wooden dial clocks were similar to those of cartel clocks, being verge escapements of eight-day

123. Drop dial English wall clock, single fusee (ie. non-striking), made c1830 by C. Aronson of London. Convex dial. Mahogany case with brass inlay. Courtesy R. Sewell.

duration and carrying two hands. Because of the very large dial size, the minute hand (and sometimes also the hour hand) would tend to have a 'tail' to counterbalance it and to avoid drag on the movement from the sheer weight of the hand. The matching-pattern hands were usually of brass.

In the last quarter of the eighteenth century, the brass dial form of English Dial clock appeared. These had circular brass dials of about 12 inches diameter (30.5cms), were almost always time-pieces only, had verge escapement, and were mechanically an enlarged form of cartel movement. Like cartel clocks, some of the earlier ones showed a mock pendulum below XII. They were cased in mahogany, with a simple narrow rim showing as a frame around the dial. Within a very few years the japanned dial was often used instead of the brass form (see Plate 123), just as it was in longcase clocks. Because the movements were timepieces only (most of them, anyway), some had tapered movement plates narrowing towards the top – less plate area being required for a clock which had no strike train.

By the end of the century, most dial clocks had gone over to the anchor escapement for greater accuracy, just as bracket clocks did. Like bracket clocks, too, the hands of these clocks follow broadly the same development of styles as in longcase clocks, with the proviso that brass hands were seldom used, steel being stronger. The backplates of dial clock movements were not engraved with decorative work, as, of course, they were completely hidden. Nor were backplates signed with an engraved name, except in very rare instances.

Once the anchor escapement form of English dial clock movement was devised, it continued in use with little modification for many years. Dial size varied from 12 inches (30.5cms) to about 14 inches (38cms), but in other respects this simple circular wall clock continued to be made for use in office, schools, railways, etc. Better-quality cases were in mahogany, but cheaper ones were made in oak.

For household use, more elegant versions were available, mostly in the form of what we usually call drop dials, or drop box versions (see Plate 123). These have a projection below the circular surround, often with a small glass window in the front so that the pendulum bob can be seen. Some drop dials were lavishly inlaid with brass or occasionally mother-of-pearl. Brass-inlaid models were usually mahogany-cased and would date from about 1800 to 1850, though rosewood was sometimes used in the 1830s and 1840s. Mother-of-pearl inlay was more a fashion of the 1840s and 1850s.

IMPORTED DIAL CLOCKS

By the middle of the nineteenth century, imported wall clocks were made to compete with native English versions. They were shipped in vast quantities from America and Germany, and drop dial wall clocks from either of these countries may well be mistaken by the beginner for English-made examples of that particular style. It is important to be able to identify one from the other, as English-made examples are considerably more valuable than imported ones.

It is believed that most were shipped in ready-cased, but it is possible that some were cased in England in English cases. Generally speaking, imported cases are recognisable by being shallower in depth, usually of lesser quality than the English equivalent, often in walnut (which English cases seldom were), and in often having a greater degree of inlay work in roundels and stringing, either in pale woods or in mother-of-pearl. The size is about the same as with English cases.

124. Typical American mahogany wall clock, mid-nineteenth century, made by Jerome & Co. This type is usually known as an Ogee clock, from the shape of the wooden moulding. Courtesy R. Sewell.

Imported clocks are mostly two-train, ie. striking clocks, while English ones are normally timepieces only. Imported clocks have their winding holes positioned quite low, almost to touch the V and VII numerals (see Plates 124, 126), whereas English examples have the winding hole (or occasionally holes) well up towards the hands' centre.

125. American mantel clock made by Jerome & Co., mid-nineteenth century, imported into Britain and sold by the thousand. Courtesy R. Sewell.

American dials are usually very thin and made of a flexible alloy. So, too, are some German dials, though some German dials are of a strong japanned iron like English ones. Some American examples have printed paper dials, these mostly being made by the Ansonia clock company, and bearing an initial A on the dial centre. American movements have pierced or skeleton plates, and do not have fusee gears. Most German examples also lack fusees, though some do have them. German movements with fusees were mostly by Winterhalder & Hoffmeyer of Schwarzwald, and bear the trade mark 'W.H. Sch.'

On very many imported examples, the wooden area surrounding the dial is of overall octagonal shape, often known at the time as an octagon clock. Imported examples sold here when new for as little as 15 shillings (£0.75), whereas English-made ones started at about £6.00. The difference in quality between the two is usually very obvious even to a beginner, once a few examples of each have been seen.

We have so far considered the sequence historically and stylistically of British clocks and later imports for the British market. But throughout we have considered typical examples, and in the next chapter we will look at some unusual and exceptional examples including, where possible, their original prices, as the price factor will help us place an extraordinary clock in a relative position to its everyday neighbour.

126. American wall clock, mid-nineteenth century, made by Ingrahams & Co., Connecticut. The case is inlaid with many fancy woods in the manner of Tonbridge ware.
Courtesy R. Sewell.

10 Quality and Original Prices

Original prices of clocks are extremely interesting when we can trace examples of them, although they are few and far between. Needless to say, it is very difficult to come across reliable examples of the original prices for lantern clocks, these being the oldest British clocks. Sometimes they are recorded in the inventories of goods left by a deceased person, but then in such cases the values may not be altogether reliable, and in any event the clocks were being valued as second-hand items.

PRICES OF LANTERN CLOCKS

In 1656, the Reverend Giles Moore, rector of Horsted Keynes in Sussex, bought a clock from Edward Barrett, the Lewes clockmaker, at a price £2 10s. 0d. (£2.50). At this date we know it must have been a pre-pendulum lantern clock, ie. a balance-wheel lantern, for there were then no other domestic clocks. The pendulum was introduced in 1658, and examples of original prices before then are very rare. With post-1658 examples of prices, even if we can establish that they *were* lantern clocks, we cannot distinguish whether they would be of the balance-wheel or pendulum type, or at least we usually cannot make this distinction.

In 1667, for example, the inventory of William Richardson of North Bierley, Yorkshire, records a 'brass clock' at £3 0s. 0d. This must have been a lantern clock, but whether a balance-wheel or a pendulum we cannot be sure.

A most interesting letter survives, sent from a London clockmaker in 1696 to a contact who wanted it for a customer, and so was probably a middleman. The clockmaker is none other than Jasper Harmer, who had been in trouble with the Clockmakers' Company for practising the craft when not trained to do so (page 26). It runs:

> For Mr Joseph Dawson in Kendall, Westmorland'
> Mr Dawson,
>   I sent yesterday ye large Clocke for ye Gentlemans Hall. It is a pendulum and goes 30 houres. If I had itt a ballance Clocke it would have gone but 16 houres and ye prise would have been but 5s. (£0.25) less yn (= *than*) this. It cost me £3 10s. 0d. (£3.50) and ye box 1s (£0.05) and I have charged no more for itt. Ye other you writt for shall bee sent next fryday by
> Yr Lo Freind,
Jaspar Harmar [sic]
> Sep 26th 1696

This is unique evidence of the difference in price between the more modern (in 1696) pendulum version of the lantern clock and the old-fashioned balance-wheel type. This clock would almost certainly have had the short bob pendulum with verge escapement; it could conceivably have been a long pendulum with anchor escapement, but this is unlikely in view of the awkwardness of transporting the separate long pendulum, which would not fit neatly into a box. The older balance-wheel version would have been less accurate as a timekeeper than the (short) pendulum version, and it is interesting to note that, despite this disadvantage, the balance type was still an available option as late as this time, almost forty years after the pendulum's introduction. It is surprising, too, that Harmer's choice of pendulum was, he says, based on the longer duration, and not on the timekeeping aspect.

The difference of five shillings (£0.25) would have been almost a week's wages to a journeyman, but presumably meant little to the ultimate purchaser of this clock. This record is interesting in other respects too, namely that it illustrates that, even at this relatively late date, clockmaking was a skill so new in Westmorland that a customer bought his clocks, via a local middleman, from London. There *were* clockmakers in Westmorland at that time, but very few, and it is indicative of the lack of confidence in the local trade that the buyer should in fact prefer to order from London. It is ironic that this confidence in the capital was obviously very misplaced, since Harmer had been banned from the trade by the Clockmakers' Company as being unqualified. Of course, the customer did not know that, nor, probably, did middleman Dawson.

As it happens, the lantern clock was a type of clock which was hardly ever made in Westmorland. In the entire recorded history of horology, not more than a couple of examples have come to light which were produced there, and not more than a couple more from Cumberland. We can be quite sure that this was a lantern clock because of the mention of the balance-wheel alternative, for no other type of clock had a balance-wheel option.

Another interesting point is that Harmer mentions that this clock runs for thirty hours and that a balance-wheel alternative would have run for only sixteen hours. The Huygens rope system, as we saw in Chapter 3, was introduced in 1658 along with the pendulum itself. Balance-wheel clocks, the only type before 1658, had two separate ropes (or chains), one each for winding the going train and the strike train.

It had long been assumed that this was the case, *ie.* that pendulum-controlled lantern clocks automatically were built using the new continuous-rope drive. But here is written confirmation of that assumption.

In practice, this would seem to have been the sensible thing to do anyway, and yet I have come across examples of lantern clocks, built with verge pendulum, which still retained the drive system of two separate weights. Why some makers persisted with this I cannot say, except that the two-rope system did offer the option of having the clock striking or not at will, by letting the strike rope run down or removing its weight. A continuous-rope lantern clock is capable of being silenced, but by far less convenient methods.

As far as we can deduce, it would seem that original prices for lantern clocks might range from £2 10s. 0d. (£2.50) to £3 10s. 0d. (£3.50). The implication is that London ones were more costly than provincial ones, and as we base the London example on the price charged by an unqualified 'ironmonger near Smithfield Bars' (a contemporary description of Harmer; see also Chapter 2), who apparently continued trading despite being banned from the trade, it seems likely that a London example by a better maker might well have cost more rather than less.

The arrival of the anchor escapement, at some date in the 1670s still disputed by different experts, made the thirty-hour longcase clock a more useful domestic timekeeper than the lantern clock, for all normal purposes. Thereafter, the only advantage which a lantern clock might offer was its potential portability, by virtue of its short pendulum being contained within the clock itself.

In view of that, one might wonder where the advantage lay for Jasper Harmer's Kendal customer in selecting a lantern clock. There may well have been some snobbery value in having a London-named clock in the house, the implication being that a clock bought from the capital was a superior product to that from a local clocksmith. Amusingly enough, in this instance the purchaser may actually have bought quite the reverse, and yet it is the local clocksmith who would have been called in to repair it when it misbehaved. At this early date, however, it is doubtful whether there would have been as many as three clockmakers within easy distance of Kendal, and their work may have been considered rustic or primitive alongside the supposed sophistication of a London product. It is also quite possible that the local merchant who acted as middleman to the ultimate customer may have been the one who suggested a London clock. It is evident that Harmer supplied him with others – 'the other you writt for shall bee sent next fryday'. So perhaps the local merchant had some remunerative arrangement with Harmer, and it is quite possible a local clockmaker may have insisted on supplying his clock directly to the customer, and not through an agent.

PRICES OF THIRTY-HOUR LONGCASE CLOCKS

We know from examples of prices gleaned here and there, that a basic single-handed thirty-hour longcase clock could be bought for as little as £2 2s. 0d. (£2.10). Those with additional 'extras' might have cost a few shillings more, but a thirty-hour one-handed longcase clock doing everything Harmer's lantern would do could have been bought for £2 10s. 0d. (£2.50) at the outside, *without* a case. Even with the extra cost of a case, the price would have risen by a mere 10s. 0d. (£0.50) if it were in painted pine, or £1 0s. 0d. in oak. So that a durable oak-cased thirty-hour single-handed clock could have been purchased for £3 0s. 0d. (£3.00) within local distance, without the extra cost and delay of transportation half-way across the land. Moreover, with its anchor escapement, the thirty-hour longcase would have kept better time than Harmer's verge pendulum lantern clock. In the light of these facts, we are forced to the conclusion that the ultimate customer was either unaware of what was available locally, or was persuaded by the merchant to let him handle it through London.

Yet another point of interest in Harmer's letter is that he describes the clock as 'ye large Clocke'. He does not state the size, but we can assess that because we know that most lantern clocks were of a standard size of roughly 14½ inches (39cms). A few were made to tiny specifications of about six inches (15cms) and even fewer to about ten inches (25.5cms). But a large clock was uncommon at any period, and was built to about seventeen and a half to eighteen inches including the top finial (46 to 47.5cms). In view of this example being larger than the normal, we must bear in mind that its price may have been a little more than one of standard size.

The thirty-hour brass dial clock in its simplest form (as we saw in Chapter 4) had a single hand, and recorded hours and quarters exactly as a lantern clock did. It struck the hours in the same manner as a lantern clock, almost always using the countwheel striking system – the only exception was that rack striking could be built-in as an optional extra by anyone who wanted to use it as a repeater.

In the South of England, the normal constructional form, especially in the earlier periods, was that of the posted movement. Some posted movements had shaped brass pillars exactly along the principles of a lantern clock. Indeed, some early thirty-hour longcase clocks actually *were* square dial lantern clocks, but housed in cases. In the North, the posted construction was seldom used, except by occasional eccentric makers such as John Sanderson of Wigton, for whom the posted movement was normal. In fact, what John Sanderson made were mostly square dial lantern clocks of large size, and it is debatable whether these ever had a case originally or whether they stood on wall brackets, for I have never seen or heard of a posted thirty-hour clock by Sanderson in its 'original' case (though many were housed in cases at a later date).

Such simple early thirty-hour longcase clocks had no 'extras' such as calendar work or a minute hand or a second hand, just as the lantern clock had none of these frills. In discussing prices, then, it is important to know just what combination of features is involved, because the basic principle, as might be expected, was that the more you had in the way of extras, the more it cost.

Examples of original prices seldom specify the make-up of the clock, and so are of limited use, as we are unclear just what features most of these priced clocks might have had. The accounts book of Samuel Roberts of Llanfair Caereinion survives for the period 1755 to 1774, being one example of a very rare type of record. Moreover, his book records briefly the make-up of the clock, its type and price, and even the customer for whom it was made. Roberts's clocks and the prices he charged for them have been the subject of a recently-published study by Pryce and Davis, *Samuel Roberts, Clock Maker*, and the authors have been able to compare actual examples of his clocks with the notebook entries. With financial assistance from the British Academy, they have been able to undertake a very much more detailed survey than my own analysis, published in 1976 in my book *Country Clocks*.

BASIC PRICES

In brief, the position is that Samuel Roberts sold his basic thirty-hour single-handed clock at £2 2s. 0d. (£2.10). A calendar feature added roughly 2s. 0d. (£0.10) extra. Repeating work added a further 5s. 0d. (£0.25). The two-handed version started at £2 9s. 0d. (£2.45) – Roberts defines these with the terminology used by other clockmakers of the day as being one 'with ye minuitts on it', because single-handed clocks, of course, did not register minutes. So, to summarise in very general terms, we can assume that such a clock could be bought for between approximately £2 0s. 0d. at the lowest end of the market and £3 0s. 0d. at the highest.

All these prices are for the clocks themselves, and do not include cases. The customer would have gone to a local joiner for his case, or would even have made one himself. A square dial case of simple cottage type for such a simple clock could have been bought for a little under 10s. 0d. (£0.50) in pine with painted finish, and for a little over that in oak. Where available, solid walnut was priced the same as oak. Arched dial casework clearly involved more time and materials, and so arched cases were a little costlier. The prices of cases would vary, as the clocks themselves did, with the individual design and any extra features, and therefore where we come across examples of clocks-and-cases with prices, we are obliged to use our imaginations to try to picture the style of case involved.

Some years ago I saw a simple thirty-hour brass dial longcase by William Roberts of Otley, which was actually dated 1758 and had the original receipt inside the door, reading: 'This clock was settlyd the 7th Oct 1758. Prise £2 3s. 6d.' (£2.17½). It is obvious from the price that the case was not included.

In fact, William Roberts lived and worked at Fewston, a village several miles from Otley (now in North Yorkshire, but at that time within the West Riding of Yorkshire). Like many rural clockmakers, Roberts would probably have taken his clocks to the nearest market to sell, which was Otley. Of course, such men could have taken along complete clocks with their cases, but it seems to have been more often the position that they took just the clocks themselves, as happened in this instance.

The inventory of the goods of George Birchall, watchmaker of Shrewsbury, who died in 1738, include 'one thirty hour Clock with the day of the Month £2 0s. 0d.' This is clearly without a case, and in any event cases were here specifically mentioned on the clocks which had them. Inventory valuations, however, are not as reliable as original receipts.

Examples of clocks which were priced inclusive of the case are found occasionally, but here a certain vagueness creeps in, because we may not know the breakdown between the two parts. In the mid-eighteenth century, John Belling of Bodmin charged £3 0s. 0d. for a thirty-hour clock in its case. The Chaplin family of Bury St Edmunds advertised clocks in 1791, these of course with the newer japanned dials, or so we assume: '30 hours with minutes and day of the month, oak or walnut, £3 13s. 6d.' (£3.67½). However, the advertisement adds that these are most often sold at £5 5s. 0d. (£5.25), which is rather puzzling unless it is simply exaggeration.

In 1815, John Hammond of Clare in Suffolk advertised '30 hours with minutes £3 13s. 6d.' (£3.67½), the very same price as the Chaplins'. In 1793, however, the Chaplins claimed to offer a cheaper range of thirty-hour clocks at £2 10s. 0d. (£2.50), but this sounds so cheap that it implies they were uncased.

ORIGINAL RECEIPTS

Very seldom does an original receipt survive, but where they do, we know exactly what the customer bought for his money. Some years ago I had a thirty-hour white dial clock made by Samuel Deacon of Barton in the Beans, Leicestershire, a well-known maker of idiosyncratic habits, and one of that very rare band whose workshop notebook survives – though in Deacon's case the book is crammed with very disorderly entries. The Deacon family still owned the workshop premises in 1951, and when it was rumoured that the property was to be sold, John Daniell, of Leicester Museum, decided to investigate whether there might be any old tools still in the premises. He was amazed to find that the original workshop set up by Samuel Deacon in 1771 was still intact, with its forge and much of its equipment. It is believed to have been abandoned when Deacon died in 1816. In the roof void he found Deacon's workshop records, which are preserved today in Leicester Records Office. Deacon's workshop was removed and re-assembled in Leicester under the care of the museum, and can be seen today as it must have looked in his lifetime.

I have personally searched, or attempted to search, Samuel Deacon's records, and they are a real mixed-up assortment of jottings in anything but chronological order. However, the point about the Deacon thirty-hour clock I mention was that it has the original receipt pasted inside the door in Deacon's own handwriting. It reads: 'Barton. July 22 1803. Mr Marven.Bot. of S.Deacon, A Clock & case for Mr Bray, best face, both, *etc.* £4 10s. 0d. Settled S.Deacon'. In this particular instance, then, we can measure and assess exactly what was supplied for the money.

By 'best face' he meant a dial of the best quality, and this japanned dial was made by James Wilson of Birmingham, whose dials were the best of their kind – best quality of japanning, best quality of artwork, and, no doubt, the most expensive on the market. We shall examine the question of japanned dials later in more detail (see Chapter 12). Obviously, in this instance Deacon himself must have already had the case purpose-made and was supplying the entire clock, which, as we have just seen, was by no means always the custom.

It would appear that Mr Marven was some sort of middleman, who was buying the clock for an ultimate customer he had for it, named Mr Bray.

PRICES OF EIGHT-DAY CLOCKS

Eight-day clocks were always more expensive than thirty-hour ones. Longcase clocks were available in the eight-day form from their very beginning. In London, which was where the pendulum was first introduced, the eight-day clock formed the majority of longcases in the first few years, and, indeed, thirty-hour longcase clocks were never very popular amongst London makers at any time. In the provinces, on the other hand, the earliest clocks were more likely to be thirty-hour, and for some rural clockmakers the thirty-hour remained their standard product for most of their lives, with only an occasional eight-day perhaps for a wealthier customer here and there.

Samuel Roberts of Llanfair Caereinion, whose notebook was mentioned earlier, is typical of many rural makers in that almost all his clocks were of thirty-hour duration. From over three hundred known clocks which he made over a span exceeding twenty years, not more than half a dozen are of longer duration than thirty hours. His basic eight-day appears to have been priced at £4 1s. 0d. (£4.05). Eight-day clocks are harder to pin down pricewise because more permutations were possible, especially if the clock had an arched dial, when it might have moonwork, rocking figures or strike/silent, and such things may not be specified in the brief description available.

An entry in a diary of 1724 records the purchase of what must have been an eight-day clock from the eccentric clockmaker, James Woolley of Codnor in Derbyshire: 'Bot. at Derby market from

Woolley of Codnor square oak clock. Paid £4 10s. 0d. (£4.50). He wanted £5.' Assuming the oak case to have been a simple one, that then puts the clock's price at roughly £4. It is difficult to imagine an eight-day selling for less than this lower limit of about £4, and many were a little more.

In the 1738 inventory of George Birchall of Shrewsbury, which was mentioned earlier, are listed 'two eight-day clocks without cases – £6 0s. 0d.' We know that inventory values are inclined to be on the low side anyway, so perhaps these were being marked down a little. Also recorded is 'one eight-day clock archt diall plate – £3 10s. 0d.' (£3.50), which shows the considerable extra price of an arched dial type. A little more puzzling is 'one eight-day clock with a black case – £3 0s. 0d.' The black case is obviously a pine case, either ebonised or painted black, but the total price of clock and case is only the same as the caseless eight-day ones mentioned earlier. Perhaps the clock itself was more modest, and, as we know, the pine case would not have been expensive.

An enlightening difference appears with the next item: 'one eight-day clock with a fineard case £5 10s. 0d. (£5.50)'. The word 'fineard' is merely an old-fashioned way of spelling 'veneered'. This case must have been in veneered walnut, which would have been highly-figured burr wood used in multi-patterned form for decorative effect (see Chapter 8). It is too early to have been mahogany, and no other woods were used as veneer in longcase work. But what a vast difference in price between black-cased at £3 0s. 0d. and burr walnut veneered at £5 10s. 0d. (£5.50). We already know that plain (solid) walnut cost no more than oak, and that oak cost only a little more than pine. But here is interesting evidence that burr walnut was much more highly valued, even in inventory terms, where prices tend to be low anyway.

In the mid-eighteenth century, John Belling of Bodmin charged £4 10s. 0d. (£4.50) for an eight-day cased clock, making the clock itself somewhere close to the basic £4. 0s. 0d. level of Sam Roberts and James Woolley. John Manby was a clockmaker and ironmonger in Skipton, Yorkshire, and some years ago I searched through some of the business records of the company, which go back patchily to about 1815. Manby sold 'a new clock & balls' to a local joiner for £4 2s. 0d. (£4.10) – the 'balls' were brass finials, which sold at roughly 1s. 6d. a set of three (£0.7½), which puts the clock itself to just over £4.00.

So, in general terms, we can look at the prices of longcase clocks of the basic type available as costing a little over £2 0s. 0d. (£2.00) for a thirty-hour, and a little over £4. 0s. 0d. (£4.00) for an eight-day.

LONG DURATION, CHIMES AND MUSIC

Once we get into the realm of clocks which were out of the ordinary, then prices soon run to much higher levels. One possibility was a longcase clock of longer than usual duration. In 1722, for instance, clockmaker William Brock of Axbridge in Somerset supplied a month clock with a five-foot pendulum, without a case, at a price of £6 6s. 0d. (£6.30). This very same price was charged by Samuel Roberts of Llanfair Caereinion in 1758 for an eight-day longcase clock chiming the quarter hours on three bells, again without a case. A quarter-chiming clock was known for short as a quarter clock. Chiming the quarters could be on any number of bells from two upwards to as many as eight (for an example, see Plate 128), or even more, depending on the complexity of the chime. The simplest form is often referred to as a ting-tang quarter chime (see Chapter 9). This usually involves

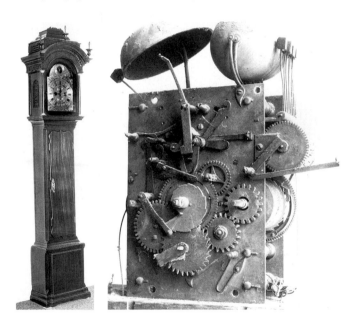

127. Superb longcase clock with choice of music or chime, by William Stumbels of Totnes, dating from the 1730s. An early use of mahogany. Height 8ft (244cms).

128. Highly complex longcase movement of the clock by Stumbels of Totnes (Plate 127), with dial removed to show wheelwork. The three-train clock with music or chime on six bells has only two winding squares, the third train being wound by the cam outside the right-hand square, a winding method unique to this maker.

two bells (apart from the hour bell, which would of course make a total of three bells), and these ring at two different pitches to give one 'ting-tang' sound at quarter past, two at half past, and so on. Some clockmakers contrived to build a ting-tang chiming clock with just the normal two trains of wheels, the strike train providing the extra power needed. More often, ting-tang chiming was operated by a separate third train of wheels. The three-bell clock supplied by Samuel Roberts and mentioned above may well have been a ting-tang quarter-chimer, chiming on two bells and striking the hour on the third.

In 1741, Thomas Moore, the Ipswich clockmaker, supplied a customer with 'a curious 8-day quarter clock in a fine walnut case 'at £16 16s. 0d. (£16.80). 'Curious' at that time meant that it was made with great care, not that it was in some way strange. Of course, we cannot assess how complicated this clock might have been, so the obvious inference that the walnut case represented £10 10s. 0d. (£10.50) of the cost may be incorrect. In any event, this would clearly have been a fine case in burr walnut veneers, not a plain case in solid wood, as we know that solid walnut was no more costly than oak, and that a simple walnut case could have been bought for less than one pound.

In 1784, William Porthouse of Penrith supplied an eight-day musical longcase clock offering a choice of seven tunes, and also including lunar work and the day of the month, at eleven guineas (£11 11s. 0d. = £11.55). We cannot be sure whether the price included a case, but if so, it was probably in oak, as it is difficult to see this price including one in mahogany. A fine mahogany case could have cost anywhere between £5 and £10 *without* its clock.

COMPLICATED CLOCKS

There were always clockmakers who were capable of producing the most amazing clocks, provided a wealthy enough customer was available to buy them. There is a danger that the novice may imagine that, because the old clockmakers lived a less sophisticated life two or three centuries ago, they were in some way simple-minded. This is far from being the case. Even from the very first days of pendulum clocks (1658), Fromanteel was able to offer longcase clocks which ran for as long as twelve months at one winding.

The better clockmakers had the mathematical ability and the engineering skills to build complicated items such as musical clocks and clocks with automated figures, clocks which showed the times of sunrise and sunset, moonrises and settings, tidal movements, and even planetary conjunctions (see Plates 35, 40, 127, 128).

A sundial, of course, registered solar time, whereas a clock averaged this out to record and display twenty-four hours exactly to each day. To set your clock to time, you had to use a sundial reading, and then add or subtract an amount, which varied according to the time of year, from zero to fourteen minutes or more. This difference between sundial time and mean time (as we

129. *Detail showing the annual calendar from a clock of c1780 by Wilkinson of Leeds, showing the Equation of Time table with the daily adjustment needed if setting up a clock.*

call clock time) was known as the 'Equation of Time', and charts were available listing adjustment rates for every day of the year. Some clocks would have an Equation Table pasted inside the door, and some had an Equation Table engraved on a calendar disc on the dial itself for constant and easy reference (see Plate 129).

Clocks which showed the Equation of Time as part of a simple calendar disc were available by the late seventeenth century, and these involved nothing very special in the way of gearing. However, some clocks were also made at this time to read both solar and mean time simultaneously and constantly, either by two sets of hands on the one dial or by two separate dials on the clock. These latter clocks were exceptionally complicated mechanically, and were produced by only a handful of makers.

Such clocks were very costly, and would have been made for royalty or nobility, being quite beyond the pocket of the 'ordinary' customer. Today these clocks are exceedingly rare items, and those known are mostly by the better London makers, who were the few who counted kings and princes amongst their clientele. But there were provincial makers, too, who could perform some of these breathtaking feats. One who comes to mind was John Williamson of Leeds, who in the late seventeenth century made a year-duration clock with strikework. This called for a tremendous store of power, and most year clocks do not strike for this reason.

HOROLOGICAL CURIOSITIES

Some clockmakers would work for many years on a masterpiece of their own invention and usually without any propsect of selling it, but they would do it as a challenge. When finished, they might charge a fee for the curious to watch it perform its functions, just as one might pay an entrance fee to a museum. Or they might attempt to sell the clock through a lottery. There are numerous examples of this in the documented history of clockmaking; sometimes the lottery raised the required sum, and sometimes it did not and had to be cancelled.

One amazing example was exhibited in 1763 by the Moore family of clockmakers of Ipswich, for an admission fee of 2s. 6d. (£0.12½), though whether it was made by them, or merely finished off by them, is in doubt. This 'clock' stood six feet square at the base and sixteen feet high, and as well as showing various astronomical features, played several pieces of music by Handel, as well as other concertos and overtures every three hours. In effect, the Moores had a small museum of clockwork, with a variety of extraordinary clocks on display.

On his death in 1833, Job Rider, the Belfast clockmaker, left behind a 'time-teller (made) with his own hands, which went for twelve years without requiring to be wound up by any individual during that long period'. The clock was self-winding by means of changes in atmospheric pressure. In practice there was little point in making clocks of extremely long duration, and when it was done it was mostly to prove that it actually was possible rather than for any practical use, since few, if any, clocks would run for years at a time without mechanical attention being required, which would involve stripping the clock down and re-starting all over again after repairing.

A clock of the 1740s is illustrated in E.L.Edwardes's book, *The Grandfather Clock*, made by John Clough of Manchester, and showing times of sunrises and sunsets together with an astrological dial registering zodiacal positions, alongside which are shown the appropriate parts of the body. It was thought propitious, in those days, that any surgery required should be carried out at the appropriate astrological time: neck and throat, Taurus; arms and shoulders, Gemini, and so on. It seems surprisingly incongruous to us today that such sophisticated mathematical abilities should go hand in hand with superstition.

Not only were there makers of great mathematical ingenuity, but many craftsmen of humble background would spend years constructing curiosities from simple materials or even waste materials. It was far from uncommon for some clockmakers to construct clocks whose wheels were made of wood, and even pinions too sometimes. Wooden clocks were traditional in parts of Germany, made from wood for cheapness, but an English-made wooden clock is rarely if ever seen today – with the exception of one or two very famous examples. Country makers, however, would often use cheap local materials – wheels from wood, or cowhorn, or old pennies, or buttons. Some of these verged on the eccentric, and were mostly made for amusement rather than as commercial items.

John Hunter of Dunfermline was a tailor by trade, and we are told in Felix Hudson's book, *Dunfermline Clockmakers*, how he made in 1790 an astronomical clock, its frame and axles of wood, showing sunrises and sunsets, the moon's daily motions, and tide rise and fall at Limekilns, as well as a hand-machine predicting the tides. His wheels were mostly made of large coat buttons!

James Gray of Edinburgh made a musical clock, which he completed in 1785, playing a choice of ten tunes, each tune three times over every third hour, while figures danced, a windmill turned, and a musician played the violin as a soldier marched on guard. The clock was to be sold by lottery at eighty guineas (£84.00) and it was sold by means of 160 tickets at 10s. 6d. (£0.52½) each. Lottery was a typical way of selling many of these very complex clocks, unless they had been specially commissioned, as they were otherwise just too costly to find a buyer.

Of course, the more functions a clock performed, the more there was to go wrong and the less were they proof against tinkering owners or inexpert repairers. I can think of one clock, today in a museum, which is so complicated that experts cannot agree first of all as to what it is supposed to do and secondly as to how to make it do it, even though most of the original parts survive. So this clock has been inoperative for the last thirty years to my knowledge, and there is some doubt as to whether the maker himself ever did finish it.

Time ultimately took its toll on many clocks and horrifying numbers must have gone onto the scrap heap in the past, which today we would have been capable of rescuing and would have thought worth the trouble. And this is a subject we turn to in the next chapter as we examine the ways in which in preserving some clocks such serious alterations were carried out as to bring them into the category of fakes.

11 MARRIAGES AND FAKES

I heard a story not long ago of a highly-skilled clock restorer (I won't say who) who acquired a very early and very rare table clock by a very famous maker. He took it apart and built an exact replica, using metals of the same composition as the original, the same tools and the same skills of the original clockmaker. Then he removed half of the parts of the first clock and substituted them with half of the parts of the clock he had just made. The result was two identical clocks, which would pass for genuine. The best experts in the world could not tell one from the other. At the worst, either would appear to be quite genuine but with some parts replaced, as might well have happened in reality over a span of time in excess of three centuries. A fake made with such dedication would be quite undetectable by you or me. Fortunately, such fakes are very rare, and happily (in one sense), they fall into a very high price bracket commercially, and would thus be way outside the pocket of most people.

The great majority of 'altered' clocks, which I lump together under the general term of fakes, are not of this nature at all. Most are clocks that were altered over the years from expediency rather than in any deliberate attempt to defraud, and consequently no trouble was taken to attempt to disguise the alterations which they actually are. With most of them, it is perfectly obvious that they have been altered, when you take the trouble to look, and when you know what to look for.

The question as to whether or not a much-altered clock is still an appealing item, and one worthy of preserving, is very much open to discussion, and certainly it would be a hard man who would advocate throwing any clock onto the scrap heap, however mutilated it might be. I happen to own the dial of a lantern clock made in 1627, which is all that survives of the original clock. Such a clock, if complete, would be a treasure. As it is, this dial is worthless, but it gives me great pleasure, and may well be as close as I shall ever get to owning a lantern clock of that age.

The point about being able to recognise a much-altered clock is to be able to avoid the pitfall of buying such a clock in error for the genuine article. Very rarely does anyone ever set out with the aim of buying a non-genuine clock. On the contrary, most people who do buy such a clock do so because they have been deceived into thinking it was a genuine one – even though if they were honest with themselves they may have been tempted into purchasing that particular example because it appeared to be a bit of a bargain, which it may well have seemed to be if viewed in comparison with a genuine one that looked 'similar'. Years of bitter experience have taught me that there are no bargains, and that in the end you only get what you pay for. It is far better for an enthusiast with limited funds to buy a good example of a very modest kind of clock, than a poor or altered example of a better type.

MARRIAGES AND FURNISHING PIECES

Alterations took place with clocks in many ways. Many quite genuine clocks have, as we have seen, been re-housed in another case at some time or other, perhaps even many years ago. Others exist today with the original dial and case, but with a replaced movement. Still others consist now of a dial, a movement, and a case from three quite separate origins, but now masquerading as a complete clock. Yet another category of these 'marriages', as such clocks are known, is the type where the clock was built-up from many separate oddments obtained from many different clocks. This latter type was often made-up in the past from the spare parts in a clockmaker's scrap box, so that what started out as an originally-constructed clock perhaps a hundred years ago, and which may have no apparent signs of alteration since its making, is in fact still a marriage of different parts of varying age, and thus not at all the same thing as a genuine period clock.

The term 'furnishing piece' is sometimes used to mean a good-looking clock which is not genuine: the same thing as a 'marriage' or a 'married' clock. The novice must be careful not to confuse this with a marriage clock, sometimes called a wedding clock, signifying a clock made as a wedding gift and often engraved with the names of the bridal pair. Auction catalogues nowadays sometimes describe a clock as 'made-up', which means just that, but another term they sometimes coin is 'composite', again meaning made from items not originally in the same clock. Auction catalogues may use a phase such as 'partly seventeenth century', or 'with alterations', or even 'restored' or 'with restorations'. Different auctioneers have different phraseology when referring to non-originality, while many make no attempt to point this out at all.

Perhaps as many as half the clocks one meets with are made-up from pieces which did not originally belong together, and the variety of different kinds of possible marriage might seem so bewildering to a novice that he may feel it would be totally impossible for him to attempt to sort the wheat from the chaff. In fact, it is quite easy to recognise a married clock if you set about the task in a systematic way, so we will examine these clocks one by one according to which type of marriage they represent.

Let us consider first those longcase clocks which were made up by a clock jobber using old parts from long-defunct clocks. These are almost always eight-day clocks with brass dials, usually arched, though square ones are always a possibility. The manufacture of genuine brass dial longcase clocks finished about

1790, after which all were white dials, with the exception of a few areas where the single-sheet brass dial clock persisted. Therefore, any brass dial longcase with the name of a nineteenth-century 'maker' is mysterious, to say the least. What sometimes happened was that an eight-day white dial clock may have had a shabby dial, or may have been regarded as inferior to a brass dial, and so quite a number had their old (original) white dials removed and new brass dials made-up, using old parts. This was a practice popular at the end of the nineteenth century and into the 1930s – it does not so much happen today. These altered clocks therefore have a certain 'age' to the dial in the form of dirt or tarnishing. Sometimes they were deliberately 'aged' behind the dial to make them look more convincing.

Many white dials had a falseplate fitting, which brass dials *never* had. It was easier for a clock jobber to fit a new dial by using an old white dial movement with its original falseplate, and this was the most common method. So examination may determine that the movement itself and the falseplate are quite genuine, and no fault will be found there. We know, however, that the very presence of the falseplate is an indication of a married clock if it has a brass dial. Many falseplates have the (white) dialmaker's name impressed on them; these can all be checked for period, and that period will often be well after brass dial clockmaking had ended.

INCOMPATIBLE STYLES
The dial will be made up using older items – *eg.* chapter ring, spandrels, maybe a seconds ring – all taken from older clocks, and once you know the styles of these features you will be able to deduce that the dial features are incompatible with each other, a whole mish-mash of conflicting periods. The dial sheet itself will probably have been made purposely to the same size as the white dial it replaced, and this dial (new in about 1900) will be of relatively thin rolled brass, not of cast brass as the originals would have been. Cast brass has a rough back surface (since it was not finished, being unseen; see Plate 25), whereas rolled brass is smooth. Cast brass also has little pitting-marks, imperfections and blow-holes from the casting, whereas rolled brass is much more perfect in finish. Rolled brass is usually thin enough to be slightly flexible, and arched brass dialsheets of cast brass are not. The dial feet may well fit correctly into the original falseplate holes, since they were positioned for this purpose, so no signs of alteration will be visible there.

Sometimes the name of the clockmaker was put onto the new (in 1900) dial, being the name from the original white dial. If so, then checking his dates may well reveal he was working far too late to be in the brass dial 'period', ie. pre-1790. Many were left without a name, and that in itself is a warning sign, since most genuine clocks *were* named.

If the dial is made from old parts, then the spandrels may not be of the right size to suit the chapter ring or dial sheet size. The engraving of numbers on the main chapter ring may be quite different in style from those on the seconds ring or calendar.

If the dial fittings were made specially at the time, then the engraving will almost certainly be of very different character from genuine eighteenth century engraving, which it purports to represent. Engraving from the late nineteenth century was almost always of uniform depth and was very flat and bland in appearance, whereas genuine eighteenth-century engraving had gradations of depth in the lettering, from deep to shallow, from heavy to fine. Also, the engraver often got the wrong numbering style or pattern, especially if he copied the numbering style from the white dial, as this would then be quite different numbering from that on a genuine brass dial of the eighteenth century. It takes a little practice to be able to recognise eighteenth century dial engraving from late nineteenth- or early twentieth-century copying, but it *is* different, and usually is very easily distinguished.

If the movement had no falseplate and the dial sheet was made new at the time of making-up the clock, then the dial feet would have been made to fit into the existing holes in the movement frontplate, so that there would be no suspiciously surplus holes. If a genuine old brass dial had been used in the making-up, then the dial feet would have had to be moved to line up with the frontplate holes, or (and this was the more usual practice) additional holes would have had to be drilled in the frontplate to receive the feet of the non-original dial (*eg.* Plate 130). So that moved dial feet (detectable by signs of the original positions or sawn-off stubs), or surplus holes in the frontplate of the movement, are immediate signs of marrying. Where a genuine old dial (with all its original fittings and matching, genuine engraving) was fitted to a different movement, there would almost always be a problem, in that the seconds hand would not fit in the right place for the seconds arbor in the movement, and the calendar, too, may well have a similar problem of misalignment. The inability of the (eight-day) clock to take a seconds feature and/ or the inoperable state of the calendar (*ie.* one which could never have worked) are two highly suspicious signs of almost certain marrying.

An old eight-day dial fitted to a different movement would very likely have caused problems with regard to the fit of the winding squares. Often the winding holes had to be enlarged or elongated in a crude and unnatural way, and this is usually fairly obvious even to a beginner. Occasionally a second set of holes was cut, leaving four winding holes but only two with an actual function – a real give-away (Plate 131). Moon dials or any other sub-dials seldom would be operable on a switched movement. Of course, the clock jobber could have repositioned all the wheels in the clock trains to make the winding arbors fit the winding holes in the replacement dial, but this meant more work, and more skilful work, and clock jobbers seldom went in for so much effort.

130. *Dial centre from a thirty-hour longcase of mid-eighteenth century date, with chapter ring and calendar disc removed. Though by a little-known provincial maker, the workmanship of the matting, with an engraved pattern through it, is of the very highest order. The 'cartwheel' nature of the dial sheet can normally be seen only from the back. The multiplicity of holes show where dial feet have been moved to fit a married-up movement. None of the holes were for chapter ring feet, as in this example it was riveted in place: see rivet stump at 9 o'clock position.*

Where a white dial was replaced by a brass one (new or old), the clock jobber would very often use the original hands from the white dial clock – they were available, they were the right length, and they fitted without any extra work being involved. As the white dial movement was almost always much later than the replacement dial purported to be, the incongruity of hands of a far-too-late design is almost always obvious. Of course, many

131. *A much altered dial, originally a thirty-hour of about 1760 with penny moon feature, almost certainly made in the Northern Pennines of the Lancs./Yorks. border area. The lettering IOHN WATSON 1777 and address MICHAELS ALY (Alley), CORNHILL, LONDON are in genuine eighteenth-century engraving and do relate to a clockmaker, but are spurious to this dial. Note the engraved dummy winding holes in the centre pattern. New winding holes have been cut close to the calendar disc, when this clock was converted to an eight-day. The new holes foul the calendar and prevent the disc turning. The movement is now German.*

genuine clocks have had their hands replaced with conveniently-available later ones, but this is just one extra pointer towards a possible marriage.

CONVERTED THIRTY-HOUR CLOCKS

Clocks with married movements are almost always eight-day clocks, that is they *became* eight-day ones. Many had originally been thirty-hour clocks, and, when such clocks began to wear excessively, it was often thought a good idea to replace the movement completely rather than repair it, and to make it an eight-day one for convenience at the same time. With this kind of marriage we have a quite genuine thirty-hour brass dial now attached to a non-original eight-day movement (see Plate 131). If the movement was once from a white dial clock with a falseplate, then the presence of the falseplate makes it instantaneously recognisable as a marriage. If there is no falseplate, then recognition as a marriage is usually very easy because no thirty-hour dial will fit onto an eight-day movement without a struggle, which enforced alterations on the clock jobber who performed the marriage. Some signs are usually very obvious on the dial itself (see Plates 130, 131).

Most eight-day clocks had a seconds dial, and most thirty-hour clocks did not. An eight-day clock without a seconds dial is unusual enough in itself to be a suspicious sign, and should lead to closer inspection for other tell-tale features. Winding holes would have to be cut into the dial, and these were usually cut imprecisely, sometimes with rough-cut edges to the holes, sometimes piercing right through an engraved pattern, and not having any ringing which some brass dial eight-days had. Most thirty-hour clocks had calendar work, and a great many of them had the mouth type of calendar, which was uncommon on eight-day clocks. Again, this feature is not a definite sign of a marriage, but is, nevertheless, a likely one. Absence of seconds dial *and* a mouth calendar on the same dial are a very unusual combination on any genuine eight-day clock, and most clocks lacking both of these features will prove to be marriages.

Most thirty-hour clocks had calendars which turned twelve-hourly by a knock-on pin method, which was simple and cheap. Most eight-day clocks had calendars which turned once in twenty-four hours, and involved an extra wheel usually positioned on the movement frontplate on the lower right, towards the five o'clock numeral on the dial. An eight-day movement, when fitted to a thirty-hour dial, can usually be made to operate the calendar on a twelve-hourly principle, but this is unusual for a genuine eight-day, and in any event the large pinion immediately behind the snail will be seen to be completely unused, whereas formerly it had its twenty-four-hour wheel connected. Furthermore, the hole where the twenty-four-hour wheel-post once fitted will be seen to be spare and unused on the movement frontplate (roughly behind the five o'clock numeral).

Most thirty-hour dials had three dial feet by which they fitted to the movement frontplate; most eight-day dials had four. To force a three-legged dial to fit onto a frontplate which formerly took four means that either the dial feet had to be moved (or some of them moved) or that extra holes had to be drilled in the frontplate, leaving some of the original holes unused. Moved dial feet or surplus holes are a sign of a marriage (see Plate 130).

It is just possible, though an unusual occurrence, for a thirty-hour movement to have been replaced by another one of thirty-hour duration, so that while thirty-hour clocks in general are far less subject to faking than eight-day ones, it is nonetheless unwise to buy even a thirty-hour clock without prior examination for such features as altered dial feet and spare frontplate holes.

FILLED HOLES
Many of the alterations just described will be over fifty years old, and often they were done as a cheaper way of repairing a clock with a faulty or worn movement. Since they were not really intended to deceive, it was less trouble to leave any signs of alteration uncamouflaged. Today, a modern clock jobber switching movements may well decide to fill empty holes, sometimes even using old yellow brass, so that the alteration goes unnoticed and the clock passes as a genuine eight-day. If this has been done, then the switch will be less easy to spot, perhaps even impossible, but many of the externally visible features will still be apparent.

White dial clocks were less often subject to having their movements changed. Indeed, with thirty-hour white dials it is very unusual, since they were, and still are, of the lowest value as a general category. Eight-day white dials, on the other hand, *do* sometimes have changed movements, and the same methods apply in identifying them as were outlined above with brass dials.

I had barely written the last paragraph when I was shown a clock bought recently at auction for close on £10,000. In its dismantled state one could clearly see what was concealed when it was assembled, namely several filled holes, and it was very obvious that the clock was made from parts of at least two others married together. This had been done skilfully, with deliberate attempts at concealing the alteration, and so in this example all external features were so well matched that the clock appeared quite genuine. As it happened, I knew about the auction and that this particular clock was in it, and, by chance, who had put the clock into it. It turned out that I also knew the buyer, *and* the restorer to whom he had shown it *after* he had bought it. Even an experienced dealer would not have been likely to spot these alterations without having the clock in pieces, which of course is impossible at an auction. The beginner has no defence against this kind of deliberate forgery, but any beginner would be foolish indeed to buy at auction in the first place, and to buy a clock in such a place at this sort of price level is just asking for trouble.

SWAPPED CASES

Many clocks today, are not in their original cases. Cases were swapped for all manner of reasons, and it is usually quite easy to identify a clock still in its original case from one which is not. Where a thirty-hour brass dial clock was 'converted' to eight-day duration by having a replacement movement fitted, as described above, it is just possible that the old, original thirty-hour case was kept. If so, the clock could be described as 'right to dial, right to case, wrong to movement'. However, in the great majority of examples with a marriage of dial to movement, it will be found that the case is also a marriage, simply because the clock has been made-up in total from old bits, including a spare case.

With most clocks, we can tell from examination whether the particular instrument under scrutiny (a genuine clock, that is, with movement 'right to dial') belongs in a particular case, or whether it is 'wrong to case'. In a very few instances we cannot tell, but almost always we can make that observation. There are a number of very simple points to look for. Even if the clock was once a thirty-hour example (later converted to eight-day) and remains in its original case, we can still identify the fact of its conversion, from tell-tale signs on the case as well as those just described on the dial and movement.

SEATBOARDS

A longcase clock movement sat on a wooden shelf called a seatboard. The seatboard was sometimes nailed to the case by being attached to the upright extensions of the case sides at the point where, for the sake of a term to use, we call them the cheeks. On some clocks, principally after about 1800, the cheeks are of pine, being blocks perhaps six inches long and maybe half an inch thick, glued, and perhaps nailed too, to the side extensions. Whether the seatboard was nailed down to the cheeks (for safety and stability) originally, or at a later time, does not really matter, because at some time most eight-day seatboards have been so fixed. Thirty-hour clocks often had the seatboard loose originally, but a great many have been nailed down at some time in the past.

For convenience of handling and moving a clock today, most people ensure that the movement, eight-day or thirty-hour, is attached to its seatboard. This might be by means of long bolts which run from below up through the board and into the movement's lower pillars, or it might be by means of seatboard hooks (which can be bought for the purpose today) that hook over the pillars and fasten with a nut underneath the seatboard. Alterations to the means of fastening the movement to its board are not important, since some dealers, myself included, will fit seatboard hooks during restoration if the clock has none, just to make subsequent handling easier. The result is that today the clock lifts off complete with seatboard, regardless of what manner was employed in the past. However, because past owners often nailed the board down to the cheeks, there are often nail- or screw-holes through seatboard ends into the cheeks. It is common sense that if there are holes in the board and not in the cheeks, or vice versa, this seatboard cannot be original to that case, more than likely indicating a swapped case.

Of course, a replaced seatboard will have no such evidence. Clock bodgers know this, and often replace seatboards knowing that most of the evidence is immediately removed. So a new (or later) seatboard on a clock is the first thing an expert looks for, as it is very often a sign of a non-original clock to case. Of course, there are occasions when an original seatboard is very badly infested with woodworm (they were often of pine), or is badly split from over-tightening of bolts, or else is badly warped and unstable, and in these instances it would be sensible practice to replace it. These occasions, however, are few, and by far the majority of replaced seatboards are there to conceal a change of case.

Sometimes another old seatboard is used in such a change, when its holes will not line up with those in the cheeks. It is usually possible to tell, simply by looking to see whether the seatboard is original to the movement, because of bolt positions, oil marks, and so on. If it *is* original to the movement and not to the case, then we have a marriage.

ALTERATIONS TO CHEEKS

To take clock A and put it into case B, even if the dial is of the same general size, will involve altering the height of the case cheeks, either by packing them higher or sawing them lower. Shortened cheeks are obvious to those who look, even if a modern saw-cut is stained to make it look old. Packings on top of the cheeks are equally obvious, and if these are new or fairly modern, then that is a suspicious sign. When the case was first made and supplied to the clockmaker, the cheeks were usually left over-length. They were sawn down to the required height by the clockmaker, once it was decided which movement was to go into it and how it would stand, to show the dial accurately in the glass of the hood door. This was a tricky thing to measure accurately first time, and so even original cuttings on the cheeks may be seen to have been attempted more than once, in an effort to locate just the right height. Sometimes errors were made, and packing, in the form of leather shims or wooden spacing wedges, was inserted on the cheek tops. Old packing is very easily recognised for what it is, and is unlikely to be confused with modern bodging. Recent packings may have been put in place instead of damaged old packings, but if this is so then the nail-holes we referred to earlier will still be visible in seatboard and cheeks, above and below the packing, and these must still line up, one with the other.

Some bodgers remove old side cheeks and replace them with new ones, thus destroying the evidence of where any nail-holes might once have been. The excuse usually given is woodworm damage, which of course could be true. However, you learn to take each such excuse with a pinch of salt, and by the time we reach three or four excuses on one particular clock, then credibility is wearing very thin.

DIAL SIZE EVIDENCE

A 12-inch dial (30.5cms) clock might be fitted into a non-original 12-inch case, or so one would expect. However, it would not fit without some alteration, as just described, to the cheeks area. But even with a case and dial of the same supposed size, there are often shades of difference in the fit. Spandrel corners that may have shown fully on one case might be covered on the other, and so swapping a clock into a different case even of the same size is not always easy. Very often, however, bodgers have tried to fit a dial to a case of a different size, and if you look for it, the evidence of that is usually very obvious. Inside most case hoods is a wooden mask of thin timber, often pine but sometimes oak, which surrounds the dial, rather like a mount does in a picture frame. On some very simple and early country clocks of rustic nature no mask was used, but most clocks have them, or once did. When the hood door is opened, the mask is the wooden frame still visible surrounding the dial.

If an 11-inch (28cms) dial is fitted into a 12-inch (30.5cms) case, there will be a gap between dial and mask, which original clocks did not have. To conceal this change, bodgers often fit a wooden bead all the way round this inner edge of the mask, and this is usually painted or stained to make it look old and match the rest of the mask. If you look for this alteration (it is best to look from the *inside* of the hood by removing it first), it is very obvious. However, as bodgers know that buyers may look for this alteration, they sometimes adopt the same policy as with seatboard cheeks, and that is to remove the old mask entirely and fit a new one tailor-made to size, thus removing the evidence. It is always possible that the old masking was badly wormed and had to be replaced, but this is a very rare occurrence, and usually new masking means a married case.

Suppose a 13-inch (33cms) dial were put into a 12-inch (30.5cms) case, then the inside mask would have to be trimmed back. If this was done carefully and the new edge was sanded down and stained for camouflage, one might imagine it would pass notice, but not so. The mask itself would be jointed at the corners, half-lapped or mitred in some way, and cutting-back in the manner described would almost always reveal some internal joint construction that was meant not to show. In any event, the line of the joint of a squared lapping joint would no longer run true to the corner, and would be visibly wrong. Again, a new mask would remove that evidence.

Sometimes a clock that was built with a square dial was altered to make it fit into an arched dial case, by adding a separate arch section, known as an added arch. The arch was often crudely soldered on or joined by rivetted tin strips, in a way which conflicts very obviously with the workmanship of the square section itself, *ie.* the original workmanship. Some central feature was often placed in the arch, such as a plate bearing the words 'Tempus Fugit', and a pair of arch spandrels from the scrap box were positioned either side. Such a clock cannot possibly be in its original case.

A few clocks were built originally with the arch as a separate section, and the novice may fear confusing this with a later added arch. Original work of this nature was mostly in the early period of the arched dial fashion, *ie.* from about 1710 to about 1740, and in any case the method by which the arch is attached tends to be of a much more professional standard. Often, too, the engraved designs may match in the arch as well as in the square sections, or the arch may carry some clearly-original feature such as a calendar or moon, whereas a bodger would not have gone to such time-consuming trouble, but would rather have made his added arch in the easiest way possible.

WEIGHT RUB MARKS

The fact that a thirty-hour clock had only one weight, and an eight-day two, is often of assistance in enabling us to recognise a swapped case. Many thirty-hour clocks, though not quite all, will have a rub mark inside the case front, just above the doortop or just below the door, or sometimes in both places. This is where the weight has rubbed over the years, and the wood can very often be felt to be quite worn away in that spot, which usually is about midway across the case front. If a case with a single weight-mark now contains an eight-day clock, it must be a marriage, because the two eight-day weights will rub, if at all, in quite different positions, approximately one-third of the way in from each side. Weights also often leave scuff-marks down the inside the clock door, plainly visible when the door is open. If the weights on any clock do not rub in the positions where it is apparent that a weight or weights once did, then something is wrong. An eight-day clock now housed in a non-original eight-day case may be detected by the fact that the weights do not bear on the existing rub-marks. The repositioning of the line ends can sometimes make a slight variance in this respect, namely in the position where the weights now drop. If line ends *have* been repositioned, this must be obvious from the seatboard, which will not only show the present lines tied off there, but also must have holes where the lines previously tied in a different position. If not, the answer again is a marriage.

PENDULUM RUB MARKS
On most cases, a rub-mark can be seen on the case backboard where the pendulum has occasionally scuffed at times when the

132. Inside a Scottish eight-day longcase of 1840, showing matching pair of thin weight-marked weights of cast iron (11lbs); flat strip steel pendulum rod; stamped brass facing to cast iron pendulum bob; scratch marks behind pendulum bob and rating nut. Note how the strike weight (on left) lags behind the going weight, a planned feature on many longcase clocks to prevent the strike running out of power first, with possible jamming of the clock if the strike should fail.

133. Pine backboard of a longcase clock c1800, showing brass-faced lead-filled pendulum bob with typical scuff marks made by the back of the bob and by the rating nut. These line up correctly here, and the apparent disparity is caused by the angle of view.

219

clock leaned too far backwards. Often two marks show, one being where the bob back has rubbed, and another, often sharper, scratch where the rating nut may have caught (see Plates 132, 133). A clock not in its original case will very probably have its pendulum at a slightly different height, so that it could never have rubbed where the old rub-marks show. This is not an infallible test, as most pendulums are of a similar length, and that of a married clock might just by chance rub in a similar place. It is surprising, however, how often this test *does* work. Of course, the bodger might have replaced the entire backboard of the case, thus removing all former evidence, just as he might with seatboards and cheeks.

LOCKS AND CATCHES

Most people would not want to lock and unlock the case door every day for access to the pull-cord of a thirty-hour clock. It follows that the majority of thirty-hour clock cases will have a turnbuckle catch, not a lock. The very opposite applies to eight-day clocks. This again is not an infallible test, but often it is possible to spot a turnbuckle-fastening eight-day clock, of which one is immediately suspicious, only to find on opening the door that there are the tell-tale thirty-hour rub-marks. Bodgers can replace a turnbuckle with a lock, but almost always the evidence of the former turnbuckle will show as scratch-marks, either on the door outside, or on the door or frame inside.

In recent years an owner may have fitted a lock on his thirty-hour clock, which originally perhaps had a turnbuckle. There is no harm in that, since weight rub-marks will confirm this was always a thirty-hour case, and in any event it was normally the position that thirty-hour cases were taken to house eight-day clocks, not so much to house other thirty-hour clocks.

LENTICLE GLASS POSITION

Some early clocks have a lenticle glass in the door, through which it was intended that the pendulum bob could be seen glinting against the light (Plates 5, 67). A bob which hangs in such a position that it does not show through the glass is enough to raise suspicions, and call for further inspection. On some cases, especially narrow ones, the pendulum may at some time have swung far enough to tap against the case sides, and in some instances an owner may have cut those sides with a gouge to stop these tapping noises from driving him insane. Does the pendulum now swing at the same point where tap-marks or gouge-cuts can be seen? If not, why not?

DEEP MOVEMENTS

Thirty-hour clocks of the birdcage type tend to be considerably deeper than plated clocks of thirty-hour or eight-day type. If the case seems unduly deep for the clock it houses, consider whether it might once have housed a birdcage thirty-hour. Likewise, if a birdcage clock is jammed in so tight that it fouls the backboard, was that case once on a plated movement clock?

STYLISTIC EVIDENCE

So far we have not mentioned the question of assessing the age of the case and comparing it with the age of the clock. This is perfectly possible, but not for a novice, and all those factors so far indicated are such as can be spotted by someone looking at his very first clock. The same goes for the question of considering the regional stylistics of a case alongside the place from which the clock purports to originate. A clock from Suffolk in a case from Lancashire would be instantly recognisable by anyone familiar with case styles as being totally incompatible, though few people are in fact so experienced.

After a while, one gets a feeling about a clock almost at first sight. The beginner cannot hope to do this, and if he thinks he does, then he is deluding himself. It takes years of experience to acquire this ability, and the collector or enthusiast who may devote an hour or two a week to his subject is still in kindergarten alongside a clock bodger who has taken a full-time course in camouflage. Experience will only come with familiarity. Examination of clocks, both in actuality and in books, is vital, though it does not take long to notice that quite a few of the books contain pictures of clocks in wrong cases, or even of clocks which are marriages of dial to movement.

It can do no harm to examine a clock which you may be thinking of buying, using every one of the various methods described above. Check for all possible alterations. If you find one such, you will almost certainly go on to find several others on the same clock. If you already own a clock at home, then practise on that one – though be prepared for the possibility of an unpleasant surprise.

The maker's name is one very important piece of evidence you will want to use in your determination as to the genuineness of a clock. How you set about finding out details of individual makers is the subject we examine in the next chapter.

12 Tracing an Individual Clockmaker

Once the recognition features have been learned, it is quite a simple matter to assess the age of a clock to within ten years. On most clocks, however, the maker's name is displayed prominently on the dial, and if that maker's dates can be looked up in a reference book, then hopefully a minimum and a maximum date will emerge, within which span the clock must fall. This principle is fine in theory, but the practice is seldom quite as straightforward as that.

The expert approaches the problem of dating and identification by first examining the clock to see that dial, movement, and case all belong together. Having done that, he then would examine individually these same components to enable him to form a view as to the clock's age. Only after having formed his own opinion on these two aspects (genuineness and apparent age) would he perhaps wish to check on any known dates for the maker, to confirm his opinions, or, perhaps, to change them.

The beginner is often short of experience, and may well try to short-circuit the system by going directly to a reference book for known dates on the maker. There are all kinds of reasons why this may not produce a correct answer, and we will examine some of those reasons later. However, as this method will work to some extent with most clocks, and as the beginner is likely to try it anyway, he will need to know which books will help him to check on the maker's life.

If he is lucky he will find that a book has been written on the clockmakers of the town in question, or more likely of the county in question. So his first step is to check this in the list of books on pages 246–8. If no book exists on the area, or if its facts on the maker are scanty, then he should try the more general books.

DICTIONARIES OF CLOCKMAKERS

The bible of the clock collector is a book called *Watchmakers and Clockmakers of the World*, compiled in the 1920s by the late G.H. Baillie, and containing about 35,000 names. In 1976, a further volume was compiled by myself, and this was enlarged in 1989 and now contains about 40,000 additional names, with dates. These two books have the same title, and are referred to as Volume One (by Baillie) and Volume Two (by myself). *Both* volumes need to be consulted, as not only does Volume Two contain many names not recorded by Baillie, but in some cases it adds further facts on a maker beyond those previously listed by Baillie. This two-volume work covers makers from the earliest times up to 1880. Most of the old clockmakers are recorded in this work, though only in brief form.

Old Clocks and Watches and their Makers by F.J. Britten is now in its ninth edition (1982), and this lists details of some 25,000 makers. Most of these makers are already in Baillie, but Britten's latest edition is especially useful for London makers, where details of apprenticeship may also be given.

British clockmakers who were working before the year 1700 are detailed in my book *The Early Clockmakers of Great Britain*. Scottish clockmakers are listed in John Smith's book *Old Scottish Clockmakers*, and those from Wales in *Clock and Watch Makers in Wales* by I.C. Peate.

If there is no county book, and the required maker fails to appear in those just listed, then your only possibility is to try the local museum and/or county records office of the region concerned, as some of these may have compiled their own local lists. Of course, it is possible for an owner to try researching a clockmaker for himself by searching such records as local parish registers, but this is too slow a process for anyone wanting to check up on a clock he is considering buying.

As I suggested before, the name alone may not be enough, even when the maker can be located in a book such as Baillie. A maker might well be listed there with a single date, such as 'circa 1790', and the clock might date many years either side of that estimate, which in any case is no more than an estimate made by the compiler. If a maker is listed as working over a known span of forty years or more, it is likely that a much closer dating is wanted. In examples where father and son followed the same trade and had the same first names, you might want to pin down the clock to whichever of perhaps as many as three men of the same name made it. If the name is a common one (as, for example, John Taylor of London) there could be a dozen or more possibilities listed, and you would still want to know which one made the clock in question. So, in the end, a knowledge of stylistic trends is essential, though admittedly it may help a beginner if the known time period can be arrived at, even approximately, from such a book, and the finer tuning of assessing the period can be tackled with that information already in mind.

A further problem with names is that a made-up clock (one made from parts of others, as was a common practice in the late nineteenth and early twentieth centuries; see Chapter 11) would not be apparent from the name alone. In such cases, one often sees a nameplate from some quite different clock, or perhaps a signed chapter ring, which has been used to make the dial look more complete. In these instances, a perfectly genuine nameplate bearing a quite genuine name of a recorded clockmaker could be misleading, even though dates for that maker can be looked up, and here again a knowledge of styles is essential to spot such a 'marriage'. One of the most obvious ways to recognise a married clock is from the conflict of contradictory stylistic features.

When using reference books such as Baillie, you must always bear in mind that the compilers were not infallible. Those entries which include the word 'circa' (or 'ca.' for short) represent the opinion of the compiler or of some informant, and such an estimate of the period of a clock may well be inaccurate. A much more sensible approach is to rely on those features which indicate the period of the clock itself – once the ability to assess its period has been learned.

If a name fails to appear in such a reference book, this need not be any reflection on the status of the maker or on the genuineness of the clock. Quite genuine clocks regularly come to light by clockmakers who happen to have escaped being recorded before. I keep a constant update of my own books by entering in new names as they arise, and barely a week passes without my noting at least two or three previously unrecorded makers.

It should also be remembered that presence of a name in such a book is in no way an indication of a 'genuine' clockmaker. Many married clocks (see Chapter 11), made up from scrap parts, carry a name of some kind, and some of these were purely invented names put on by the assembler of the clock to give it a more authentic appearance. This type of 'maker's' name has also often found its way into these books. If used correctly, these books can be a most helpful guide to dating, but if used wrongly they can prove far more misleading than helpful.

UNSIGNED CLOCKS

Some clocks are unsigned and carry no maker's name on the dial. There were often reasons why this was so at the time, though these reasons may not be apparent to us today. With lantern clocks, for instance, a good many were, and still are, unsigned, and a sensible collector learns to use his own assessment of the quality of an item and to judge it on its own merits rather than by its maker's name. A discerning collector would not be dissuaded from buying a lantern clock just because it had no maker's name. The less discerning, however, have always felt that there was some sort of comfort in the clock's having a name, especially what they believe to be a 'good' name. To accommodate them, therefore, many lantern clocks, which once were unsigned, have 'acquired' names. The practice still occurs today, and those who study such things in detail can witness an unsigned clock being sold through an auction, perhaps, and then re-surfacing some time later proudly bearing a name, and often a prestigious name at that.

This practice of adding a faked name occurs not only on lantern clocks, but on longcases and other types too. If one follows such famous names as Thomas Tompion and Joseph Knibb at auction, it is surprising not only how many clocks by these people come to light in a year, but how many either fail to sell or sell at an absurdly low price (for such makers), and the reason is that many are either outright fakes or carry faked names.

Some clocks were unsigned originally because they were made by one maker to be retailed by another. This happened particularly with lantern clocks, but to a much lesser extent with longcase clocks. Some longcase brass dial clocks are unsigned, but a small minority. One type of clock that was often unnamed was made by certain Quaker clockmakers, who regarded it as a sign of vanity to proclaim themselves as the makers. So some unsigned clocks were therefore made by Quakers, and with experience these can often be recognised. This is not at all the same thing, however, as deducing that an unsigned clock was Quaker-made, though one does often see such clocks passed off as being Quaker work in an attempt at giving them some sort of provenance.

NAMES ON WHITE DIALS

White dial clocks were almost always lettered with the name of the maker (or retailer) on the dial. Today, however, a great many appear to be unsigned at first sight, whereas close examination will frequently reveal that faint traces of the name remain. Over the years owners have often over-cleaned the dials to the point where the name has become very faint or even completely worn away. It is unwise to regard a white dial clock as having no maker's name unless very careful inspection has been carried out. There is a knack in managing to read a worn name, and this only comes with experience. It is all a matter of holding the dial in the right light and at the right angle and patiently deciphering the faint letters. The use of ultraviolet light in a darkened room can often make an 'invisible' name legible as if by magic. A skilled restorer can re-letter a dial exactly as it was done first and this is regarded as standard restoration practice.

The re-lettering of dials, of course, gives the forger a chance to falsely endow clocks with a prestigious name, so one has to be wary of this, and it is by no means easy to recognise when this has happened. I have seen clocks with white dials purporting to be by Jonas Barber of Winster, Westmorland, who is a maker highly regarded today, especially in his own area, which were quite spuriously re-lettered and were not made by Barber at all. This maker happens to have had certain highly uncommon factors within his movements which make them easily identifiable as being his work, once his methods are known, but with makers whose work does not have distinctive features of constructional style, it may well be impossible to tell if the re-lettering is genuine or faked.

NAMES OF DIALMAKERS

The name of the maker is not the only important signature which may help identification and dating. With white dial clocks, there is very often a second name, that of the dialmaker, whose name was usually imprinted on the back of the dial or on its iron falseplate. The known working periods of the dialmakers (which can be checked in my book *White Dial Clocks, the Complete Guide*) can be compared datewise alongside that of the clockmaker, and obviously the two must tally. So the name of the dialmaker is a very important secondary check to establish the age of the clock. While there were very many dialmakers, the great bulk of the market was supplied by only a few. The names and periods of those most commonly met with are:

Osborne and Wilson. Birmingham. Partners 1772–1777.
Osborne (Thomas and widow and son). Birmingham. 1777–1813.
Wilson, James. Birmingham. 1777–1809.
Wilkes (father and son). Birmingham. 1820–52.
Finnemore (various in family). Birmingham. 1812–1852.
Owen (various). Birmingham. 1803–22.
Walker and Hughes. Birmingham. 1810–1835.
Wright, Benjamin. Birmingham. circa. 1805–circa 1820.

When the clock has a falseplate, it is usually possible to make out the impressed dialmaker's name on the falseplate itself by peering into the movement from the side, especially if a torch is used. Not all falseplates are impressed with a name, but most are. If the clock has no falseplate, or if the falseplate carries no name, then the dialmaker's name can often be seen on the back of the calendar wheel (with a mouth type of calendar) or on the back of the moon wheel (with a moondial clock). In these latter places the name may be harder to spot unless the dial is removed, whereupon it becomes much easier. Falseplates were used only with white dials. If a brass dial clock has a falseplate, it is a made-up clock.

NAMES OF OWNERS
Some clocks carried the name of the first owner on the dial, as well as that of the maker. This might be the case with a clock made as a present for a wedding, for instance, or perhaps for some other special event. In these instances, the year will often be included as well. Some individual makers, and even several makers within a certain region, might have made a regular habit of lettering the names of the first owners on the dial. William Porthouse of Penrith was a maker who did this regularly, and I have recorded about thirty clocks where this maker did this – *eg.* Thomas and Ann Harrison 1749, William and Elizabeth Wagstaffe 1752. Research proved that many were actually for wedding occasions, and presumably the couple wished to have the event commemorated in this way. The presence of the first owner's name on a dial is usually regarded as a bonus, especially if it carries the date as well, for then the exact age of the clock is known.

One unusual way of lettering the first owner's name was to use his name instead of numerals. This was done with both clocks and watches, though it is an uncommon practice. The name needed to have twelve letters in it, or to be spaced round the numbers in such a way as to fit the 1–12 sequence. A clock by William Petherick of St Austell carries the name, instead of numerals, of 'Henry Udy 1781'. A watch of 1790 by William Swaine of Woodbridge has the name 'Jeptha Waller' instead of numerals.

The owner's name is usually an obvious extra feature, and is easily recognised as such. There are occasions, however, when the *only* name on the dial is that of the first owner, and then we may well mistake it for that of the maker and fail to locate it in the basic reference books. Of course, it is very difficult to know whether this has happened, and if so, when.

STRANGE NAMES

Some names on dials prove both fascinating and puzzling, and sometimes clockmakers with unusual names played on that fact. One maker named Obadiah Orange Lemmon worked at Battle in Sussex, and signed his clocks enigmatically 'Orange Lemmon Battle'. Samuel Reeve the clockmaker worked at Stonham, a village in Suffolk, where he died in 1718, and lived at the Magpie Inn. He signed his clocks 'Sam Reeve, Stonham Py', and his successor, Samuel Hart, did the same, signing as 'Sam Hart, Stonham Py'.

Some names were just plain unusual: Agrippa Wadge of Callington, Digory Henwood of Fowey, John Pentecost Job of Truro, Jury Cramp of Horsham come to mind, and Mark Anthony Dempster of Richmond, Yorkshire, who carried on the tradition by naming his children Mark Anthony, Julius Caesar and Marcus Brutus! A few makers deliberately played on their names, with such instances as 'Fear of Bristol', 'A. Seagull, Hull', and 'A. Body, Battle'.

ALIASES

There are examples enough in the history of clockmaking of those in the trade who deliberately wished to conceal their names – criminals wanted for running off with the master's stock or even his wife, runaway apprentices. Some such makers may well account for the number of clocks made without any names at all, probably sold anonymously at markets and fairs to help the maker escape detection. One notorious example was the clockmaker Thomas Norweb, a man who kept moving, having worked for a short spell in the 1760s at Wetherby, Selby, Brigg, Louth, Wrawby (Lincolnshire), and perhaps at other places too. His descendants discovered, when tracing their ancestry with the assistance of the memoirs of his widow (written when she was in a debtor's prison), some very unusual aspects of his background. Most curious of all was the fact that the name Norweb does not exist at all prior to Thomas of that ilk, and that is because it was an invented name, being an anagram of Browne. It is supposed that he made up his surname to help him leave his murky (and still unknown) past behind him. So researching a maker can often provide some interesting surprises, and can be a fascinating pursuit in its own right.

There will always be some names on clocks which will prove mystifying, and sometimes this may be because they were intended so to be. The regulations of membership imposed by the many town and city guilds, which controlled the crafts until the mid-nineteenth century, were such as to forbid anyone to trade within their territories unless he were a member. Those who tried to do so were prosecuted, and so some makers attempted to escape the system and the danger of prosecution by selling the clocks (or watches) they made with invented names. The practice of putting an invented name on an item was known as early as the first half of the seventeenth century, and even though the item itself may be quite genuine, it could prove that the name is a faked one, in which case no amount of research is likely to discover anything about the supposed maker.

13 RESTORATION

Restoration of most clocks simply involves the complete disman-
tling of the movement and dial to single-piece components,
cleaning, polishing, and re-assembling. At the same time, any
faulty or rusted parts are made good and any damage is repaired.
Such work is a highly-skilled business, and should not be
undertaken by amateurs. I have seen some so-called restorers
dangle a complete movement in a tin of paraffin by a piece of
string, leave it there for twenty-four hours, and then hang on an
extra heavy weight with no pendulum, thus forcing the clock to
rattle into shape with a sound not unlike a distant machine gun.
This, obviously, is not recommended practice, and fortunately
happens less often today, since the high price of most clocks forces
owners to seek out a real restorer, who will handle their clock with
care and skill.

As far as mechanics are concerned, there is no merit in dirt, and
no one would quarrel with the principle of cleaning clock
movements. Most clocks therefore have their movement parts
cleaned and polished during restoration, and this is quite normal
practice with one exception, which I will come to below. The
question of whether or not to clean clock dials is a much more
controversial matter.

BRASS DIAL CLOCKS
When a brass dial clock was new, its dial was brightly polished,
and most engraved areas were silvered on the surface in order to
show up the black wax-filled numerals more clearly. Matted areas,
such as a dial centre, could not be silvered, so in practice we are
talking of those engraved areas which were inscribed onto a
polished ground. Principal of these were the chapter ring, seconds
chapter ring, calendar ring, and, on some clocks, the engraved dial
centre and such items as a nameplate. Some of the very earliest
bracket clocks had chapter rings of solid silver, and perhaps the
practice of silvering was in a way a continuation of that principle.
The silvering was done by applying a solution of silver chloride
as a paste, then lacquering it against tarnishing, whereupon the
resulting finish would last for something like twenty years. As the
engraving was filled with black wax (or occasionally red wax, or
blue, for special effect), the silvering paste was rejected from the
engraved pattern and numerals, leaving the lettering to stand out
boldly against the silver-white background.

Once the lacquer deteriorates then the dial begins to tarnish,
and many clocks which one sees today have a dial blackened from
perished silvering, or else appear brightly polished, with metal
cream trapped in every crevice. In that condition, the appearance

may in fact be one of age, but the effect is nothing like that which was originally intended. Some owners are afraid to have the dial professionally cleaned and polished, as they feel they may be losing the original finish of the clock, but of course the surface condition is anything but original.

Some dials have been polished by owners for many years, and today show no signs at all of silvering, to the point where owners cannot think that their clock ever was given that finish in the first place. In fact, when a clock is stripped down for cleaning, there is almost always some faint trace of silvering remaining, which shows that the clock actually was once so treated.

Those who wish to leave their clock dials in dirty or tarnished condition are free to do so, but it is accepted practice amongst restorers, dealers, collectors, and even informed museums to clean and re-silver as appropriate. Those who imagine that, by leaving the clock dial dirty, they may be preserving something of the original silvering have failed to take into account the fact that the clock will have been re-silvered numerous times in its past life anyway, and what remains today is a trace of old *re*-silvering.

There is a point to be made that constant cleaning of dials by professionals (which involves some abrasive treatment necessary to give a key to the silvering) will eventually wear the engraving thin and faint. One can see this worn engraving regularly on some clock dials, which is a pity, for their appearance is nothing like that of a clock with a good, boldly-engraved dial. Such worn engraving is perhaps more the result of over-enthusiastic amateur work. I have watched amateurs honing away with emery discs on dirty chapter rings, using power tools, and destroying much of the brass surface as they did so, which is another reason why restoration is best left to those whose livelihood depends on it.

On the other hand, a dirty dial which is left exposed to the elements (*ie.* unlacquered) will often be affected by atmospheric etching, causing discolouring and even pitting of the surface to the point that, when it does go for restoration at some future date, much more abrasion will be needed to attempt to clean it.

LANTERN CLOCKS

There is one category of clock where the usual rules of cleaning may not apply, and that is with lantern clocks. Here attitudes vary somewhat. All would agree that the essential bearing surfaces need to be cleaned and bushed where necessary, *eg.* pivots, pinions, wheel teeth. But today some owners prefer to leave the parts themselves unpolished, sometimes including the dial and outer 'case' parts. One reason for this is that it is sometimes thought that this condition shows the clock's age better (though this could be said of longcase clocks, too, if one wished to argue that point). Perhaps more important is the fact that from sheer age lantern clocks have had more repairs, restorations, replaced wheels, and so on, than most other clocks, including sometimes recently-performed repairs. Polishing to some extent conceals these repairs, and thus makes the task of assessment so much more tricky for a potential buyer.

With lantern clocks, therefore, a sort of compromise is often arrived at, and this is a principle I usually follow myself. Bearing surfaces are cleaned to remove the possibility of aggravated wear and tear, but other parts are often left in an unpolished state. This means that any new part is obviously new and is not concealed. After all, there is no shame in the fact that a three-hundred-year-old clock has had to have some worn-out part replaced, and most buyers accept that as being to some degree inevitable, as long as they can see what has actually been done.

Lacquering is normally limited to the dial only. Not only does it help combat atmospheric etching, but it keeps the dial bright and clean, and removes the necessity for owners to attack it with metal polish (thus exposing the hands to possible damage). It is not normal practice to lacquer the clock plates, and certainly not the wheels, since either may cause shreds of lacquer to peel into the wheelwork and accentuate wear.

CASEWORK RESTORATION

Restoration of clock casework is the same in principle as with other antique furniture. Many clocks have suffered at the feet from damp floors, and a good number have had their feet removed, or have even been sawn short in the base on account of rot. Replaced feet are not regarded as a problem on longcase clocks, and perhaps half the clocks one meets with have them. As long as the replacements are in a compatible style, it is not a serious detriment, though obviously original feet are preferred. If the replaced feet are themselves of some considerable age, then few people can recognise them from the originals.

The base of the clock itself (*ie.* the section between the feet and the trunk) generally suffered less than the feet. A replaced base was considered a serious detriment until recently. However, as clocks become ever harder to find, a more tolerant attitude is usually adopted today. A country pine case, or even an oak one, may well have had its base seriously shortened, to the point where it stands ludicrously low. This could even result in a thirty-hour clock running for less than twenty-four hours, or an eight-day clock needing winding every sixth day. If the clock is a good one, as early ones often are, then one has no alternative but to replace a shortened base. A good cabinet-maker can usually blend in the cut of the wood and the colouring to match the rest. It is still a defect, but not one that should prevent anyone from buying what might otherwise be a highly-desirable clock.

The hoods of some clocks have also been cut down to get a tall clock into a room that would otherwise have been too small for it.

This can be a more difficult problem to deal with, especially if the hood originally had a swan-neck pediment. It is very difficult to join onto a cut-down swan-neck, as the joint will usually be obvious. Such a fault is regarded as a more serious one than a shortened base, and might well deter some buyers, even if it has been carefully restored. It is also often a problem to know just what shape the original swan-neck followed, and replacement of such a part is often little more than a guessing game as to its outline; and an inelegant outline can mar a clock badly in overall balance and proportion. These two factors are very important in assessing its value.

BACKBOARDS
The backboards of some clocks have suffered from damp, rot, woodworm, or all three. Some clocks had oak backboards – principally London clocks and some from the North-west (Lancashire in particular). Oak backboards were stronger, and seldom have these problems. On the great majority of longcase clocks at all periods, the backboards were of pine, a soft wood, much prone to attack from woodworm. Old pine backboards almost always have a few wormholes somewhere, but they can be treated, and unless the infestation is bad or has weakened the timber seriously, this should not be a problem.

Occasionally, other woods were used for backboards – chestnut and fruitwood being the principal alternatives to pine. Both these woods suffer from worm attack, sometimes to an even greater degree than pine. If the backboard is badly wormed, then it may be necessary to replace the entire backing. This is something collectors do not like, but may be forced to accept. Certainly, a strong replacement is better than a crumbling original. If wormholes show on the surface, then there is often a honeycombed interior which is sometimes so bad that pieces can be snapped off with the fingers.

WOODWORM
Oak is immune to woodworm attack, except in special circumstances, eg. where weakened by damp, as on the feet of a clock, or in a sapwood streak, which tends to show as a yellow stripe in darker surrounds. If a sapwood streak happens to run down the front of an oak clock, this can mar the appearance. Oak might also show worm attack if used as a thin veneer onto a softwood backing (such as pine), but in longcase work oak was virtually never used as veneer.

English walnut was prone to worm attack, whether the wood was in solid form, or, more especially, if used as veneer onto pine. American walnut, usually used in solid form in the second half of the eighteenth-century, is subject to woodworm, but less so than English walnut, which was superseded as native supplies were exhausted. Mahogany is immune to worm except when it has been softened by damp, or when used in veneer form onto a softwood backing. Many nineteenth-century longcases have considerable mahogany veneer used onto pine, and worm infestation in the pine basewood will often show holes through the mahogany veneer.

Many buyers are put off by woodworm, often because they do not understand the nature of the problem. The holes in woodwormed timber are the flight-holes where the beetle has eaten its way out and flown away. A new clean hole is very obvious, and often has a powdery sawdust spilling from it. This dust can keep spilling out for years, long after the infestation is dead, so dust need not be a cause for alarm. What one has to watch out for, however, are new flight-holes, which tend to suggest that the infestation is still active. To help recognise new holes, if and when they appear, owners and dealers sometimes wax over the old flight-holes, effectively filling them with wax polish. This is not so much to discourage woodworm as to make it apparent when any new holes occur, thus indicating the infestation is still active.

Woodwormed timber can be treated with a proprietary fluid, which can be painted on the surface (ensure you paint both sides of a backboard), but it will smell strongly for days afterwards, so it is best to do this in an outbuilding. Better still is to use the fluid in an injection can, which looks a little like an oilcan, and has a long thin nozzle by means of which fluid can be poured into the tunnels. It is best to avoid treating a polished (exterior) surface of a clock case, as the finish might be harmed, and in any case the polish will impede the absorption of the liquid into the wood.

It is unlikely that woodworm will be attracted to an antique clock unless they are already living in it. These beetles like new timber, such as household floorboards, and a householder has much more cause to worry about them infesting the loft timbers than his clock. They usually infest areas which cannot easily be polished and dusted, which in longcase clocks means principally the backboard or the softwood glue blocks inside the case. Naturally, one cannot wax and shine an unplaned backboard, but an occasional application of wax to the backboard may well deter the beetles. In adult form the woodworm is a tiny shell-backed beetle. They can often be seen flying in through open windows in spring and summer, when most householders mistake them for midges and ignore them.

One possibility is to hang those little fly-killing sachets or lanterns inside the clock case, perhaps inside the base and well out of the way of the weights. This makes the clock case into a small gas chamber, and the vapours kill all living insects such as flies or woodworm. What they would do to people I cannot imagine.

WHITE DIAL RESTORATION

The question of whether or not to 'restore' white dials is one which troubles some collectors. Should they be left in the condition they have now arrived at, that is, with all the signs of wear and tear of two centuries or more – in other words in the 'original' condition as we now find them? The problem, of course, is that the condition they are in today is often anything but original. An example of just such a tired dial is shown here (Plate 134), the clockmaker's name (Wm. Snow, Padside) being barely visible. Over the years, successive owners have tried to clean the dial, usually by wiping with a wet cloth and some cleaning agent such as a kitchen liquid. The cleaning has removed almost all the fine blackwork, which originally was done in a very thin paint, almost as thin as ink.

134. *Twelve-inch white dial from a thirty-hour clock c1780-90, showing faded artwork and maker's name barely legible. Crude attempts at touching in the numerals have made it even worse. The crazing shows clearly. Dialmaker James Wilson of Birmingham.*

To make matters worse, some past owner of this particular clock has tried to touch in the hour numerals with black paint, and the result looks very unsightly. The dial can be seen to be quite dirty in parts, and the dirt causes the craze-marks, which all these dials have to some degree, to show more prominently. Chips and bump-marks show here and there where the white japanned surface has broken – just below the centre hole, for instance. The original gilt around the calendar mouth has worn away, the minute numbers remain only as faint shadows, and the two original circles which formed the 'chapter ring' are invisible except on close inspection. The flowers themselves survive, as the oil painting is more resistant to abuse than the blackwork, but even on the flowers the fine stalk lines, originally in black, have washed away.

135. *The same dial after cleaning and expert restoration. The original background remains and faint crazing still shows, but less obviously than when dirty. The clockmaker is William Snow of Padside, Yorkshire. This numbering pattern is typical of almost all white dial clocks from this first period (1770-1800).*

Today, it is recognised practice to clean and restore such dials, provided that it is restored faithfully. The result can be seen in Plate 135. Attempts at removing the over-touched hour numerals have not completely removed evidence of that earlier abuse – a shadow remains on, for example, the V numeral and beside the lighter crossbar on IX and X. After professional cleaning, however, the dial is brighter, and therefore the crazing shows less, so that although the dial shows some signs of its age, it does now look as it was meant to look when William Snow first bought his dial from the Birmingham dialmaker James Wilson.

The fine blackwork visible in the restored dial barely shows at all in the earlier photograph. However, when the dial was handled in a good light and angled to catch the correct reflections, all those features could be made out quite clearly, so that it was not restored by guesswork but by lettering faithfully over the original faded work.

Most of the photographs in this book were taken after similar restoration had been carried out, and this is the manner in which most dealers and collectors like to see their clocks restored today. A visit to a saleroom will soon enable the inexperienced to see dials in their unrestored state. Restoring such a dial is highly skilled work, and it is not something that should be attempted by a novice, or more harm than good may result.

It is unwise to let anyone attempt such restoration who is not experienced at it, and it is a good idea to ask to see photographs or examples of a restorer's work first. Re-touching such a dial does not mean re-painting the background and starting anew, as one sometimes sees. It is essential to keep the character of the original, and almost always the original groundpaint, complete with craze-marks. Occasionally a dial may be found in very poor condition, with rust coming through the japanned surface, or perhaps blisters or bubbles in the japanwork, sometimes shelling off and crumbling to the touch. It is pointless to attempt to seal over this decaying surface. Instead, a skilled restorer will break off any loose sections, remove the rust, and will then match in by painting over the missing part and blending it almost invisibly into the good area. If this is done well it is almost impossible to detect.

If you do not have the services of a good dial restorer available to you, it might be worth trying a specialist clock dealer, who may be willing to get it done for you – though he might not be too obliging if you have bought the clock against him at auction and then ask him to sort out the problems which you can't deal with. If you cannot find a good dial restorer, the best thing is to leave well alone.

RE-PAINTED DIALS
Be very wary of a dial which has been re-painted in its entirety, *ie*. background and all. If this has happened, you have no way of

knowing whether the name on the dial is the name that was always there. Nor can you even tell if the dial has always been of that style or apparent age. A poor quality dial of 1860 can come out from 'restoration' looking like a high class dial of 1780, and might have acquired in the process all manner of features it never had before. I can think of one instance of which I know where all the restored dials come out with rocking ships in the arch, to be sold to the gullible with a taste for boats.

The novice may feel incapable of judging whether the background is original or re-painted. However, after looking at a number of clocks, it is usually a very easy matter to spot the difference in a Dulux white gloss background! The original grounds are often of a blue/green tint, especially in the eighteenth century. Almost all original grounds will show crazing to some degree, and this will usually be especially obvious around the points where the dial feet are fixed, as strain there will have caused crazed patterns to radiate from those points. However, the faker can work craze patterns into his new ground too, though seldom as convincingly as genuine crazing. If you are apprehensive of the whole problem, as you should be, then go to a specialist dealer and let him show you the genuine article and explain it to you. That is why they are there.

Whether you buy your clock already fully restored, or have it restored after purchase, you will eventually reach the point where you will want to set up your clock to have it running. Even if it is installed for you by the vendor, there will come a time when you will have to move it yourself and you will need to know how to go about this. It is this topic we look at in the next chapter.

14 SETTING UP YOUR CLOCK
AND CARING FOR IT

Those clocks which are not sensitive to levels, such as carriage clocks, can be picked up and set down again at will without requiring any adjustment. With pendulum clocks, however, this is not quite the case. If one such has been dismantled for moving and set up again at the same level, then there is no problem, but levels are often a matter of personal opinion or judgement, and this is where the beginner has trouble in getting his clock to run.

We must all surely be familiar with the situation where a mantel clock has to be propped up on one side by a couple of coins in order to make it run, even though the mantel itself might be judged to be level with a spirit-level. The reason for this is because the crutch setting has been disturbed, probably by carrying the clock with its pendulum in place, the result being that the pendulum bumped from side to side during moving and bent the crutch arm out of its correct position. The crutch (the forked arm through which the pendulum hangs) cannot be *seen* to be in its correct setting. Rather, it is a matter of trying the clock and correcting its stance a little at a time until the 'right' position is found for the level of the surface in question.

REMOVING THE PENDULUM
In moving any pendulum clock, the pendulum should be taken off *before* transporting the clock in its entirety. With a spring-driven clock, such as a bracket clock or spring dial clock, this will result in the clock rattling away at high speed until the pendulum is replaced. No harm should result in this provided the pendulum is removed for only a short time, as in moving the clock between rooms in a house. If the pendulum is to be left off for any length of time, such as in moving house, then a small folded piece of paper wedged between the crutch and the movement backplate will hold the crutch still until the whole has been re-assembled.

Some bracket clocks have a special carrying nut, which screws through the pendulum rod to hold it firmly and safely in place during carrying. In such cases the pendulum does not need to be removed, but simply screwed tight with its carrying nut.

Any clock owner will sooner or later need to know how to set his pendulum clock 'in beat' by adjusting the crutch arm. This is most easily done in a longcase clock, because both crutch and pendulum are easily reached and can be seen with the clock hood removed. The principle is the same, however, for any other pendulum clock, though with a bracket clock or a spring wall clock the working space may be restricted, and it may be more a matter of feeling your way than of seeing it.

DISMANTLING

A longcase clock should be dismantled for moving. If a longcase clock is moved fully assembled, then damage is likely to occur. At the very least, the crutch will be bent out of position or broken, and the suspension spring (by which the pendulum hangs) is also liable to break. Moving a clock in this manner is the major cause of a well-running clock failing to work after house-moving.

To dismantle a longcase clock, the weight(s) should be removed, and the pendulum also, after first having taken the hood off for access, of course. With an eight-day clock it is as well to wind the clock to within two or three inches of maximum (but not right to the top), and to apply masking tape to hold the lines neatly in place on the barrel. This is far easier than carrying the clock with long lengths of line trailing, and it saves the risk of the lines becoming trapped between the wheels, when they can be very time-consuming to untangle. If the pulleys are wound right to the top (*ie.* up against the seatboard), you may find it difficult to get them back in place again when re-assembling, as they will be jammed too tightly against the board.

The majority of longcase movements are fastened to the wooden board which they sit on (the seatboard), usually by special bolts known as seatboard hooks. This means that the movement, complete with its attached seatboard, will lift clear of the case's upright side-pieces – occasionally a screw or nail may hold the seatboard down for safety. In removing the pendulum and the movement, care should be taken not to bend the crutch, and it is unwise to rest the movement on its back, as in most instances this will immediately bend the crutch completely out of its setting, or may even break it. The safest way is to carry the movement face down on a cushion or soft pad such as foam rubber. Care must be taken, when lifting it off the pad, not to catch the hands.

When re-assembling, first of all put the case in the required position in such a way that it rests firmly against the wall. If the skirting board is thick, this may mean packing the backboard at the top with a small packing piece – a matchbox could be sellotaped in place. The front feet may then need packing up slightly so that the case is wedged firmly back to the wall to prevent it from swaying. A clock which is free to sway is likely to stop frequently. If you wish to screw the clock to the wall, as was often done in the past, it is best not to insert the screw till it has run satisfactorily for two or three weeks, so that you are sure the clock is happily level.

LEVELLING

Put the hood onto the case without the movement inside it at this stage. You now need to check that the case is visually 'level'. It is often useful to use a spirit-level on an easily accessible area, such as the ledge immediately in front of the hood door. If you level it in this way, you have some means of checking that level again at a later date – if, for example, the clock should settle itself into the carpet pile, or if you move it to a different room or a different house.

Once you are satisfied that the case is firm and level, then put the movement into place and re-hang the weights and pendulum. Don't forget to remove the masking tape from the barrels (sellotape usually refuses to stick to gutlines, especially if they are oily, but masking tape will normally stick). Push the pendulum to one side and see if the clock runs. If it does not, or if it runs for only a short time, then the clock is probably out of beat, which means that the crutch position will need setting. The level you have so far been checking has been the level of the *case*, and you now need to set your crutch position so that the clock will run with the case truly level.

CRUTCH SETTING

When a clock is in beat, it will tick evenly as the pendulum swings from side to side. A clock which is out of beat will tick unevenly (if at all), like someone limping rather than walking. If you then observe the swing of the pendulum, you will notice that it swings with a longer, heavier beat to one side than to the other. This is most obvious in the last few beats as a clock is about to stop. To correct this, *ie.* to set the clock in beat, bend the crutch slightly in the direction of the heaviest swing. If the clock ticks heaviest as the pendulum swings to the right, then bend the crutch to the right, seen as you face the clock.

The crutch should be bent in its stem, which is made of soft steel and will bend (usually) without too much trouble. Avoid trying to bend it at the top joint, or you may break the joint. You may need to have several attempts, bending the crutch just a little each time. If you bend it too far, or if it is already bent far out of position, the clock may fail to tick at all, in which case set off by bending the crutch to what would appear to be a roughly central position. Once it ticks, even if only briefly, you have a starting-point to work from.

At about five minutes to each hour, a longcase clock will be heard to warn as it lifts a lever preparatory to striking the hour. A clock which is slightly out of beat will often stop at the warning time – as the clock is struggling to run anyway, the action of lifting the strike lever is too much for it. So if the clock stops at around five minutes to, this is usually a sign that the clock is almost in beat, but not quite. It is not necessary, indeed not advisable, to remove the pendulum in order to bend the crutch to re-set it.

Setting a bracket clock or wall clock in beat involves exactly the same procedure, although you will of course be working in a more confined space.

CASE CARE

Care of a wooden clock case is exactly the same as for any other piece of antique furniture. Regular waxing and polishing (any kind of wax will do) helps to feed the wood, which may help it resist drying out or shrinking. An old-fashioned wax (of beeswax and turpentine) will help build up the patina, although it is hard work to apply it and one application every six months or so is plenty. Regular waxing between times with any sort of modern wax or spray will do the wood no harm.

OILING

The clock itself should require no maintenance other than an occasional oiling. A spot of oil the size of a pinhead should be applied to the end of each arbor at the point where it meets the plates of the clock, so there are in fact four oiling-points per arbor – one inside the backplate, one outside it, and two similar points on the frontplate. Special clock oil can be bought, but any light machine oil will do, such as sewing-machine oil. A long piece of thin wire may be needed to reach these oiling-points. Too much oil will simply dribble where it is not wanted, and on no account should the teeth of the wheels or pinions be oiled, or these may cause dust and grit to adhere and thus aggravate wear.

A clock will need cleaning at least once every twenty years, and this needs to be done by an experienced professional restorer. A dirty clock may still continue to work even though sadly in need of a clean, but the life of a clock is being shortened by running it in dirty condition, and it is a false economy.

WEIGHT LINES

Weight lines for an eight-day longcase clock are made of catgut, and will normally be replaced during cleaning, after which they should last for another twenty years. Thirty-hour clocks driven by rope will need to have the rope replaced after about ten years, as it tends to fray. Special ropes of an open weave are made for the purpose – a piece of old clothes-line is not the answer, as it will slip. Any clock restorer can get you a new rope, which you should be able to fit yourself in a few minutes. Cut the two loose ends to fit snugly together and then stitch loosely through them with thin nylon, rubbing a little carpet glue into the ends to stop them fraying, otherwise loose strands may catch in the wheelwork. Catgut lines for eight-day clocks are not expensive, but you may have to have a restorer fit these for you. Wire lines are not recommended nor are those of nylon or fishing line.

We have now run through a brief history of the origins and development of clocks made and sold in Britain. By now you should understand how to recognise the various types when you come across them and, hopefully, how to assess their ages and even qualities. If you have read this book before buying a clock, then you would be well advised to read it again, and a few other books too, as it may be too late *after* you have made your purchase. Reading about clocks before you buy one is not only a sensible safeguard against making a serious mistake, but should also add to the pleasure of selection, as you will be viewing from a more informed standpoint.

If you are an experienced collector, who reads this book as he reads all the others, I hope you will have found something here which was new to you. For the novice and the experienced reader alike I hope this book will have increased the pleasure you derive from the world of clocks.

APPENDIX A

SOCIETIES

Antiquarian Horological Society, New House, High Street, Ticehurst, East Sussex TN5 7AL.
British Horological Institute, Upton Hall, Newark, Nottinghamshire.

APPENDIX B

USEFUL MAGAZINES

Antiquarian Horology (quarterly). Antiquarian Horological Society, New House, Ticehurst, East Sussex TN5 7AL.
Clocks Magazine (monthly). From newsagents or by subscription to Select Subscriptions Ltd, 5 River Park Estate, Berkhampstead HP4 1HL.
Horological Journal (monthly). British Horological Institute, Upton Hall, Newark, Nottinghamshire.

APPENDIX C

NOTABLE MUSEUM COLLECTIONS

Basingstoke, Hants. Museum and Art Gallery, Old Town Hall, Market Place
Birmingham. The Museum of Science and Industry, Newhall Street
Bradford. Bowling Hall Museum, Bowling Hall Road
Bury St Edmunds, Suffolk. The Gershom-Parkington Collection, 8 Angel Hill
Cambridge. Fitzwilliam Museum, Trumpington Street
Coventry. Herbert Art Gallery and Museum, Jordan Well
Dumfries. Dumfries Burgh Museum, The Observatory, Corberry Hill
Leeds. Abbey House Museum, Kirstall
Leicester. Newarke Houses Museum, The Newarke
Liverpool. Liverpool City Museums, William Brown Street
London. The British Museum, Great Russell Street, WC1
   Clockmakers' Company Museum, Guildhall, Basinghall Street, EC2
   London Museum, Kensington Palace, The Broad Walk, W8
   National Maritime Museum, Romney Road, Greenwich, SE10
   Science Museum, Exhibition Road, South Kensington, SW7
   Victoria and Albert Museum, Cromwell Road, South Kensington, SW7
Norwich. Bridewell Museum, Bridewell Alley
Oxford. Museum of the History of Science, Broad Street
Port Sunlight. The Lady Lever Art Gallery, Port Sunlight Village, Wirral
Prescot. Prescot Museum of Clock and Watch-Making, 34, Church Street
Waddesdon. Waddesdon Manor, Waddesdon, near Aylesbury
York. Castle Museum, Tower Street

BIBLIOGRAPHY

Here follows a list of reference books which will be useful in tracing a clockmaker and in identifying the age and style of a clock.

Allan, Charles. *Old Stirling Clockmakers (& St Ninians)* (published privately, Stirling, 1990).

Baillie, G.H. *Watchmakers and Clockmakers of the World, Volume One* (NAG Press, 1976) (see also Loomes).

Barder, R.C.R. *English Country Grandfather Clocks* (David & Charles, 1983).

Barker, D. *The Arthur Negus Guide to Clocks* (Hamlyn, 1980).

Bates, Keith. *Clockmakers of Northumberland & Durham* (Pendulum Publications, 1980).

Beeson, C.F.C. *Clockmaking in Oxfordshire* (Museum of the History of Science, 1989).

Bellchambers, J.K. *Somerset Clockmakers* (Antiquarian Horological Society).

Bellchambers, J.K. *Devonshire Clockmakers* (The Devonshire Press Ltd, 1962).

Brown, H.M. *Cornish Clocks & Clockmakers* (David & Charles, 1970).

Bruton, Eric. *The Longcase Clock* (Hart-Davis, 1970).

Bruton, Eric. *The Wetherfield Collection of Clocks* (NAG Press, 1981).

Daniel, John. *Leicestershire Clockmakers* (Leicestershire Museums, 1975).

Dawson, P., Drover & Parkes. *Early English Clocks* (Antique Collectors' Club, 1982).

Dowler, Graham. *Gloucestershire Clock & Watchmakers* (Phillimore, 1984).

Edwardes, E.L. *The Grandfather Clock* (Sherrat, 1980).

Edwardes, E.L. *The Story of the Pendulum Clock* (Sherrat, 1977).

Elliott, D.J. *Shropshire Clocks & Clockmakers* (Phillimore, 1979).

Haggar, A.L. & Miller, L.F. *Suffolk Clocks & Clockmakers* (Antiquarian Horological Society, 1974).

Hana, W.F.J. *English Lantern Clocks* (Blandford Press, 1979).

Hudson, Felix. *Scottish Clockmakers* (F. Hudson, Dunfermline, 1982).

Hughes, R.G. *Derbyshire Clock & Watch Makers* (Derby Museum, 1976).

Lee, R.A. *The Knibb Family Clockmakers* (Manor House Publications, 1963).

Legg, Edward. *Clock & Watchmakers of Buckinghamshire* (Bradwell Abbey Field Centre, 1976).

Lloyd, H. Alan. *Old Clocks* (Benn, 1958).

Loomes, Brian. *Antique British Clocks, A Buyer's Guide* (Robert Hale, 1991).

Loomes, Brian. *Antique British Clocks Illustrated* (Robert Hale, 1992).

Loomes, Brian. *Complete British Clocks* (David & Charles, 1978).

Loomes, Brian. *Country Clocks & their London Origins* (David & Charles, 1976).

Loomes, Brian. *The Early Clockmakers of Great Britain* (NAG Press, 1982).

Loomes, Brian. *Grandfather Clocks & their Cases* (David & Charles, 1985).

Loomes, Brian. *Lancashire Clocks & Clockmakers* (David & Charles, 1975).

Loomes, Brian. *Watchmakers & Clockmakers of the World, Volume Two* (NAG Press, 1976 (revised 1989)).

Loomes, Brian. *Westmorland Clocks & Clockmakers* (David & Charles, 1974).

Loomes, Brian. *White Dial Clocks (the Complete Guide)* (David & Charles, 1981).

Loomes, Brian. *Yorkshire Clockmakers (revised edition)* (George Kelsall, 1985).

McKenna, Joseph. *Watch & Clockmakers of Warwickshire* (Pendulum Press, 1985).

McKenna, Joseph. *Watch & Clockmakers of Birmingham* (Pendulum Press, 1986).

Mason, Bernard. *Clock & Watch Making in Colchester* (Country Life, 1969).

Mather, H. *Clock & Watchmakers of Nottinghamshire* (The Friends of Nottingham Museum, 1979).

Moore, Nicholas. *Chester Clocks & Clockmakers* (Chester Museum, 1970s).

Norgate, J. & M. & Hudson, F. *Dunfermline Clockmakers* (F. Hudson, 1982).

Peate, I. *Clock & Watch Makers in Wales* (Welsh Folk Museum, 1960).

Penfold, John. *The Clockmakers of Cumberland* (Brant Wright Associates, 1977).

Penman, L. *The Clock Repairer's Handbook* (David & Charles/Arco, 1985).

Ponsford, Clive, N. *Devon Clocks & Clockmakers* (David & Charles, 1985).

Ponsford, C.N. & Authers, W.P. *Clocks & Clockmakers of Tiverton* (W.P. Authers, 1977).

Ponsford, Clive N. *Time in Exeter* (Headwell Vale Books, 1978).

Pryce, W.T.R. & Davies, T. Alun. *Samuel Roberts, Clockmaker* (Welsh Folk Museum, 1985).

Robinson, T. *The Longcase Clock* (Antique Collectors' Club, 1981).

Rose, Ronald E. *English Dial Clocks* (Antique Collectors' Club, 1978).

Royer-Collard, F.B. *Skeleton Clocks* (NAG Press, 1969).

Seaby, W.A. *Clockmakers of Warwick & Leamington* (Warwick Museum, 1981).

Smith, E. *Striking and Chiming Clocks* (David & Charles/Arco, 1985).

Smith, John. *Old Scottish Clockmakers* (E.P. Publishing Ltd, 1975).

Snell, Michael. *Clocks & Clockmakers of Salisbury* (Hobnob Press, 1986).

Symonds, R.W. Thomas. *Tompion: his Life & Work* (Spring Books, 1968).

Tebbutt, Laurence. *Stamford Clocks and Watches* (Dolby Bros Ltd, 1975).

Treherne, A.A. *Nantwich Clockmakers* (Nantwich Museum, 1986).

Tribe, T. & Whatmoor, P. *Dorset Clocks & Clockmakers* (Tanat Books, 1981).

Tyler, E.J. *The Clockmakers of Sussex* (Watch & Clock Book Society, 1986).

Vernon, J. *The Grandfather Clock Maintenance Manual* (David & Charles/Van Nostrand Rheinhold, 1983).

Walker, J.E.S. *Hull & East Riding Clocks* (Hornsea Museum Publications, 1982).

Wallace, William. *Time in Hamilton* (published privately, 1981).

White, George. *English Lantern Clocks* (Antique Collectors' Club, 1989).

INDEX